Data Mining with R
Learning with Case Studies

Chapman & Hall/CRC
Data Mining and Knowledge Discovery Series

SERIES EDITOR
Vipin Kumar
University of Minnesota
Department of Computer Science and Engineering
Minneapolis, Minnesota, U.S.A

AIMS AND SCOPE

This series aims to capture new developments and applications in data mining and knowledge discovery, while summarizing the computational tools and techniques useful in data analysis. This series encourages the integration of mathematical, statistical, and computational methods and techniques through the publication of a broad range of textbooks, reference works, and handbooks. The inclusion of concrete examples and applications is highly encouraged. The scope of the series includes, but is not limited to, titles in the areas of data mining and knowledge discovery methods and applications, modeling, algorithms, theory and foundations, data and knowledge visualization, data mining systems and tools, and privacy and security issues.

PUBLISHED TITLES

UNDERSTANDING COMPLEX DATASETS:
DATA MINING WITH MATRIX DECOMPOSITIONS
David Skillicorn

COMPUTATIONAL METHODS OF FEATURE
SELECTION
Huan Liu and Hiroshi Motoda

CONSTRAINED CLUSTERING: ADVANCES IN
ALGORITHMS, THEORY, AND APPLICATIONS
Sugato Basu, Ian Davidson, and Kiri L. Wagstaff

KNOWLEDGE DISCOVERY FOR
COUNTERTERRORISM AND LAW ENFORCEMENT
David Skillicorn

MULTIMEDIA DATA MINING: A SYSTEMATIC
INTRODUCTION TO CONCEPTS AND THEORY
Zhongfei Zhang and Ruofei Zhang

NEXT GENERATION OF DATA MINING
Hillol Kargupta, Jiawei Han, Philip S. Yu,
Rajeev Motwani, and Vipin Kumar

DATA MINING FOR DESIGN AND MARKETING
Yukio Ohsawa and Katsutoshi Yada

THE TOP TEN ALGORITHMS IN DATA MINING
Xindong Wu and Vipin Kumar

GEOGRAPHIC DATA MINING AND
KNOWLEDGE DISCOVERY, SECOND EDITION
Harvey J. Miller and Jiawei Han

TEXT MINING: CLASSIFICATION, CLUSTERING,
AND APPLICATIONS
Ashok N. Srivastava and Mehran Sahami

BIOLOGICAL DATA MINING
Jake Y. Chen and Stefano Lonardi

INFORMATION DISCOVERY ON ELECTRONIC
HEALTH RECORDS
Vagelis Hristidis

TEMPORAL DATA MINING
Theophano Mitsa

RELATIONAL DATA CLUSTERING: MODELS,
ALGORITHMS, AND APPLICATIONS
Bo Long, Zhongfei Zhang, and Philip S. Yu

KNOWLEDGE DISCOVERY FROM DATA STREAMS
João Gama

STATISTICAL DATA MINING USING SAS
APPLICATIONS, SECOND EDITION
George Fernandez

INTRODUCTION TO PRIVACY-PRESERVING DATA
PUBLISHING: CONCEPTS AND TECHNIQUES
Benjamin C. M. Fung, Ke Wang, Ada Wai-Chee Fu,
and Philip S. Yu

HANDBOOK OF EDUCATIONAL DATA MINING
Cristóbal Romero, Sebastian Ventura,
Mykola Pechenizkiy, and Ryan S.J.d. Baker

DATA MINING WITH R: LEARNING WITH
CASE STUDIES
Luís Torgo

Chapman & Hall/CRC
Data Mining and Knowledge Discovery Series

Data Mining with R
Learning with Case Studies

Luís Torgo

CRC Press
Taylor & Francis Group
Boca Raton London New York

CRC Press is an imprint of the
Taylor & Francis Group, an **informa** business
A CHAPMAN & HALL BOOK

Chapman & Hall/CRC
Taylor & Francis Group
6000 Broken Sound Parkway NW, Suite 300
Boca Raton, FL 33487-2742

Library of Congress Cataloging-in-Publication Data

Torgo, Luís.
    Data mining with R : learning with case studies / Luís Torgo.
        p. cm. -- (Chapman & Hall/CRC data mining and knowledge discovery series)
    Includes bibliographical references and index.
    ISBN 978-1-4398-1018-7 (hardback)
    1. Data mining--Case studies. 2. R (Computer program language) I. Title.

QA76.9.D343T67 2010
006.3'12--dc22
                                           2010036935

Visit the Taylor & Francis Web site at
http://www.taylorandfrancis.com

and the CRC Press Web site at
http://www.crcpress.com

Contents

Preface

The main goal of this book is to introduce the reader to the use of R as a tool for data mining. R is a freely downloadable[1] language and environment for statistical computing and graphics. Its capabilities and the large set of available add-on packages make this tool an excellent alternative to many existing (and expensive!) data mining tools.

One of the key issues in data mining is size. A typical data mining problem involves a large database from which one seeks to extract useful knowledge. In this book we will use MySQL as the core database management system. MySQL is also freely available[2] for several computer platforms. This means that one is able to perform "serious" data mining without having to pay any money at all. Moreover, we hope to show that this comes with no compromise of the quality of the obtained solutions. Expensive tools do not necessarily mean better tools! R together with MySQL form a pair very hard to beat as long as one is willing to spend some time learning how to use them. We think that it is worthwhile, and we hope that at the end of reading this book you are convinced as well.

The goal of this book is not to describe all facets of data mining processes. Many books exist that cover this scientific area. Instead we propose to introduce the reader to the power of R and data mining by means of several case studies. Obviously, these case studies do not represent all possible data mining problems that one can face in the real world. Moreover, the solutions we describe cannot be taken as complete solutions. Our goal is more to introduce the reader to the world of data mining using R through practical examples. As such, our analysis of the case studies has the goal of showing examples of knowledge extraction using R, instead of presenting complete reports of data mining case studies. They should be taken as examples of possible paths in any data mining project and can be used as the basis for developing solutions for the reader's own projects. Still, we have tried to cover a diverse set of problems posing different challenges in terms of size, type of data, goals of analysis, and the tools necessary to carry out this analysis. This hands-on approach has its costs, however. In effect, to allow for every reader to carry out our described steps on his/her computer as a form of learning with concrete case studies, we had to make some compromises. Namely, we cannot address extremely large problems as this would require computer resources that are not available to

---

[1]Download it from http://www.R-project.org.
[2]Download it from http://www.mysql.com.

everybody. Still, we think we have covered problems that can be considered large and have shown how to handle the problems posed by different types of data dimensionality.

We do not assume any prior knowledge about R. Readers who are new to R and data mining should be able to follow the case studies. We have tried to make the different case studies self-contained in such a way that the reader can start anywhere in the document. Still, some basic R functionalities are introduced in the first, simpler case studies, and are not repeated, which means that if you are new to R, then you should at least start with the first case studies to get acquainted with R. Moreover, the first chapter provides a very short introduction to R and MySQL basics, which should facilitate the understanding of the following chapters. We also do not assume any familiarity with data mining or statistical techniques. Brief introductions to different data mining techniques are provided as necessary in the case studies. It is not an objective of this book to provide the reader with full information on the technical and theoretical details of these techniques. Our descriptions of these tools are given to provide a basic understanding of their merits, drawbacks, and analysis objectives. Other existing books should be considered if further theoretical insights are required. At the end of some sections we provide "further readings" pointers that may help find more information if required. In summary, our target readers are more users of data analysis tools than researchers or developers. Still, we hope the latter also find reading this book useful as a form of entering the "world" of R and data mining.

The book is accompanied by a set of freely available R source files that can be obtained at the book's Web site.[3] These files include all the code used in the case studies. They facilitate the "do-it-yourself" approach followed in this book. We strongly recommend that readers install R and try the code as they read the book. All data used in the case studies is available at the book's Web site as well. Moreover, we have created an R package called DMwR that contains several functions used in the book as well as the datasets already in R format. You should install and load this package to follow the code in the book (details on how to do this are given in the first chapter).

---

[3]http://www.liaad.up.pt/~ltorgo/DataMiningWithR/.

Acknowledgments

I would like to thank my family for all the support they give me. Without them I would have found it difficult to embrace this project. Their presence, love, and caring provided the necessary comfort to overcome the ups and downs of writing a book. The same kind of comfort was given by my dear friends who were always ready for an extra beer when necessary. Thank you all, and now I hope I will have more time to share with you.

I am also grateful for all the support of my research colleagues and to LIAAD/INESC Porto LA as a whole. Thanks also to the University of Porto for supporting my research. Part of the writing of this book was financially supported by a sabbatical grant (SFRH/BSAB/739/2007) of FCT.

Finally, thanks to all students and colleagues who helped in proofreading drafts of this book.

Luis Torgo
Porto, Portugal

List of Figures

List of Tables

Chapter 1

Introduction

R is a programming language and an environment for statistical computing. It is similar to the S language developed at AT&T Bell Laboratories by Rick Becker, John Chambers and Allan Wilks. There are versions of R for the Unix, Windows and Mac families of operating systems. Moreover, R runs on different computer architectures like Intel, PowerPC, Alpha systems and Sparc systems. R was initially developed by Ihaka and Gentleman (1996), both from the University of Auckland, New Zealand. The current development of R is carried out by a core team of a dozen people from different institutions around the world. R development takes advantage of a growing community that cooperates in its development due to its open source philosophy. In effect, the source code of every R component is freely available for inspection and/or adaptation. This fact allows you to check and test the reliability of anything you use in R. There are many critics to the open source model. Most of them mention the lack of support as one of the main drawbacks of open source software. It is certainly not the case with R! There are many excellent documents, books and sites that provide free information on R. Moreover, the excellent R-help mailing list is a source of invaluable advice and information, much better than any amount of money could ever buy! There are also searchable mailing lists archives that you can (and should!) use before posting a question. More information on these mailing lists can be obtained at the R Web site in the section "Mailing Lists".

Data mining has to do with the discovery of useful, valid, unexpected, and understandable knowledge from data. These general objectives are obviously shared by other disciplines like statistics, machine learning, or pattern recognition. One of the most important distinguishing issues in data mining is size. With the widespread use of computer technology and information systems, the amount of data available for exploration has increased exponentially. This poses difficult challenges to the standard data analysis disciplines: One has to consider issues like computational efficiency, limited memory resources, interfaces to databases, etc. All these issues turn data mining into a highly interdisciplinary subject involving tasks not only of typical data analysts but also of people working with databases, data visualization on high dimensions, etc.

R has limitations with handling enormous datasets because all computation is carried out in the main memory of the computer. This does not mean that we will not be able to handle these problems. Taking advantage of the highly flexible database interfaces available in R, we will be able to perform data mining on large problems. Being faithful to the open source philosophy, we will use the excellent MySQL database management system.[1] MySQL is also available for quite a large set of computer platforms and operating systems. Moreover, R has a package that enables an easy interface to MySQL (package RMySQL (James and DebRoy, 2009)).

In summary, we hope that at the end of reading this book you are convinced that you can do data mining on large problems without having to spend any money at all! That is only possible due to the generous and invaluable contribution of lots of people who build such wonderful tools as R and MySQL.

1.1 How to Read This Book?

The main spirit behind the book is

Learn by doing it!

The book is organized as a set of case studies. The "solutions" to these case studies are obtained using R. All necessary steps to reach the solutions are described. Using the book Web site[2] and the book-associated R package (DMwR), you can get all code included in the document, as well as all data of the case studies. This should facilitate trying them out by yourself. Ideally, you should read this document beside your computer and try every step as it is presented to you in the document. R code is shown in the book using the following font:

```
> R.version
```

```
              _
platform      i486-pc-linux-gnu
arch          i486
os            linux-gnu
system        i486, linux-gnu
status
major         2
minor         10.1
year          2009
month         12
day           14
svn rev       50720
language      R
version.string R version 2.10.1 (2009-12-14)
```

---

[1] Free download at http://www.mysql.com
[2] http://www.liaad.up.pt/~ltorgo/DataMiningWithR/.

R commands are entered at R command prompt, ">". Whenever you see this prompt you can interpret it as R waiting for you to enter a command. You type in the commands at the prompt and then press the ENTER key to ask R to execute them. This may or may not produce some form of output (the result of the command) and then a new prompt appears. At the prompt you may use the arrow keys to browse and edit previously entered commands. This is handy when you want to type commands similar to what you have done before as you avoid typing them again.

Still, you can take advantage of the code provided at the book Web site to cut and paste between your browser or editor and the R console, thus avoiding having to type all commands described in the book. This will surely facilitate your learning experience and improve your understanding of its potential.

1.2   A Short Introduction to R

The goal of this section is to provide a brief introduction to the key issues of the R language. We do not assume any familiarity with computer programming. Readers should be able to easily follow the examples presented in this section. Still, if you feel some lack of motivation to continue reading this introductory material, do not worry. You may proceed to the case studies and then return to this introduction as you get more motivated by the concrete applications.

R is a functional language for statistical computation and graphics. It can be seen as a dialect of the S language (developed at AT&T) for which John Chambers was awarded the 1998 Association for Computing Machinery (ACM) Software award that mentioned that this language "forever altered how people analyze, visualize and manipulate data".

R can be quite useful just by using it in an interactive fashion at its command line. Still, more advanced uses of the system will lead the user to develop his own functions to systematize repetitive tasks, or even to add or change some functionalities of the existing add-on packages, taking advantage of being open source.

1.2.1   Starting with R

In order to install R in your system, the easiest way is to obtain a binary distribution from the R Web site[3] where you can follow the link that takes you to the CRAN (Comprehensive R Archive Network) site to obtain, among other things, the binary distribution for your particular operating system/architecture. If you prefer to build R directly from the sources, you can get instructions on how to do it from CRAN.

---

[3]http://www.R-project.org.

After downloading the binary distribution for your operating system you just need to follow the instructions that come with it. In the case of the Windows version, you simply execute the downloaded file (R-2.10.1-win32.exe)[4] and select the options you want in the following menus. In some operating systems you may need to contact your system administrator to fulfill the installation task due to lack of permissions to install software.

To run R in Windows you simply double-click the appropriate icon on your desktop, while in Unix versions you should type R at the operating system prompt. Both will bring up the R console with its prompt ">".

If you want to quit R you can issue the command q() at the prompt. You will be asked if you want to save the current workspace. You should answer yes only if you want to resume your current analysis at the point you are leaving it, later on.

Although the set of tools that comes with R is by itself quite powerful, it is natural that you will end up wanting to install some of the large (and growing) set of add-on packages available for R at CRAN. In the Windows version this is easily done through the "Packages" menu. After connecting your computer to the Internet you should select the "Install package from CRAN..." option from this menu. This option will present a list of the packages available at CRAN. You select the one(s) you want, and R will download the package(s) and self-install it(them) on your system. In Unix versions, things may be slightly different depending on the graphical capabilities of your R installation. Still, even without selection from menus, the operation is simple.[5] Suppose you want to download the package that provides functions to connect to MySQL databases. This package name is RMySQL.[6] You just need to type the following command at R prompt:

```
> install.packages('RMySQL')
```

The install.packages() function has many parameters, among which there is the repos argument that allows you to indicate the nearest CRAN mirror.[7] Still, the first time you run the function in an R session, it will prompt you for the repository you wish to use.

One thing that you surely should do is install the package associated with this book, which will give you access to several functions used throughout the book as well as datasets. To install it you proceed as with any other package:

```
> install.packages('DMwR')
```

---

[4]The actual name of the file changes with newer versions. This is the name for version 2.10.1.

[5]Please note that the following code also works in Windows versions, although you may find the use of the menu more practical.

[6]You can get an idea of the functionalities of each of the R packages in the R FAQ (frequently asked questions) at CRAN.

[7]The list of available mirrors can be found at http://cran.r-project.org/mirrors.html.

If you want to know the packages currently installed in your computer, you can issue

```
> installed.packages()
```

This produces a long output with each line containing a package, its version information, the packages it depends, and so on. A more user-friendly, although less complete, list of the installed packages can be obtained by issuing

```
> library()
```

The following command can be very useful as it allows you to check whether there are newer versions of your installed packages at CRAN:

```
> old.packages()
```

Moreover, you can use the following command to update all your installed packages:

```
> update.packages()
```

R has an integrated help system that you can use to know more about the system and its functionalities. Moreover, you can find extra documentation at the R site. R comes with a set of HTML files that can be read using a Web browser. On Windows versions of R, these pages are accessible through the HELP menu. Alternatively, you can issue help.start() at the prompt to launch a browser showing the HTML help pages. Another form of getting help is to use the help() function. For instance, if you want some help on the plot() function, you can enter the command "help(plot)" (or alternatively, ?plot). A quite powerful alternative, provided you are connected to the Internet, is to use the RSiteSearch() function that searches for key words or phrases in the mailing list archives, R manuals, and help pages; for example,

```
> RSiteSearch('neural networks')
```

Finally, there are several places on the Web that provide help on several facets of R, such as the site http://www.rseek.org/.

1.2.2   R Objects

There are two main concepts behind the R language: objects and functions. An object can be seen as a storage space with an associated name. Everything in R is stored in an object. All variables, data, functions, etc. are stored in the memory of the computer in the form of named objects.

Functions are a special type of R objects designed to carry out some operation. They usually take some arguments and produce a result by means of executing some set of operations (themselves usually other function calls). R already comes with an overwhelming set of functions available for us to use, but as we will see later, the user can also create new functions.

Content may be stored in objects using the assignment operator. This operator is denoted by an angle bracket followed by a minus sign (<-):[8]

```
> x <- 945
```

The effect of the previous instruction is thus to store the number 945 on an object named **x**.

By simply entering the name of an object at the R prompt one can see its contents:[9]

```
> x
```

```
[1] 945
```

The rather cryptic "[1]" in front of the number 945 can be read as "this line is showing values starting from the first element of the object." This is particularly useful for objects containing several values, like vectors, as we will see later.

Below you will find other examples of assignment statements. These examples should make it clear that this is a destructive operation as any object can only have a single content at any time t. This means that by assigning some new content to an existing object, you in effect lose its previous content:

```
> y <- 39
> y
```

```
[1] 39
```

```
> y <- 43
> y
```

```
[1] 43
```

You can also assign numerical expressions to an object. In this case the object will store the result of the expression:

```
> z <- 5
> w <- z^2
> w
```

```
[1] 25
```

```
> i <- (z * 2 + 45)/2
> i
```

---

[8]You may actually also use the = sign but this is not recommended as it may be confused with testing for equality.

[9]Or an error message if we type the name incorrectly, a rather frequent error!

```
[1] 27.5
```

This means that we can think of the assignment operation as "calculate whatever is given on the right side of the operator, and assign (store) the result of this calculation to the object whose name is given on the left side".

If you only want to know the result of some arithmetic operation, you do not need to assign the result of an expression to an object. In effect, you can use R prompt as a kind of calculator:

```
> (34 + 90)/12.5
```

```
[1] 9.92
```

Every object you create will stay in the computer memory until you delete it. You may list the objects currently in the memory by issuing the `ls()` or `objects()` command at the prompt. If you do not need an object, you may free some memory space by removing it:

```
> ls()
```

```
[1] "i" "w" "x" "y" "z"
```

```
> rm(y)
> rm(z, w, i)
```

Object names may consist of any upper- and lower-case letters, the digits 0 to 9 (except in the beginning of the name), and also the period, ".", which behaves like a letter. Note that names in R are *case sensitive*, meaning that `Color` and `color` are two distinct objects. This is in effect a frequent cause of frustration for beginners who keep getting "object not found" errors. If you face this type of error, start by checking the correctness of the name of the object causing the error.

1.2.3 Vectors

The most basic data object in R is a vector. Even when you assign a single number to an object (like in `x <- 45.3`), you are creating a vector containing a single element. All objects have a *mode* and a *length*. The mode determines the kind of data stored in the object. Vectors are used to store a set of elements of the same atomic data type. The main atomic types are *character*,[10] *logical*, *numeric*, or *complex*. Thus you may have vectors of characters, logical values (T or F or `FALSE` or `TRUE`),[11] numbers, and complex numbers. The length of an object is the number of elements in it, and can be obtained with the function `length()`.

---

[10]The *character* type is in effect a set of characters, which are usually known as strings in some programming languages, and not a single character as you might expect.

[11]Recall that R is case sensitive; thus, for instance, `True` is not a valid logical value.

Most of the time you will be using vectors with length larger than 1. You can create a vector in R, using the c() function, which combines its arguments to form a vector:

```
> v <- c(4, 7, 23.5, 76.2, 80)
> v

[1]   4.0  7.0 23.5 76.2 80.0

> length(v)

[1] 5

> mode(v)

[1] "numeric"
```

All elements of a vector must belong to the same mode. If that is not true, R will force it by type coercion. The following is an example of this:

```
> v <- c(4, 7, 23.5, 76.2, 80, "rrt")
> v

[1] "4"    "7"    "23.5" "76.2" "80"    "rrt"
```

All elements of the vector have been converted to character mode. Character values are strings of characters surrounded by either single or double quotes.

All vectors may contain a special value called NA. This represents a missing value:

```
> u <- c(4, 6, NA, 2)
> u

[1]   4   6  NA   2

> k <- c(T, F, NA, TRUE)
> k

[1]  TRUE FALSE    NA  TRUE
```

You can access a particular element of a vector through an index between square brackets:

```
> v[2]

[1] "7"
```

The example above gives you the second element of the vector **v**. You will learn in Section 1.2.7 that we may use vectors of indexes to obtain more powerful indexing schemes.

You can also change the value of one particular vector element by using the same indexing strategies:

```
> v[1] <- "hello"
> v
```

```
[1] "hello" "7"      "23.5"  "76.2"  "80"     "rrt"
```

R allows you to create empty vectors like this:

```
> x <- vector()
```

The length of a vector can be changed by simply adding more elements to it using a previously nonexistent index. For instance, after creating the empty vector x, you could type

```
> x[3] <- 45
> x
```

```
[1] NA NA 45
```

Notice how the first two elements have an unknown value, NA. This sort of flexibility comes with a cost. Contrary to other programming languages, in R you will not get an error if you use a position of a vector that does not exists:

```
> length(x)
```

```
[1] 3
```

```
> x[10]
```

```
[1] NA
```

```
> x[5] <- 4
> x
```

```
[1] NA NA 45 NA  4
```

To shrink the size of a vector, you can take advantage of the fact that the assignment operation is destructive, as we have mentioned before. For instance,

```
> v <- c(45, 243, 78, 343, 445, 44, 56, 77)
> v
```

```
[1]   45 243  78 343 445  44  56  77
```

```
> v <- c(v[5], v[7])
> v
```

```
[1] 445  56
```

Through the use of more powerful indexing schemes to be explored in Section 1.2.7, you will be able delete particular elements of a vector in an easier way.

1.2.4   Vectorization

One of the most powerful aspects of the R language is the vectorization of several of its available functions. These functions operate directly on each element of a vector. For instance,

```
> v <- c(4, 7, 23.5, 76.2, 80)
> x <- sqrt(v)
> x
```

```
[1] 2.000000 2.645751 4.847680 8.729261 8.944272
```

The function `sqrt()` calculates the square root of its argument. In this case we have used a vector of numbers as its argument. Vectorization leads the function to produce a vector of the same length, with each element resulting from applying the function to the respective element of the original vector.

You can also use this feature of R to carry out vector arithmetic:

```
> v1 <- c(4, 6, 87)
> v2 <- c(34, 32.4, 12)
> v1 + v2
```

```
[1] 38.0 38.4 99.0
```

What if the vectors do not have the same length? R will use a *recycling rule* by repeating the shorter vector until it fills in the size of the larger vector. For example,

```
> v1 <- c(4, 6, 8, 24)
> v2 <- c(10, 2)
> v1 + v2
```

```
[1] 14  8 18 26
```

It is just as if the vector `c(10,2)` was `c(10,2,10,2)`. If the lengths are not multiples, then a warning is issued:

```
> v1 <- c(4, 6, 8, 24)
> v2 <- c(10, 2, 4)
> v1 + v2
```

```
[1] 14  8 12 34
Warning message:
In v1 + v2 :
  longer object length is not a multiple of shorter object length
```

Yet, the recycling rule has been used, and the operation was carried out (it is a warning, not an error!).

As mentioned, single numbers are represented in R as vectors of length 1. This is very handy for operations like the one shown below:

```
> v1 <- c(4, 6, 8, 24)
> 2 * v1
```

```
[1]  8 12 16 48
```

Notice how the number 2 (actually the vector c(2)!) was recycled, resulting in multiplying all elements of v1 by 2. As we will see, this recycling rule is also applied with other objects, such as arrays and matrices.

1.2.5   Factors

Factors provide an easy and compact form of handling categorical (nominal) data. Factors have *levels* that are the possible values they can take. Factors are particularly useful in datasets where you have nominal variables with a fixed number of possible values. Several graphical and summarization functions that we will explore in the following chapters take advantage of this type of information. Factors allow you to use and show the values of your nominal variables as they are, which is clearly more interpretable for the user, while internally R stores these values as numeric codes that are considerably more memory efficient.

Let us see how to create factors in R. Suppose you have a vector with the sex of ten individuals:

```
> g <- c("f", "m", "m", "m", "f", "m", "f", "m", "f", "f")
> g
```

```
[1] "f" "m" "m" "m" "f" "m" "f" "m" "f" "f"
```

You can transform this vector into a factor by entering

```
> g <- factor(g)
> g
```

```
[1] f m m m f m f m f f
Levels: f m
```

Notice that you do not have a character vector anymore. Actually, as mentioned above, factors are represented internally as numeric vectors.[12] In this example, we have two levels, 'f' and 'm', which are represented internally as 1 and 2, respectively. Still, you do not need to bother about this as you can use the "original" character values, and R will also use them when showing you the factors. So the coding translation, motivated by efficiency reasons, is transparent to you.

Suppose you have five extra individuals whose sex information you want to store in another factor object. Suppose that they are all males. If you still want the factor object to have the same two levels as object g, you must use the following:

---

[12]You can confirm it by typing mode(g).

```
> other.g <- factor(c("m", "m", "m", "m", "m"), levels = c("f",
+       "m"))
> other.g
```

```
[1] m m m m m
Levels: f m
```

Without the `levels` argument; the factor `other.g` would have a single level ('m').

As a side note, this is one of the first examples of one of the most common things in a functional programming language like R, which is function composition. In effect, we are applying one function (`factor()`) to the result of another function (`c()`). Obviously, we could have first assigned the result of the `c()` function to an object and then call the function `factor()` with this object. However, this is much more verbose and actually wastes some memory by creating an extra object, and thus one tends to use function composition quite frequently, although we incur the danger of our code becoming more difficult to read for people not so familiarized with this important notion of function composition.

One of the many things you can do with factors is to count the occurrence of each possible value. Try this:

```
> table(g)
```

```
g
f m
5 5
```

```
> table(other.g)
```

```
other.g
f m
0 5
```

The `table()` function can also be used to obtain cross-tabulation of several factors. Suppose that we have in another vector the age category of the ten individuals stored in vector **g**. You could cross-tabulate these two vectors as follows:

```
> a <- factor(c('adult','adult','juvenile','juvenile','adult','adult',
+            'adult','juvenile','adult','juvenile'))
> table(a,g)
```

```
         g
a         f m
  adult   4 2
  juvenile 1 3
```

A short side note: You may have noticed that sometimes we have a line starting with a "+" sign. This occurs when a line is getting too big and you decide to change to a new line (by hitting the ENTER key) before the command you are entering finishes. As the command is incomplete, R starts the new line with the continuation prompt, the "+" sign. You should remember that these signs are not to be entered by you! They are automatically printed by R (as is the normal prompt ">").

Sometimes we wish to calculate the marginal and relative frequencies for this type of contingency tables. The following gives you the totals for both the sex and the age factors of this dataset:

```
> t <- table(a, g)
> margin.table(t, 1)

a
   adult juvenile
      6        4

> margin.table(t, 2)

g
f m
5 5
```

The "1" and "2" in the functions represent the first and second dimensions of the table, that is, the rows and columns of t.

For relative frequencies with respect to each margin and overall, we do

```
> prop.table(t, 1)

          g
a                 f         m
   adult     0.6666667 0.3333333
   juvenile 0.2500000 0.7500000

> prop.table(t, 2)

          g
a           f   m
   adult     0.8 0.4
   juvenile 0.2 0.6

> prop.table(t)

          g
a           f   m
   adult     0.4 0.2
   juvenile 0.1 0.3
```

Notice that if we wanted percentages instead, we could simply multiply these function calls by 100.

1.2.6 Generating Sequences

R has several facilities to generate different types of sequences. For instance, if you want to create a vector containing the integers between 1 and 1,000, you can simply type

```
> x <- 1:1000
```

which creates a vector called x containing 1,000 elements—the integers from 1 to 1,000.

You should be careful with the precedence of the operator ":". The following examples illustrate this danger:

```
> 10:15 - 1
```

```
[1]   9 10 11 12 13 14
```

```
> 10:(15 - 1)
```

```
[1] 10 11 12 13 14
```

Please make sure you understand what happened in the first command (remember the recycling rule!).

You may also generate decreasing sequences such as the following:

```
> 5:0
```

```
[1] 5 4 3 2 1 0
```

To generate sequences of real numbers, you can use the function seq(). The instruction

```
> seq(-4, 1, 0.5)
```

```
 [1] -4.0 -3.5 -3.0 -2.5 -2.0 -1.5 -1.0 -0.5  0.0  0.5  1.0
```

generates a sequence of real numbers between −4 and 1 in increments of 0.5. Here are a few other examples of the use of the function seq():[13]

```
> seq(from = 1, to = 5, length = 4)
```

```
[1] 1.000000 2.333333 3.666667 5.000000
```

```
> seq(from = 1, to = 5, length = 2)
```

```
[1] 1 5
```

```
> seq(length = 10, from = -2, by = 0.2)
```

---

[13]You may want to have a look at the help page of the function (typing, for instance, '?seq'), to better understand its arguments and variants.

```
[1] -2.0 -1.8 -1.6 -1.4 -1.2 -1.0 -0.8 -0.6 -0.4 -0.2
```

You may have noticed that in the above examples the arguments used in the function calls were specified in a different way—by first indicating the name of the parameter and then the value we want to use for that specific parameter. This is very handy when we have functions with lots of parameters, most with default values. These defaults allow us to avoid having to specify them in our calls if the values suit our needs. However, if some of these defaults do not apply to our problem, we need to provide alternative values. Without the type of specification by name shown in the above examples, we would need to use the specification by position. If the parameter whose default we want to change is one of the last parameters of the function, the call by position would require the specification of all previous parameters values, even though we want to use their default values.[14] With the specification by name we avoid this trouble as this allows us to change the order of the parameters in our function calls, as they are being specified by their names.

Another very useful function to generate sequences with a certain pattern is the function **rep()**:

```
> rep(5, 10)

[1] 5 5 5 5 5 5 5 5 5 5

> rep("hi", 3)

[1] "hi" "hi" "hi"

> rep(1:2, 3)

[1] 1 2 1 2 1 2

> rep(1:2, each = 3)

[1] 1 1 1 2 2 2
```

The function **gl()** can be used to generate sequences involving factors. The syntax of this function is **gl(k,n)**, where **k** is the number of levels of the factor, and **n** is the number of repetitions of each level. Here are two examples,

```
> gl(3, 5)

[1] 1 1 1 1 1 2 2 2 2 2 3 3 3 3 3
Levels: 1 2 3

> gl(2, 5, labels = c("female", "male"))
```

---

[14] Actually, we can simply use commas with empty values until we reach the wanted position, as in **seq(1,4,40)**.

```
[1] female female female female female male   male   male   male   male
Levels: female male
```

Finally, R has several functions that can be used to generate random sequences according to different probability density functions. The functions have the generic structure *rfunc*(n, par1, par2, ...), where *func* is the name of the probability distribution, n is the number of data to generate, and par1, par2, ... are the values of some parameters of the density function that may be required. For instance, if you want ten randomly generated numbers from a normal distribution with zero mean and unit standard deviation, type

```
> rnorm(10)
```

```
[1] -0.74350857  1.14875838  0.26971256  1.06230562 -0.46296225
[6] -0.89086612 -0.12533888 -0.08887182  1.27165411  0.86652581
```

while if you prefer a mean of 10 and a standard deviation of 3, you should use

```
> rnorm(4, mean = 10, sd = 3)
```

```
[1]  5.319385 15.133113  8.449766 10.817147
```

To get five numbers drawn randomly from a Student t distribution with 10 degrees of freedom, type

```
> rt(5, df = 10)
```

```
[1] -1.2697062  0.5467355  0.7979222  0.4949397  0.2497204
```

R has many more probability functions, as well as other functions for obtaining the probability densities, the cumulative probability densities, and the quantiles of these distributions.

1.2.7   Sub-Setting

We have already seen examples of how to get one element of a vector by indicating its position inside square brackets. R also allows you to use vectors within the brackets. There are several types of index vectors. Logical index vectors extract the elements corresponding to true values. Let us see a concrete example:

```
> x <- c(0, -3, 4, -1, 45, 90, -5)
> x > 0
```

```
[1] FALSE FALSE  TRUE FALSE  TRUE  TRUE FALSE
```

The second instruction of the code shown above is a logical condition. As x is a vector, the comparison is carried out for all elements of the vector (remember the famous recycling rule!), thus producing a vector with as many logical values as there are elements in x. If we use this vector of logical values to index x, we get as a result the positions of x that correspond to the true values:

```
> x[x > 0]

[1]  4 45 90
```

This reads as follows: Give me the positions of x for which the following logical expression is true. Notice that this is another example of the notion of function composition, which we will use rather frequently. Taking advantage of the logical operators available in R, you can use more complex logical index vectors, as for instance,

```
> x[x <= -2 | x > 5]

[1] -3 45 90 -5

> x[x > 40 & x < 100]

[1] 45 90
```

As you may have guessed, the "|" operator performs logical disjunction, while the "&" operator is used for logical conjunction.[15] This means that the first instruction shows us the elements of x that are either less than or equal to −2, or greater than 5. The second example presents the elements of x that are both greater than 40 and less than 100.

R also allows you to use a vector of integers to extract several elements from a vector. The numbers in the vector of indexes indicate the positions in the original vector to be extracted:

```
> x[c(4, 6)]

[1] -1 90

> x[1:3]

[1]  0 -3  4

> y <- c(1, 4)
> x[y]

[1]  0 -1
```

---

[15]There are also other operators, && and ||, to perform these operations. These alternatives evaluate expressions from left to right, examining only the first element of the vectors, while the single character versions work element-wise.

Alternatively, you can use a vector with negative indexes to indicate which elements are to be excluded from the selection:

```
> x[-1]
[1] -3  4 -1 45 90 -5
> x[-c(4, 6)]
[1]  0 -3  4 45 -5
> x[-(1:3)]
[1] -1 45 90 -5
```

Note the need for parentheses in the previous example due to the precedence of the ":" operator.

Indexes can also be formed by a vector of strings, taking advantage of the fact that R allows you to name the elements of a vector, through the function names(). Named elements are sometimes preferable because their positions are easier to memorize. For instance, imagine you have a vector of measurements of a chemical parameter obtained at five different places. You could create a named vector as follows:

```
> pH <- c(4.5, 7, 7.3, 8.2, 6.3)
> names(pH) <- c("area1", "area2", "mud", "dam", "middle")
> pH
```

```
 area1  area2    mud    dam middle
   4.5    7.0    7.3    8.2    6.3
```

In effect, if you already know the names of the positions in the vector at the time of its creation, it is easier to proceed this way:

```
> pH <- c(area1 = 4.5, area2 = 7, mud = 7.3, dam = 8.2, middle = 6.3)
```

The vector pH can now be indexed using the names shown above:

```
> pH["mud"]
```

```
mud
7.3
```

```
> pH[c("area1", "dam")]
```

```
area1    dam
  4.5    8.2
```

Finally, indexes may be empty, meaning that all elements are selected. An empty index represents the absence of a restriction on the selection process. For instance, if you want to fill in a vector with zeros, you could simply do "x[] <- 0". Please notice that this is different from doing "x <- 0". This latter case would assign to x a vector with one single element (zero), while the former (assuming that x exists before, of course!) will fill in all current elements of x with zeros. Try both!

1.2.8 Matrices and Arrays

Data elements can be stored in an object with more than one dimension. This may be useful in several situations. Arrays store data elements in several dimensions. Matrices are a special case of arrays with two single dimensions. Arrays and matrices in R are nothing more than vectors with a particular attribute that is the *dimension*. Let us see an example. Suppose you have the vector of numbers c(45,23,66,77,33,44,56,12,78,23). The following would "organize" these ten numbers as a matrix:

```
> m <- c(45, 23, 66, 77, 33, 44, 56, 12, 78, 23)
> m

[1] 45 23 66 77 33 44 56 12 78 23

> dim(m) <- c(2, 5)
> m

     [,1] [,2] [,3] [,4] [,5]
[1,]   45   66   33   56   78
[2,]   23   77   44   12   23
```

Notice how the numbers were "spread" through a matrix with two rows and five columns (the dimension we have assigned to m using the dim() function). Actually, you could simply create the matrix using the simpler instruction:

```
> m <- matrix(c(45, 23, 66, 77, 33, 44, 56, 12, 78, 23), 2,
+     5)
```

You may have noticed that the vector of numbers was spread in the matrix by columns; that is, first fill in the first column, then the second, and so on. You can fill the matrix by rows using the following parameter of the function matrix():

```
> m <- matrix(c(45, 23, 66, 77, 33, 44, 56, 12, 78, 23), 2,
+     5, byrow = T)
> m

     [,1] [,2] [,3] [,4] [,5]
[1,]   45   23   66   77   33
[2,]   44   56   12   78   23
```

As the visual display of matrices suggests, you can access the elements of a matrix through a similar indexing scheme as in vectors, but this time with two indexes (the dimensions of a matrix):

```
> m[2, 3]

[1] 12
```

You can take advantage of the sub-setting schemes described in Section 1.2.7 to extract elements of a matrix, as the following examples show:

```
> m[-2, 1]
```

```
[1] 45
```

```
> m[1, -c(3, 5)]
```

```
[1] 45 23 77
```

Moreover, if you omit any dimension, you obtain full columns or rows of the matrix:

```
> m[1, ]
```

```
[1] 45 23 66 77 33
```

```
> m[, 4]
```

```
[1] 77 78
```

Notice that, as a result of sub-setting, you may end up with a vector, as in the two above examples. If you still want the result to be a matrix, even though it is a matrix formed by a single line or column, you can use the following instead:

```
> m[1, , drop = F]
```

```
     [,1] [,2] [,3] [,4] [,5]
[1,]   45   23   66   77   33
```

```
> m[, 4, drop = F]
```

```
     [,1]
[1,]   77
[2,]   78
```

Functions cbind() and rbind() may be used to join together two or more vectors or matrices, by columns or by rows, respectively. The following examples should illustrate this:

```
> m1 <- matrix(c(45, 23, 66, 77, 33, 44, 56, 12, 78, 23), 2,
+       5)
> m1
```

```
     [,1] [,2] [,3] [,4] [,5]
[1,]   45   66   33   56   78
[2,]   23   77   44   12   23
```

```
> cbind(c(4, 76), m1[, 4])
```

```
      [,1] [,2]
[1,]     4   56
[2,]    76   12

> m2 <- matrix(rep(10, 20), 4, 5)
> m2

      [,1] [,2] [,3] [,4] [,5]
[1,]    10   10   10   10   10
[2,]    10   10   10   10   10
[3,]    10   10   10   10   10
[4,]    10   10   10   10   10

> m3 <- rbind(m1[1, ], m2[3, ])
> m3

      [,1] [,2] [,3] [,4] [,5]
[1,]    45   66   33   56   78
[2,]    10   10   10   10   10
```

You can also give names to the columns and rows of matrices, using the functions colnames() and rownames(), respectively. This facilitates memorizing the data positions.

```
> results <- matrix(c(10, 30, 40, 50, 43, 56, 21, 30), 2, 4,
+       byrow = T)
> colnames(results) <- c("1qrt", "2qrt", "3qrt", "4qrt")
> rownames(results) <- c("store1", "store2")
> results

       1qrt 2qrt 3qrt 4qrt
store1   10   30   40   50
store2   43   56   21   30

> results["store1", ]

1qrt 2qrt 3qrt 4qrt
  10   30   40   50

> results["store2", c("1qrt", "4qrt")]

1qrt 4qrt
  43   30
```

Arrays are extensions of matrices to more than two dimensions. This means that they have more than two indexes. Apart from this they are similar to matrices and can be used in the same way. Similar to the matrix() function, there is an array() function to facilitate the creation of arrays. The following is an example of its use:

```
> a <- array(1:24, dim = c(4, 3, 2))
> a

, , 1

     [,1] [,2] [,3]
[1,]   1    5    9
[2,]   2    6   10
[3,]   3    7   11
[4,]   4    8   12

, , 2

     [,1] [,2] [,3]
[1,]   13   17   21
[2,]   14   18   22
[3,]   15   19   23
[4,]   16   20   24
```

You can use the same indexing schemes to access elements of an array. Make sure you understand the following examples.

```
> a[1, 3, 2]

[1] 21

> a[1, , 2]

[1] 13 17 21

> a[4, 3, ]

[1] 12 24

> a[c(2, 3), , -2]

     [,1] [,2] [,3]
[1,]   2    6   10
[2,]   3    7   11
```

The recycling and arithmetic rules also apply to matrices and arrays, although they are tricky to understand at times. Below are a few examples:

```
> m <- matrix(c(45, 23, 66, 77, 33, 44, 56, 12, 78, 23), 2,
+       5)
> m

     [,1] [,2] [,3] [,4] [,5]
[1,]   45   66   33   56   78
[2,]   23   77   44   12   23
```

```
> m * 3

     [,1] [,2] [,3] [,4] [,5]
[1,]  135  198   99  168  234
[2,]   69  231  132   36   69

> m1 <- matrix(c(45, 23, 66, 77, 33, 44), 2, 3)
> m1

     [,1] [,2] [,3]
[1,]   45   66   33
[2,]   23   77   44

> m2 <- matrix(c(12, 65, 32, 7, 4, 78), 2, 3)
> m2

     [,1] [,2] [,3]
[1,]   12   32    4
[2,]   65    7   78

> m1 + m2

     [,1] [,2] [,3]
[1,]   57   98   37
[2,]   88   84  122
```

R also includes operators and functions for standard matrix algebra that have different rules. You may obtain more information on this by looking at Section 5 of the document "An Introduction to R" that comes with R.

1.2.9   Lists

R lists consist of an ordered collection of other objects known as their *components*. Unlike the elements of vectors, list components do not need to be of the same type, mode, or length. The components of a list are always numbered and may also have a name attached to them. Let us start by seeing a simple example of how to create a list:

```
> my.lst <- list(stud.id=34453,
+               stud.name="John",
+               stud.marks=c(14.3,12,15,19))
```

The object my.lst is formed by three components. One is a number and has the name stud.id, the second is a character string having the name stud.name, and the third is a vector of numbers with name stud.marks.

To show the contents of a list you simply type its name as any other object:

```
> my.lst
```

```
$stud.id
[1] 34453

$stud.name
[1] "John"

$stud.marks
[1] 14.3 12.0 15.0 19.0
```

You can extract individual elements of lists using the following indexing schema:

```
> my.lst[[1]]

[1] 34453

> my.lst[[3]]

[1] 14.3 12.0 15.0 19.0
```

You may have noticed that we have used double square brackets. If we had used `my.lst[1]` instead, we would obtain a different result:

```
> my.lst[1]

$stud.id
[1] 34453
```

This latter notation extracts a sub-list formed by the first component of `my.lst`. On the contrary, `my.lst[[1]]` extracts the value of the first component (in this case, a number), which is not a list anymore, as you can confirm by the following:

```
> mode(my.lst[1])

[1] "list"

> mode(my.lst[[1]])

[1] "numeric"
```

In the case of lists with named components (as the previous example), we can use an alternative way of extracting the value of a component of a list:

```
> my.lst$stud.id

[1] 34453
```

The names of the components of a list are, in effect, an attribute of the list, and can be manipulated as we did with the names of elements of vectors:

```
> names(my.lst)
```

```
[1] "stud.id"      "stud.name"    "stud.marks"
```

```
> names(my.lst) <- c("id", "name", "marks")
> my.lst
```

```
$id
[1] 34453
```

```
$name
[1] "John"
```

```
$marks
[1] 14.3 12.0 15.0 19.0
```

Lists can be extended by adding further components to them:

```
> my.lst$parents.names <- c("Ana", "Mike")
> my.lst
```

```
$id
[1] 34453
```

```
$name
[1] "John"
```

```
$marks
[1] 14.3 12.0 15.0 19.0
```

```
$parents.names
[1] "Ana"   "Mike"
```

You can check the number of components of a list using the function `length()`:

```
> length(my.lst)
```

```
[1] 4
```

You can remove components of a list as follows:

```
> my.lst <- my.lst[-5]
```

You can concatenate lists using the `c()` function:

```
> other <- list(age = 19, sex = "male")
> lst <- c(my.lst, other)
> lst
```

```
$id
[1] 34453

$name
[1] "John"

$marks
[1] 14.3 12.0 15.0 19.0

$parents.names
[1] "Ana"  "Mike"

$age
[1] 19

$sex
[1] "male"
```

Finally, you can unflatten all data in a list using the function `unlist()`. This will create a vector with as many elements as there are data objects in a list. This will coerce different data types to a common data type,[16] which means that most of the time you will end up with everything being character strings. Moreover, each element of this vector will have a name generated from the name of the list component that originated it:

```
> unlist(my.lst)
           id            name         marks1          marks2        marks3
      "34453"          "John"         "14.3"            "12"          "15"
        marks4 parents.names1 parents.names2
          "19"           "Ana"         "Mike"
```

1.2.10   Data Frames

Data frames are the data structure most indicated for storing data tables in R. They are similar to matrices in structure as they are also bi-dimensional. However, contrary to matrices, data frames may include data of a different type in each column. In this sense they are more similar to lists, and in effect, for R, data frames are a special class of lists.

We can think of each row of a data frame as an observation (or case), being described by a set of variables (the named columns of the data frame).

You can create a data frame as follows:

```
> my.dataset <- data.frame(site=c('A','B','A','A','B'),
+ season=c('Winter','Summer','Summer','Spring','Fall'),
+ pH = c(7.4,6.3,8.6,7.2,8.9))
> my.dataset
```

---

[16]Because vector elements must have the same type (*c.f.* Section 1.2.3).

```
  site season  pH
1    A Winter 7.4
2    B Summer 6.3
3    A Summer 8.6
4    A Spring 7.2
5    B   Fall 8.9
```

Elements of data frames can be accessed like a matrix:

```
> my.dataset[3, 2]
```

```
[1] Summer
Levels: Fall Spring Summer Winter
```

Note that the "season" column has been coerced into a factor because all its elements are character strings. Similarly, the "site" column is also a factor. This is the default behavior of the **data.frame()** function.[17]

You can use the indexing schemes described in Section 1.2.7 with data frames. Moreover, you can use the column names for accessing full columns of a data frame:

```
> my.dataset$pH
```

```
[1] 7.4 6.3 8.6 7.2 8.9
```

You can perform some simple querying of the data in the data frame, taking advantage of the sub-setting possibilities of R, as shown on these examples:

```
> my.dataset[my.dataset$pH > 7, ]
```

```
  site season  pH
1    A Winter 7.4
3    A Summer 8.6
4    A Spring 7.2
5    B   Fall 8.9
```

```
> my.dataset[my.dataset$site == "A", "pH"]
```

```
[1] 7.4 8.6 7.2
```

```
> my.dataset[my.dataset$season == "Summer", c("site", "pH")]
```

```
  site  pH
2    B 6.3
3    A 8.6
```

---

[17]Check the help information on the **data.frame()** function to see examples of how you can use the I() function, or the **stringsAsFactors** parameter to avoid this coercion.

You can simplify the typing of these queries using the function `attach()`, which allows you to access the columns of a data frame directly without having to use the name of the respective data frame. Let us see some examples of this:

```
> attach(my.dataset)
> my.dataset[site=='B', ]

  site season  pH
2    B Summer 6.3
5    B   Fall 8.9

> season
```

```
[1] Winter Summer Summer Spring Fall
Levels: Fall Spring Summer Winter
```

The inverse of the function `attach()` is the function `detach()` that disables these facilities:

```
> detach(my.dataset)
> season
```

```
Error: Object "season" not found
```

Whenever you are simply querying the data frame, you may find it simpler to use the function `subset()`:

```
> subset(my.dataset, pH > 8)

  site season  pH
3    A Summer 8.6
5    B   Fall 8.9

> subset(my.dataset, season == "Summer", season:pH)

  season  pH
2 Summer 6.3
3 Summer 8.6
```

Notice however that, contrary to the other examples seen above, you may not use this sub-setting strategy to change values in the data. So, for instance, if you want to sum 1 to the pH values of all summer rows, you can only do it this way:

```
> my.dataset[my.dataset$season == 'Summer','pH'] <-
+     my.dataset[my.dataset$season == 'Summer','pH'] + 1
```

You can add new columns to a data frame in the same way you did with lists:

```
> my.dataset$NO3 <- c(234.5, 256.6, 654.1, 356.7, 776.4)
> my.dataset

  site season  pH   NO3
1    A Winter 7.4 234.5
2    B Summer 7.3 256.6
3    A Summer 9.6 654.1
4    A Spring 7.2 356.7
5    B   Fall 8.9 776.4
```

The only restriction to this addition is that new columns must have the same number of rows as the existing data frame; otherwise R will complain. You can check the number of rows or columns of a data frame with these two functions:

```
> nrow(my.dataset)
```

```
[1] 5
```

```
> ncol(my.dataset)
```

```
[1] 4
```

Usually you will be reading your datasets into a data frame, either from some file or from a database. You will seldom type the data using the `data.frame()` function as above, particularly in a typical data mining scenario. In the next chapters describing our data mining case studies, you will see how to import this type of data into data frames. In any case, you may want to browse the "R Data Import/Export" manual that comes with R to check all the different possibilities that R has.

R has a simple spreadsheet-like interface that can be used to enter small data frames. You can edit an existent data frame by typing

```
> my.dataset <- edit(my.dataset)
```

or you may create a new data frame with,

```
> new.data <- edit(data.frame())
```

You can use the names vector to change the name of the columns of a data frame:

```
> names(my.dataset)
```

```
[1] "site"   "season" "pH"      "NO3"
```

```
> names(my.dataset) <- c("area", "season", "pH", "NO3")
> my.dataset
```

```
  area season  pH   NO3
1    A Winter 7.4 234.5
2    B Summer 7.3 256.6
3    A Summer 9.6 654.1
4    A Spring 7.2 356.7
5    B   Fall 8.9 776.4
```

As the names attribute is a vector, if you just want to change the name of one particular column, you can type

```
> names(my.dataset)[4] <- "PO4"
> my.dataset
```

```
  area season  pH   PO4
1    A Winter 7.4 234.5
2    B Summer 7.3 256.6
3    A Summer 9.6 654.1
4    A Spring 7.2 356.7
5    B   Fall 8.9 776.4
```

Finally, R comes with some "built-in" data sets that you can use to explore some of its potentialities. Most of the add-on packages also come with datasets. To obtain information on the available datasets, type

```
> data()
```

To use any of the available datasets, you can proceed as follows:

```
> data(USArrests)
```

This instruction "creates" a data frame called USArrests, containing the data of this problem that comes with R.

1.2.11   Creating New Functions

R allows the user to create new functions. This is a useful feature, particularly when you want to automate certain tasks that you have to repeat over and over. Instead of writing the instructions that perform this task every time you want to execute it, you encapsulate them in a new function and then simply use it whenever necessary.

R functions are objects as the structures that you have seen in the previous sections. As an object, a function can store a value. The "value" stored in a function is the set of instructions that R will execute when you call this function. Thus, to create a new function, one uses the assignment operator to store the contents of the function in an object name (the name of the function).

Let us start with a simple example. Suppose you often want to calculate the standard error of a mean associated to a set of values. By definition, the standard error of a sample mean is given by

$$\text{standard error} = \sqrt{\frac{s^2}{n}}$$

where s^2 is the sample variance and n the sample size.

Given a vector of values, we want a function to calculate the respective standard error. Let us call this function **se**. Before proceeding to create the function we should check whether there is already a function with this name in R. If that is the case, then it would be better to use another name, not to "hide" the other R function from the user.[18] To check the existence of that function, it is sufficient to type its name at the prompt:

```
> se
```

```
Error: Object "se" not found
```

The error printed by R indicates that we are safe to use that name. If a function (or any other object) existed with the name "se", R would have printed its content instead of the error.

The following is a possible way to create our function:

```
> se <- function(x) {
+     v <- var(x)
+     n <- length(x)
+     return(sqrt(v/n))
+ }
```

Thus, to create a function object, you assign to its name something with the general form

```
function(<set of parameters>) { <set of R instructions> }
```

After creating this function, you can use it as follows:

```
> se(c(45,2,3,5,76,2,4))
```

```
[1] 11.10310
```

If we need to execute several instructions to implement a function, like we did for the function **se()**, we need to have a form of telling R when the function body starts and when it ends. R uses the curly braces as the syntax elements that start and finish a group of instructions.

The value returned by any function can be "decided" using the function **return()** or, alternatively, R returns the result of the last expression that was evaluated within the function. The following function illustrates this and also the use of parameters with default values,

---

[18]You do not have to worry about overriding the definition of the R function. It will continue to exist, although your new function with the same name will be on top of the search path of R, thus "hiding" the other standard function.

```
> basic.stats <- function(x,more=F) {
+    stats <- list()
+
+    clean.x <- x[!is.na(x)]
+
+    stats$n <- length(x)
+    stats$nNAs <- stats$n-length(clean.x)
+
+    stats$mean <- mean(clean.x)
+    stats$std <- sd(clean.x)
+    stats$med <- median(clean.x)
+    if (more) {
+      stats$skew <- sum(((clean.x-stats$mean)/stats$std)^3) /
+                    length(clean.x)
+      stats$kurt <- sum(((clean.x-stats$mean)/stats$std)^4) /
+                    length(clean.x) - 3
+    }
+    unlist(stats)
+ }
```

This function has a parameter (`more`) that has a default value (`F`). This means that you can call the function with or without setting this parameter. If you call it without a value for the second parameter, the default value will be used. Below are examples of these two alternatives:

```
> basic.stats(c(45, 2, 4, 46, 43, 65, NA, 6, -213, -3, -45))

       n       nNAs      mean       std      med
11.00000   1.00000  -5.00000  79.87768  5.00000

> basic.stats(c(45, 2, 4, 46, 43, 65, NA, 6, -213, -3, -45),
+     more = T)

        n        nNAs       mean        std        med       skew       kurt
11.000000   1.000000  -5.000000  79.877684   5.000000  -1.638217   1.708149
```

The function `basic.stats()` also introduces a new instruction of R: the instruction `if()`. As the name indicates this instruction allows us to condition the execution of certain instructions to the truth value of a logical test. In the case of this function, the two instructions that calculate the kurtosis and skewness of the vector of values are only executed if the variable `more` is true; otherwise they are skipped.

Another important instruction is the `for()`. This instruction allows us to repeat a set of commands several times. Below is an example of the use of this instruction:

```
> f <- function(x) {
+    for(i in 1:10) {
+      res <- x*i
```

```
+       cat(x,'*',i,'=',res,'\n')
+    }
+ }
```

Try to call f() with some number (e.g. f(5)). The instruction for in this function says to R that the instructions "inside of it" (delimited by the curly braces) are to be executed several times. Namely, they should be executed with the variable "i" taking different values at each repetition. In this example, "i" should take the values in the set 1:10, that is, 1, 2, 3, ..., 10. This means that the two instructions inside the for are executed ten times, each time with i set to a different value. The set of values specified in front of the word **in** can be any vector, and the values need not be a sequence or numeric.

The function cat() can be used to output the contents of several objects to the screen. Namely, character strings are written as themselves (try cat('hello!')), while other objects are written as their content (try y <- 45 and then cat(y)). The string "\n" makes R change to the next line.

1.2.12 Objects, Classes, and Methods

One of the design goals of R is to facilitate the manipulation of data so that we can easily perform the data analysis tasks we have. In R, data is stored on objects. As mentioned, everything in R is an object, from simple numbers to functions or more elaborate data structures. Every R object belongs to a *class*. Classes define the abstract characteristics of the objects that belong to them. Namely, they specify the attributes or properties of these objects and also their behaviors (or methods). For instance, the matrix class has specific properties like the dimension of the matrices and it also has specific behavior for some types of operations. In effect, when we ask R the content of a matrix, R will show it with a specific format on the screen. This happens because there is a specific print method associated with all objects of the class matrix. In summary, the class of an object determines (1) the methods that are used by some general functions when applied to these objects, and also (2) the representation of the objects of that class. This representation consists of the information that is stored by the objects of this class.

R has many predefined classes of objects, together with associated methods. On top of this we can also extend this list by creating new classes of objects or new methods. These new methods can be both for these new classes or for existing classes. New classes are normally created after existing classes, usually by adding some new pieces of information to their representation.

The representation of a class consists of a set of *slots*. Each slot has a name and an associated class that determines the information that it stores. The operator "@" can be used to access the information stored in a slot of an object. This means that x@y is the value of the slot y of the object x. This obviously assumes that the class of objects to which x belongs has a slot of information named y.

Another important notion related to classes is the notion of inheritance between classes. This notion establishes relationships between the classes that allow us to indicate that a certain new class extends an existing one by adding some extra information. This extension also implies that the new class inherits all the methods of the previous class, which facilitates the creation of new classes, as we do not start from scratch. In this context, we only need to worry about implementing the methods for the operations where the new class of objects differs from the existing one that it extends.

Finally, another very important notion is that of polymorphism. This notion establishes that some functions can be applied to different classes of objects, producing the results that are adequate for the respective class. In R, this is strongly related to the notion of generic functions. Generic functions implement a certain, very general, high-level operation. For instance, as we will see, the function `plot()` can be used to obtain a graphical representation of an object. This is its general goal. However, this graphical representation may actually be different depending on the type of object. It is different to plot a set of numbers, than to plot a linear regression model, for instance. Polymorphism is the key to implementing this without disturbing the user. The user only needs to know that there is a function that provides a graphical representation of objects. R and its inner mechanisms handle the job of *dispatching* these general tasks for the class-specific functions that provide the graphical representation for each class of objects. All this method-dispatching occurs in the background without the user needing to know the "dirty" details of it. What happens, in effect, is that as R knows that `plot()` is a generic function, it will search for a plot method that is specific for the class of objects that were included in the `plot()` function call. If such a method exists, it will use it; otherwise it will resort to some default plotting method. When the user decides to create a new class of objects he needs to decide if he wants to have specific methods for his new class of objects. So if he wants to be able to plot objects of the new class, then he needs to provide a specific plot method for this new class of objects that "tells" R how to plot these new objects.

These are the basic details on classes and methods in R. The creation of new classes and respective methods is outside the scope of this book. More details can be obtained in many existing books on programming with R, such as, the excellent book *Software for Data Analysis* by Chambers (2008).

1.2.13 Managing Your Sessions

When you are using R for more complex tasks, the command line typing style of interaction becomes a bit limited. In these situations it is more practical to write all your code in a text file and then ask R to execute it. To produce such a file, you can use your favorite text editor (like Notepad, Emacs, etc.) or, in case you are using the Windows version of R, you can use the script editor available in the File menu. After creating and saving the file, you can issue the following command at R prompt to execute all commands in the file:

```
> source('mycode.R')
```

This assumes that you have a text file called "mycode.R"[19] in the current working directory of R. In Windows versions the easiest way to change this directory is through the option "Change directory" of the "File" menu. In Unix versions you may use the functions getwd() and setwd() respectively, to, check and change the current working directory.

When you are using the R prompt in an interactive fashion you may wish to save some of the objects you create for later use (such as some function you have typed in). The following example saves the objects named f and my.dataset in a file named "mysession.RData":

```
> save(f,my.dataset,file='mysession.RData')
```

Later, for instance in a new R session, you can load these objects by issuing

```
> load('mysession.RData')
```

You can also save all objects currently in R workspace,[20] by issuing

```
> save.image()
```

This command will save the workspace in a file named ".RData" in the current working directory. This file is automatically loaded when you run R again from this directory. This kind of effect can also be achieved by answering Yes when quitting R (*see* Section 1.2.1).

Further readings on R

The online manual *An Introduction to R* that comes with every distribution of R is an excellent source of information on the R language. The "Contributed" subsection of the "Documentation" section at the R Web site, includes several free books on different facets of R.

1.3   A Short Introduction to **MySQL**

This section provides a very brief introduction to MySQL. MySQL is not necessary to carry out all the case studies in this book. Still, for larger data mining projects, the use of a database management system like MySQL can be crucial.

MySQL can be downloaded at no cost from the Web site http://www.mysql.com. As R, MySQL is available for different operating systems, such as Linux and Windows. If you wish to install MySQL on your computer, you should download it from the MySQL Web site and follow its installation instructions. Alternatively, you can also access any MySQL server that is installed on another computer to which you have network access.

---

[19]The extension ".R" is not mandatory.
[20]These can be listed issuing ls(), as mentioned before.

You can use a client program to access MySQL on your local computer or over the network. There are many different MySQL client programs at the MySQL Web site. MySQL comes with a console-type client program, which works in a command-by-command fashion, like the R console. Alternatively, you have graphical client programs that you can install to use MySQL. In particular, the MySQL Query Browser is a freely available and quite a nice example of such programs that you may consider installing on your computer.

To access a MySQL server installed on your computer using the console-type client, you can issue the following command at your operating system prompt:

```
$> mysql -u myuser -p

Password: ********

mysql>
```

or, in case of a remote server, something like

```
$> mysql -h myserver.xpto.pt -u myuser -p

Password: ********

mysql>
```

We are assuming that the server has a user named "myuser" and that the server is password protected. If all this sounds strange to you, you should either talk with your system administrator about MySQL, or learn a bit more about this software using the user manual that comes with every installation, or by reading a book (e.g., DuBois, 2000).

After entering MySQL, you can either use existent database or create a new one. The latter can be done as follows in the MySQL console-type client:

```
mysql> create database contacts;

Query OK, 1 row affected (0.09 sec)
```

To use this newly created database or any other existing database, you issue

```
mysql> use contacts;

Database changed
```

A database is formed by a set of tables containing the data concerning some entities. You can create a table as follows:

```
mysql> create table people(
    -> id INT primary key,
    -> name CHAR(30),
    -> address CHAR(60));
```

```
Query OK, 1 row affected (0.09 sec)
```

Note the continuation prompt of MySQL ("->").

To populate a table with data, you can either insert each record by hand or use one of the MySQL import statements to read in data contained, for instance, in a text file.

A record can be inserted in a table as follows:

```
mysql> insert into people
    -> values(1,'John Smith','Strange Street, 34, Unknown City');

Query OK, 1 row affected (0.35 sec)
```

You can list the records in a given table using the SELECT statement, of which we provide a few examples below.

```
mysql> select * from people;

+----+------------+----------------------------------+
| id | name       | address                          |
+----+------------+----------------------------------+
|  1 | John Smith | Strange Street, 34, Unknown City |
+----+------------+----------------------------------+
1 row in set (0.04 sec)


mysql> select name, address from people;

+------------+----------------------------------+
| name       | address                          |
+------------+----------------------------------+
| John Smith | Strange Street, 34, Unknown City |
+------------+----------------------------------+
1 row in set (0.00 sec)


mysql> select name from people where id >= 1 and id < 10;

+------------+
| name       |
+------------+
| John Smith |
+------------+
1 row in set (0.00 sec)
```

After you finish working with MySQL, you can leave the console-type client by issuing the "quit" statement.

Further readings on MySQL

Further information on MySQL can be obtained from the free user's manual that comes with MySQL. This manual illustrates all aspects of MySQL, from installation to the technical specifications of the SQL language used in MySQL. The book *MySQL* by DuBois (2000), one of the active developers of MySQL, is also a good general reference on this DBMS.

Chapter 2

Predicting Algae Blooms

This case study will introduce you to some basic tasks of data mining: data pre-processing, exploratory data analysis, and predictive model construction. For this initial case study we have selected a small problem by data mining standards. Namely, we are addressing the problem of predicting the frequency occurrence of several harmful algae in water samples. If you are not familiar with the R language and you have not read the small introduction provided in Section 1.2 of Chapter 1, you may feel the need to review that section as you work through this case study.

2.1 Problem Description and Objectives

High concentrations of certain harmful algae in rivers constitute a serious ecological problem with a strong impact not only on river lifeforms, but also on water quality. Being able to monitor and perform an early forecast of algae blooms is essential to improving the quality of rivers.

With the goal of addressing this prediction problem, several water samples were collected in different European rivers at different times during a period of approximately 1 year. For each water sample, different chemical properties were measured as well as the frequency of occurrence of seven harmful algae. Some other characteristics of the water collection process were also stored, such as the season of the year, the river size, and the river speed.

One of the main motivations behind this application lies in the fact that chemical monitoring is cheap and easily automated, while the biological analysis of the samples to identify the algae that are present in the water involves microscopic examination, requires trained manpower, and is therefore both expensive and slow. As such, obtaining models that are able to accurately predict the algae frequencies based on chemical properties would facilitate the creation of cheap and automated systems for monitoring harmful algae blooms.

Another objective of this study is to provide a better understanding of the factors influencing the algae frequencies. Namely, we want to understand how these frequencies are related to certain chemical attributes of water samples as well as other characteristics of the samples (like season of the year, type of river, etc.).

2.2   Data Description

The data available for this problem was collected in the context of the ERU-DIT[1] research Network and used in the COIL 1999 international data analysis competition. It is available from several sources, such as in the UCI Machine Learning Repository of data sets.[2]

There are two main datasets for this problem. The first consists of data for 200 water samples. To be more precise, each observation in the available datasets is in effect an aggregation of several water samples collected from the same river over a period of 3 months, during the same season of the year.

Each observation contains information on 11 variables. Three of these variables are nominal and describe the season of the year when the water samples to be aggregated were collected, as well as the size and speed of the river in question. The eight remaining variables are values of different chemical parameters measured in the water samples forming the aggregation, namely:

- Maximum pH value

- Minimum value of O_2 (oxygen)

- Mean value of Cl (chloride)

- Mean value of NO_3^- (nitrates)

- Mean value of NH_4^+ (ammonium)

- Mean of PO_4^{3-} (orthophosphate)

- Mean of total PO_4 (phosphate)

- Mean of chlorophyll

Associated with each of these parameters are seven frequency numbers of different harmful algae found in the respective water samples. No information is given regarding the names of the algae that were identified.

The second dataset contains information on 140 extra observations. It uses the same basic structure but it does not include information concerning the seven harmful algae frequencies. These extra observations can be regarded as a kind of test set. The main goal of our study is to predict the frequencies of

---

[1]http://www.erudit.de/erudit/.
[2]http://archive.ics.uci.edu/ml/.

the seven algae for these 140 water samples. This means that we are facing a predictive data mining task. This is one among the diverse set of problems tackled in data mining. In this type of task, our main goal is to obtain a model that allows us to predict the value of a certain target variable given the values of a set of predictor variables. This model may also provide indications on which predictor variables have a larger impact on the target variable; that is, the model may provide a comprehensive description of the factors that influence the target variable.

2.3 Loading the Data into R

We will consider two forms of getting the data into R: (1) one by simply taking advantage of the package accompanying the book that includes data frames with the datasets ready for use; and (2) the other by going to the book Web site, downloading the text files with the data, and then loading them into R. The former is obviously much more practical. We include information on the second alternative for illustrative purposes on how to load data into R from text files.

If you want to follow the easy path, you simply load the book package,[3] and you immediately have a data frame named `algae` available for use. This data frame contains the first set of 200 observations mentioned above.

```
> library(DMwR)
> head(algae)
```

	season	size	speed	mxPH	mnO2	Cl	NO3	NH4	oPO4	PO4	Chla
1	winter	small	medium	8.00	9.8	60.800	6.238	578.000	105.000	170.000	50.0
2	spring	small	medium	8.35	8.0	57.750	1.288	370.000	428.750	558.750	1.3
3	autumn	small	medium	8.10	11.4	40.020	5.330	346.667	125.667	187.057	15.6
4	spring	small	medium	8.07	4.8	77.364	2.302	98.182	61.182	138.700	1.4
5	autumn	small	medium	8.06	9.0	55.350	10.416	233.700	58.222	97.580	10.5
6	winter	small	high	8.25	13.1	65.750	9.248	430.000	18.250	56.667	28.4

	a1	a2	a3	a4	a5	a6	a7
1	0.0	0.0	0.0	0.0	34.2	8.3	0.0
2	1.4	7.6	4.8	1.9	6.7	0.0	2.1
3	3.3	53.6	1.9	0.0	0.0	0.0	9.7
4	3.1	41.0	18.9	0.0	1.4	0.0	1.4
5	9.2	2.9	7.5	0.0	7.5	4.1	1.0
6	15.1	14.6	1.4	0.0	22.5	12.6	2.9

A data frame can be seen as a kind of matrix or table with named columns,

---

[3]Please note that you will have to install the package as it does not come with the standard installation of R. Check Section 1.2.1 (page 3) to know how to do this.

which is the ideal data structure for holding data tables in R. The `head()` function shows us the first six lines of any data frame.

Alternatively, you may use the text files available in the "Data" section of the book Web site. The "Training data" link contains the 200 water samples in a file named "Analysis.txt", while the "Test data" link points to the "Eval.txt" file that contains the 140 test samples. There is an additional link that points to a file ("Sols.txt") that contains the algae frequencies of the 140 test samples. This last file will be used to check the performance of our predictive models and will be taken as unknown information for now. The files have the values for each observation in a different line. Each line of the training and test files contains the values of the variables (according to the description given on Section 2.2) separated by spaces. Unknown values are indicated with the string "XXXXXXX".

The first thing to do is to download the three files from the book Web site and store them in some directory on your hard disk (preferably on the current working directory of your running R session, which you may check issuing the command `getwd()` at the prompt).

After downloading the data files into a local directory, we can start by loading into R the data from the "Analysis.txt" file (the training data, i.e. the data that will be used to obtain the predictive models). To read the data from the file it is sufficient to issue the following command:[4]

```
> algae <- read.table('Analysis.txt',
+           header=F,
+           dec='.',
+           col.names=c('season','size','speed','mxPH','mnO2','Cl',
+           'NO3','NH4','oPO4','PO4','Chla','a1','a2','a3','a4',
+           'a5','a6','a7'),
+           na.strings=c('XXXXXXX'))
```

The parameter `header=F` indicates that the file to be read does not include a first line with the variables names. `dec='.'` states that the numbers use the '.' character to separate decimal places. These two previous parameter settings could have been omitted as we are using their default values. `col.names` allows us to provide a vector with the names to give to the variables whose values are being read. Finally, `na.strings` serves to indicate a vector of strings that are to be interpreted as unknown values. These values are represented internally in R by the value NA, as mentioned in Section 1.2.3.

R has several other functions that can be used to read data contained in text files. You may wish to type "`?read.table`" to obtain further information on this and other related functions. Moreover, R has a manual that you may want to browse named "R Data Import/Export"; it describes the different possibilities R includes for reading data from other applications.

---

[4]We assume that the data files are in the current working directory of R. If not, use the command "setwd()" to change this, or use the "Change dir..." option in the "File" menu of Windows versions.

The result of the instruction above is a data frame. Each line of this data frame contains an observation of our dataset. For instance, we can see the first 5 observations using the instruction `algae[1:5,]`.[5] In Section 1.2.7 (page 16) we have described alternative ways of extracting particular elements of R objects like data frames.

2.4 Data Visualization and Summarization

Given the lack of further information on the problem domain, it is wise to investigate some of the statistical properties of the data, so as to get a better grasp of the problem. Even if that was not the case, it is always a good idea to start our analysis with some kind of exploratory data analysis similar to the one we will show below.

A first idea of the statistical properties of the data can be obtained through a summary of its descriptive statistics:

```
> summary(algae)

    season          size         speed          mxPH               mnO2
 autumn:40     large :45    high  :84    Min.    :5.600    Min.    : 1.500
 spring:53     medium:84    low   :33    1st Qu.:7.700    1st Qu.: 7.725
 summer:45     small :71    medium:83    Median :8.060    Median : 9.800
 winter:62                               Mean    :8.012    Mean    : 9.118
                                         3rd Qu.:8.400    3rd Qu.:10.800
                                         Max.    :9.700    Max.    :13.400
                                         NA's    :1.000    NA's    : 2.000

       Cl                  NO3                 NH4                 oPO4
 Min.    :  0.222    Min.    : 0.050    Min.    :    5.00    Min.    :  1.00
 1st Qu.: 10.981    1st Qu.: 1.296    1st Qu.:   38.33    1st Qu.: 15.70
 Median : 32.730    Median : 2.675    Median :  103.17    Median : 40.15
 Mean    : 43.636    Mean    : 3.282    Mean    :  501.30    Mean    : 73.59
 3rd Qu.: 57.824    3rd Qu.: 4.446    3rd Qu.:  226.95    3rd Qu.: 99.33
 Max.    :391.500    Max.    :45.650    Max.    :24064.00    Max.    :564.60
 NA's    : 10.000    NA's    : 2.000    NA's    :    2.00    NA's    :  2.00

      PO4                 Chla                 a1                  a2
 Min.    :  1.00    Min.    :  0.200    Min.    : 0.00    Min.    : 0.000
 1st Qu.: 41.38    1st Qu.:  2.000    1st Qu.: 1.50    1st Qu.: 0.000
 Median :103.29    Median :  5.475    Median : 6.95    Median : 3.000
 Mean    :137.88    Mean    : 13.971    Mean    :16.92    Mean    : 7.458
 3rd Qu.:213.75    3rd Qu.: 18.308    3rd Qu.:24.80    3rd Qu.:11.375
 Max.    :771.60    Max.    :110.456    Max.    :89.80    Max.    :72.600
 NA's    :  2.00    NA's    : 12.000
      a3                  a4                  a5                  a6
```

---

[5] You can get a similar result with `head(algae)`, as we have seen before.

```
Min.    : 0.000    Min.    : 0.000    Min.    : 0.000    Min.    : 0.000
1st Qu.: 0.000    1st Qu.: 0.000    1st Qu.: 0.000    1st Qu.: 0.000
Median : 1.550    Median : 0.000    Median : 1.900    Median : 0.000
Mean    : 4.309    Mean    : 1.992    Mean    : 5.064    Mean    : 5.964
3rd Qu.: 4.925    3rd Qu.: 2.400    3rd Qu.: 7.500    3rd Qu.: 6.925
Max.    :42.800    Max.    :44.600    Max.    :44.400    Max.    :77.600

        a7
Min.    : 0.000
1st Qu.: 0.000
Median : 1.000
Mean    : 2.495
3rd Qu.: 2.400
Max.    :31.600
```

This simple instruction immediately gives us a first overview of the statistical properties of the data.[6] In the case of nominal variables (which are represented by factors in R data frames), it provides frequency counts for each possible value.[7] For instance, we can observe that there are more water samples collected in winter than in the other seasons. For numeric variables, R gives us a series of statistics like their mean, median, quartiles information and extreme values. These statistics provide a first idea of the distribution of the variable values (we return to this issue later on). In the event of a variable having some unknown values, their number is also shown following the string NAs. By observing the difference between medians and means, as well as the inter-quartile range (3rd quartile minus the 1st quartile),[8] we can get an idea of the skewness of the distribution and also its spread. Still, most of the time, this information is better captured graphically. Let us see an example:

```
> hist(algae$mxPH, prob = T)
```

This instruction shows us the histogram of the variable *mxPH*. The result appears in Figure 2.1. With the parameter `prob=T` we get probabilities for each interval of values,[9] while omitting this parameter setting would give us frequency counts.

Figure 2.1 tells us that the values of variable *mxPH* apparently follow a distribution very near the normal distribution, with the values nicely clustered around the mean value. A more precise check of this hypothesis can be

---

[6] An interesting alternative with similar objectives is the function `describe()` in package Hmisc (Harrell Jr, 2009).

[7] Actually, if there are too many, only the most frequent are shown.

[8] If we order the values of a variable, the 1st quartile is the value below which there are 25% of the data points, while the 3rd quartile is the value below which there are 75% of the cases, thus implying that between these two values we have 50% of our data. The inter-quartile range is defined as the 3rd quartile minus the 1st quartile, thus being a measure of the spread of the variable around its central value (larger values indicate larger spread).

[9] The areas of the rectangles should sum to one (and not the height of the rectangles as some people might expect).

Histogram of algae$mxPH

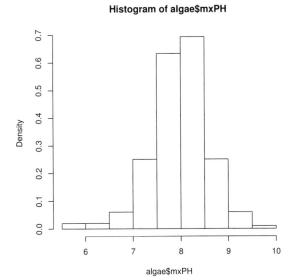

FIGURE 2.1: The histogram of variable *mxPH*.

obtained using normal Q-Q plots. The function `qq.plot()`, in the `car` (Fox, 2009) package, obtains this type of plot, the result of which is shown in Figure 2.2, together with a slightly more sophisticated version of the histogram. The graphs were obtained with the following code:

```
> library(car)
> par(mfrow~c(1,2))
> hist(algae$mxPH, prob=T, xlab='',
+       main='Histogram of maximum pH value',ylim=0:1)
> lines(density(algae$mxPH,na.rm=T))
> rug(jitter(algae$mxPH))
> qq.plot(algae$mxPH,main='Normal QQ plot of maximum pH')
> par(mfrow=c(1,1))
```

After loading the package,[10] the code starts with a call to the `par()` function that can be used to set several parameters of the R graphics system. In this case we are dividing the graphics output window into a one line per two columns area, with the goal of obtaining two graphs side by side on the same figure. We then obtain the first graph, which is again a histogram of the variable *mxPH*, except that this time we specify an empty X-axis label, we change

---

[10] A word of warning on the use of the function `library()` to load packages. This is only possible if the package is installed on your computer. Otherwise an error will be issued by R. If that is the case, you will need to install the package using any of the methods described in Section 1.2.1.

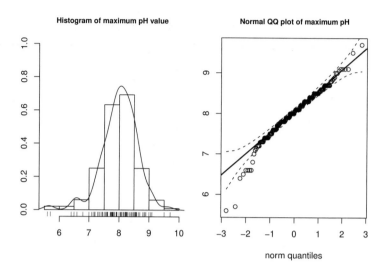

FIGURE 2.2: An "enriched" version of the histogram of variable *MxPH* (left) together with a normal Q-Q plot (right).

the title of the graph, and we provide other limits for the Y-axis. The next instruction plots a smooth version of the histogram (a kernel density estimate[11] of the distribution of the variable), while the following plots the real values of the variable near the X-axis, thus allowing easy spotting of outliers.[12] For instance, we can observe that there are two values significantly smaller than all others. This kind of data inspection is very important as it may identify possible errors in the data sample, or even help to locate values that are so awkward that they may only be errors, or at least we would be better off by disregarding them in posterior analysis. The second graph shows a Q-Q plot obtained with the `qq.plot()` function, which plots the variable values against the theoretical quantiles of a normal distribution (solid black line). The function also plots an envelope with the 95% confidence interval of the normal distribution (dashed lines). As we can observe, there are several low values of the variable that clearly break the assumptions of a normal distribution with 95% confidence.

You should also note the extensive use of function composition in the previous example, with several functions being called with the result of other

---

[11] The `na.rm=T` parameter setting is used in several functions as a way of indicating that NA values should not be considered in the function calculation. This is necessary in several functions because it is not their default behavior, and otherwise an error would be generated.

[12] Actually, this contains two function calls, the `rug()` function performs the plotting, while the `jitter()` function is used to randomly perturb slightly the original values to plot, so that we almost eliminate the possibility of two values being equal, thus avoiding ticks over each other that would "hide" some values from the visual inspection.

functions. Every time you have difficulties in understanding this type of instruction, you can always call them separately, one at a time, to fully understand what they produce.

Another example (Figure 2.3) showing this kind of data inspection can be achieved with the following instructions, this time for variable *oPO4*:

```
> boxplot(algae$oPO4, ylab = "Orthophosphate (oPO4)")
> rug(jitter(algae$oPO4), side = 2)
> abline(h = mean(algae$oPO4, na.rm = T), lty = 2)
```

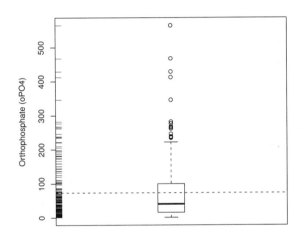

FIGURE 2.3: An "enriched" box plot for *orthophosphate*.

The first instruction draws a box plot of variable *oPO4*. Box plots provide a quick summarization of some key properties of the variable distribution. Namely, there is a box whose vertical limits are the 1st and 3rd quartiles of the variable. This box has a horizontal line inside that represents the median value of the variable. Let r be the inter-quartile range. The small horizontal dash above the box is the largest observation that is less than or equal to the 3rd quartile plus $1.5 \times r$. The small horizontal dash below the box is the smallest observation that is greater than or equal to the 1st quartile minus $1.5 \times r$. The circles below or above these small dashes represent observations that are extremely low (high) compared to all others, and are usually considered outliers. This means that box plots give us plenty of information regarding not only the central value and spread of the variable, but also eventual outliers.

The second instruction was described before (the only difference being the place where the data is plotted), while the third uses the function `abline()` to draw a horizontal line[13] at the mean value of the variable, which is obtained using the function `mean()`. By comparing this line with the line inside the box indicating the median, we can conclude that the presence of several outliers has distorted the value of the mean as a statistic of centrality (i.e., indicating the more common value of the variable).

The analysis of Figure 2.3 shows us that the variable *oPO4* has a distribution of the observed values clearly concentrated on low values, thus with a positive skew. In most of the water samples, the value of *oPO4* is low, but there are several observations with high values, and even with extremely high values.

Sometimes when we encounter outliers, we are interested in inspecting the observations that have these "strange" values. We will show two ways of doing this. First, let us do it graphically. If we plot the values of variable *NH4*, we notice a very large value. We can identify the respective water sample by:

```
> plot(algae$NH4, xlab = "")
> abline(h = mean(algae$NH4, na.rm = T), lty = 1)
> abline(h = mean(algae$NH4, na.rm = T) + sd(algae$NH4, na.rm = T),
+     lty = 2)
> abline(h = median(algae$NH4, na.rm = T), lty = 3)
> identify(algae$NH4)
```

The first instruction plots all values of the variable. The calls to the `abline()` function draw three informative lines, one with the mean value, another with the mean plus one standard deviation, and the other with the median. They are not necessary for this identification task. The last instruction is interactive and allows the user to click on the plotted dots with the left mouse button. For every clicked dot, R will write the respective row number in the `algae` data frame.[14] The user can finish the interaction by clicking the right mouse button.

If we want to inspect the respective observations in the `algae` data frame, then we better proceed in the following way:

```
> plot(algae$NH4, xlab = "")
> clicked.lines <- identify(algae$NH4)
> algae[clicked.lines, ]
```

As you may have guessed before, the function `identify()`, gives as a result the number of the lines corresponding to the clicked points in the graph and thus we may take advantage of this fact to index the `algae` data frame, thus obtaining the full information on these observations.

We can also perform this inspection without graphics, as shown below:

---

[13] The parameter `lty=2` is used to obtain a dashed line.

[14] The position where you click relatively to the point determines the side where R writes the row number. For instance, if you click on the right of the dot, the row number will be written on the right.

```
> algae[algae$NH4 > 19000, ]
```

This instruction illustrates another form of indexing a data frame, using a logical expression as a row selector (see Section 1.2.7 for more examples of this). The output of this instruction may seem a bit strange. This results from the fact that there are some observations with NA values in variable *NH4*. For these observations, R is unable to know the result of the comparison and thus the NAs. We can avoid this behavior by issuing instead the instruction `algae[!is.na(algae$NH4) & algae$NH4 > 19000,]`. The call to the function `is.na()` produces a vector of Boolean values (TRUE or FALSE). An element of this vector is TRUE when *NH4* is NA. This vector has as many elements as there are rows in the data frame `algae`. The construction `!is.na(algae$NH4)` thus returns a vector of Boolean values that are TRUE in positions corresponding to rows where *NH4* is known, because '!' is the logical negation operator. In summary, this alternative call would give us the rows of the data frame that have known values in *NH4* and are greater than 19,000.

Let us now explore a few examples of another type of data inspection. These examples use the `lattice` (Sarkar, 2010) package of R, which provides a large set of impressive graphics tools implementing the ideas behind Trellis graphics (Cleveland, 1993).

Suppose we would like to study the distribution of the values of, say, algal *a1*. We could use any of the possibilities discussed before. However, if we wanted to study how this distribution depends on other variables, new tools are required.

Conditioned plots are graphical representations that depend on a certain factor. A factor is a nominal variable with a set of finite values. For instance, we can obtain a set of box plots for the variable *a1*, for each value of the variable *size* (*see* Figure 2.4). Each of the box plots was obtained using the subset of water samples that have a certain value of the variable *size*. These graphs allow us to study how this nominal variable may influence the distribution of the values of *a1*. The code to obtain the box plots is

```
> library(lattice)
> bwplot(size ~ a1, data=algae, ylab='River Size',xlab='Algal A1')
```

The first instruction loads in the `lattice` package. The second obtains a box plot using the `lattice` version of these plots. The first argument of this instruction can be read as "plot *a1* for each value of *size*". The remaining arguments have obvious meanings.

Figure 2.4 allows us to observe that higher frequencies of algal *a1* are expected in smaller rivers, which can be valuable knowledge.

An interesting variant of this type of plot that gives us more information on the distribution of the variable being plotted, are box-percentile plots, which are available in package `Hmisc`. Let us see an example of its use with the same algal *a1* against the size of rivers:

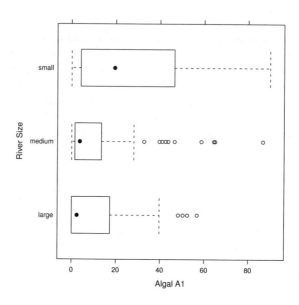

FIGURE 2.4: A conditioned box plot of Algal *a1*.

```
> library(Hmisc)
> bwplot(size ~ a1, data=algae,panel=panel.bpplot,
+        probs=seq(.01,.49,by=.01), datadensity=TRUE,
+        ylab='River Size',xlab='Algal A1')
```

The result of this call is shown in Figure 2.5. The dots are the mean value of the frequency of the algal for the different river sizes. Vertical lines represent the 1st quartile, median, and 3rd quartile, in that order. The graphs show us the actual values of the data with small dashes, and the information of the distribution of these values is provided by the quantile plots. These graphs thus provide much more information than standard box plots like the one shown in Figure 2.4. For instance, we can confirm our previous observation that smaller rivers have higher frequencies of this alga, but we can also observe that the value of the observed frequencies for these small rivers is much more widespread across the domain of frequencies than for other types of rivers.

This type of conditioned plot is not restricted to nominal variables, nor to a single factor. You can carry out the same kind of conditioning study with continuous variables as long as you previously "discretized" them. Let us see an example by observing the behavior of the frequency of algal *a3* conditioned by *season* and *mnO2*, this latter being a continuous variable. Figure 2.6 shows such a graph and the code to obtain it is the following:

```
> minO2 <- equal.count(na.omit(algae$mnO2),
+                      number=4,overlap=1/5)
```

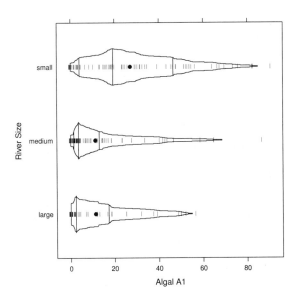

FIGURE 2.5: A conditioned box percentile plot of Algal *a1*.

```
> stripplot(season ~ a3|minO2,
+           data=algae[!is.na(algae$mnO2),])
```

The first instruction uses function `equal.count()` to create a factorized version of the continuous variable *mnO2*. The parameter `number` sets the number of desired bins, while the parameter `overlap` sets the overlap between the bins near their respective boundaries (this means that certain observations will be assigned to adjacent bins). The bins are created such that they contain an equal number of observations. You may have noticed that we did not use `algae$mnO2` directly. The reason is the presence of NA values in this variable. This would cause problems in the subsequent graphics function. We have used the function `na.omit()` that removes any NA value from a vector.[15]

The second line contains the call to the graphics function `stripplot()`. This is another graphical function of the `lattice` package. It creates a graph containing the actual values of a variable, in different strips depending on another variable (in this case the *season*). Different graphs are then drawn for each bin of the variable *mnO2*. The bins are ordered from left to right and from bottom up. This means that the bottom-left plot corresponds to lower values of *mnO2*.[16] The existence of NA values in *mnO2* also has some impact on the data to be used for drawing the graph. Instead of using the

---

[15]Later, in Section 2.5 we will see a better solution to this.
[16]You can check the actual values of the created intervals by printing the created discretized version of the variable.

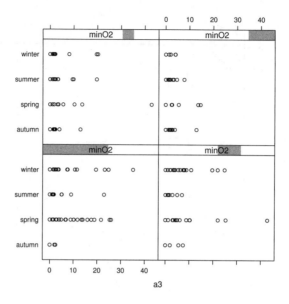

FIGURE 2.6: A conditioned strip plot of Algal *a3* using a continuous variable.

parameter `data=algae` (as for creating Figure 2.4), we had to "eliminate" the rows corresponding to samples with NA values in *mnO2*.

Further readings on data summarization and visualization

Most standard statistics books will include some sections on providing summaries of data. A simple and well-written book is *Statistics for Technology* by Chatfield (1983). This book has simple examples and is quite informal. Another good source of information is the book *Introductory Statistics with R* by Dalgaard (2002). For data visualization, the book *Visualizing Data* by Cleveland (1993) is definitely a must. This is an outstanding book that is clearly worth its value. A more formal follow-up of this work is the book *The Elements of Graphing Data* (Cleveland, 1995). A more recent and outstanding contribution is the *Handbook of Data Visualization* edited by Chen et al. (2008). Finally, more oriented toward R we have the book *R Graphics* by Murrell (2006).

2.5   Unknown Values

There are several water samples with unknown values in some of the variables. This situation, rather common in real-world problems, may preclude the use of certain techniques that are not able to handle missing values.

Whenever we are handling a dataset with missing values, we can follow several strategies. The most common are

- Remove the cases with unknowns.

- Fill in the unknown values by exploring the correlations between variables.

- Fill in the unknown values by exploring the similarity between cases.

- Use tools that are able to handle these values.

The last alternative is the most restrictive, as it limits the set of tools one can use. Still, it may be a good option whenever we are confident in the merit of the strategies used by those data mining tools to handle missing values.

In the following subsections we will show examples of how to implement these strategies in R. If you decide to try the code given in these sections, you should be aware that they are not complementary. This means that as you go into another method of dealing with missing values, you should read in again the original data to have all the unknown cases again, as each section handles them in a different way. The easiest form of doing this is to execute the following code:

```
> library(DMwR)
> data(algae)
```

2.5.1 Removing the Observations with Unknown Values

The option of removing the cases with unknown values is very easy to implement, and can also be a reasonable choice when the proportion of cases with unknowns is small with respect to the size of the available dataset.

Before eliminating all observations with at least one unknown value in some variable, it is always wise to have a look, or at least count them:

```
> algae[!complete.cases(algae),]
...
...
> nrow(algae[!complete.cases(algae),])
[1] 16
```

The function `complete.cases()` produces a vector of Boolean values with as many elements as there are rows in the `algae` data frame, where an element is TRUE if the respective row is "clean" of NA values (i.e., is a complete observation). Thus the above instruction shows the water samples with some NA values because the '!' operator performs logical negation, as was mentioned before.

In order to remove these 16 water samples from our data frame, we can simply do

```
> algae <- na.omit(algae)
```

Even if we decide not to use this drastic method of removing all cases with some unknown value, we can remove some observations because the number of unknown values is so high that they are almost useless, and even complex methods of filling in these values will be too unreliable. Note that if you have executed the previous command, you should read in the data again, as this instruction has removed all unknowns, so the next statements would not make sense! Looking at the cases with unknowns we can see that both the samples 62 and 199 have six of the eleven explanatory variables with unknown values. In such cases, it is wise to simply ignore these observations by removing them:

```
> algae <- algae[-c(62, 199), ]
```

In problems where the visual inspection of all the cases with unknowns is unfeasible due to their number, we need to be able to find the rows with a large number of NAs. The following code gives you the number of unknown values in each row of the **algae** dataset:

```
> apply(algae, 1, function(x) sum(is.na(x)))
```

The function **apply()** belongs to a set of very powerful functions of R. These functions are sometimes known as meta-functions and allow applying other functions to objects under certain conditions. In the case of the function **apply()**, we can use it to apply any function to one of the dimensions of a multidimensional object. Using the **apply()** function we are executing a function on all rows of the data frame.[17] This function, specified on the third argument of **apply()**, will be called with each row of the data frame. The function we have provided is in this case a temporary function. It is temporary because it only exists within the call of the **apply()**. Alternatively, we could have supplied the name of a "normal" function. The temporary function basically calculates the number of NAs on the object x, its argument. It takes advantage of the fact that a TRUE value in R is equivalent to the number 1, and the FALSE to the value 0, which means that when you sum a vector of Boolean values, you obtain how many TRUEs exist in the vector.

Based on this code we can create a function that gives us the rows in **algae** that have a certain number of unknowns. Such function is available in the book package and you can use it as follows:

```
> data(algae)
> manyNAs(algae, 0.2)
```

```
[1]   62 199
```

---

[17]The 1 on the second argument stands for the first dimension of the object in the first argument, i.e., the rows.

The call to `data()` is only necessary if you have previously removed the rows with lots of unknowns. The `manyNAs()` function gives you the row numbers that, in this case, have more than 20% of the columns with an NA. In the second argument you can alternatively supply the exact number of columns that you want to consider as the limit. So, an alternative to the code given before that does not require you to know the number of the rows with lots of unknowns is

```
> algae <- algae[-manyNAs(algae), ]
```

In this case we have used the default value of the second argument of `manyNAs()`, which is 0.2.

2.5.2 Filling in the Unknowns with the Most Frequent Values

An alternative to eliminating the cases with unknown values is to try to find the most probable value for each of these unknowns. Again, several strategies can be followed, with different trade-offs between the level of approximation and the computational complexity of the method.

The simplest and fastest way of filling in the unknown values is to use some statistic of centrality. These statistics reflect the most frequent value of a variable distribution; thus they are a natural choice for this strategy. Several statistics of centrality exist, like the mean, the median, the mode, etc. The choice of the most adequate value depends on the distribution of the variable. For approximately normal distributions, where all observations are nicely clustered around the mean, this statistic is the best choice. However, for skewed distributions, or for variables with outliers, the mean can be disastrous. Skewed distributions have most values clustered near one of the sides of the range of values of the variable; thus the mean is clearly not representative of the most common value. On the other hand, the presence of outliers (extreme values) may distort the calculation of the mean,[18] thus leading to similar representativeness problems. Therefore, it is not wise to use the mean without a previous inspection of the distribution of the variable using, for instance, some of the graphical tools of R (e.g., Figure 2.2). For skewed distributions or for variables with outliers, the median is a better statistic of centrality.

For instance, the sample `algae[48,]` does not have a value in the variable *mxPH*. As the distribution of this variable is nearly normal (compare with Figure 2.2) we could use its mean value to fill in the "hole". This could be done by

```
> algae[48, "mxPH"] <- mean(algae$mxPH, na.rm = T)
```

---

[18]The mean of the vector `c(1.2,1.3,0.4,0.6,3,15)` is 3.583.

where the function `mean()` gives the mean value of any vector of numbers, and `na.rm=T` disregards any NA values in this vector from the calculation.[19]

Most of the time we will be interested in filling in all unknowns of a column instead of working on a case-by-case basis as above. Let us see an example of this with the variable *Chla*. This variable is unknown on 12 water samples. Moreover, this is a situation were the mean is a very poor representative of the most frequent value of the variable. In effect, the distribution of *Chla* is skewed to lower values, and there are a few extreme values that make the mean value (13.971) highly unrepresentative of the most frequent value. Therefore, we will use the median to fill in all the unknowns in this column,

```
> algae[is.na(algae$Chla), "Chla"] <- median(algae$Chla, na.rm = T)
```

The function `centralImputation()`, available in the book package, fills in all unknowns in a dataset using a statistic of centrality. This function uses the median for numeric columns and uses the most frequent value (the mode) for nominal variables. You may use it as follows:

```
> data(algae)
> algae <- algae[-manyNAs(algae), ]
> algae <- centralImputation(algae)
```

While the presence of unknown values may impair the use of some methods, filling in their values using a strategy as above is usually considered a bad idea. This simple strategy, although extremely fast, and thus appealing for large datasets, may introduce a large bias in the data, which can influence our posterior analysis. However, unbiased methods that find the optimal value to fill in an unknown are extremely complex and may not be adequate for some large data mining problems.

2.5.3   Filling in the Unknown Values by Exploring Correlations

An alternative for getting less biased estimators of the unknown values is to explore the relationships between variables. For instance, using the correlation between the variable values, we could discover that a certain variable is highly correlated with *mxPH*, which would enable us to obtain other, more probable values for the sample number 48, which has an unknown on this variable. This could be preferable to the use the mean as we did above.

To obtain the variables correlation we can issue the command

```
> cor(algae[, 4:18], use = "complete.obs")
```

The function `cor()` produces a matrix with the correlation values between

---

[19]Without this 'detail' the result of the call would be NA because of the presence of NA values in this column.

the variables (we have avoided the first 3 variables/columns because they are nominal). The `use="complete.obs"` setting tells R to disregard observations with NA values in this calculation. Values near 1 (-1) indicate a strong positive (negative) linear correlation between the values of the two respective variables. Other R functions could then be used to approximate the functional form of this linear correlation, which in turn would allow us to estimate the values of one variable from the values of the correlated variable.

The result of this `cor()` function is not very legible but we can put it through the function `symnum()` to improve this:

```
> symnum(cor(algae[,4:18],use="complete.obs"))

      mP mO Cl NO NH o P Ch a1 a2 a3 a4 a5 a6 a7
mxPH 1
mnO2    1
Cl         1
NO3          1
NH4            ,  1
oPO4     .  .       1
PO4      .  .     *  1
Chla .              1
a1         .      . .   1
a2    .             .     1
a3                        1
a4    .             .        1
a5                              1
a6         .  .          .  1
a7                                 1
attr(,"legend")
[1] 0 ' ' 0.3 '.' 0.6 ',' 0.8 '+' 0.9 '*' 0.95 'B' 1
```

This symbolic representation of the correlation values is more legible, particularly for large correlation matrices.

In our data, the correlations are in most cases irrelevant. However, there are two exceptions: between variables *NH4* and *NO3*, and between *PO4* and *oPO4*. These two latter variables are strongly correlated (above 0.9). The correlation between *NH4* and *NO3* is less evident (0.72) and thus it is risky to take advantage of it to fill in the unknowns. Moreover, assuming that you have removed the samples 62 and 199 because they have too many unknowns, there will be no water sample with unknown values on *NH4* and *NO3*. With respect to *PO4* and *oPO4*, the discovery of this correlation[20] allows us to fill in the unknowns on these variables. In order to achieve this we need to find the form of the linear correlation between these variables. This can be done as follows:

---

[20] According to domain experts, this was expected because the value of total phosphates (*PO4*) includes the value of orthophosphate (*oPO4*).

```
> data(algae)
> algae <- algae[-manyNAs(algae), ]
> lm(PO4 ~ oPO4, data = algae)

Call:
lm(formula = PO4 ~ oPO4, data = algae)

Coefficients:
(Intercept)              oPO4
     42.897             1.293
```

The function `lm()` can be used to obtain linear models of the form $Y = \beta_0 + \beta_1 X_1 + \ldots + \beta_n X_n$. We will describe this function in detail in Section 2.6. The linear model we have obtained tells us that $PO4 = 42.897 + 1.293 \times oPO4$. With this formula we can fill in the unknown values of these variables, provided they are not both unknown.

After removing the sample 62 and 199, we are left with a single observation with an unknown value on the variable $PO4$ (sample 28); thus we could simply use the discovered relation to do the following:

```
> algae[28, "PO4"] <- 42.897 + 1.293 * algae[28, "oPO4"]
```

However, for illustration purposes, let us assume that there were several samples with unknown values on the variable $PO4$. How could we use the above linear relationship to fill all the unknowns? The best would be to create a function that would return the value of $PO4$ given the value of $oPO4$, and then apply this function to all unknown values:

```
> data(algae)
> algae <- algae[-manyNAs(algae), ]
> fillPO4 <- function(oP) {
+       if (is.na(oP))
+            return(NA)
+       else return(42.897 + 1.293 * oP)
+ }
> algae[is.na(algae$PO4), "PO4"] <- sapply(algae[is.na(algae$PO4),
+       "oPO4"], fillPO4)
```

We first create a function called `fillPO4()` with one argument, which is assumed to be the value of $oPO4$. Given a value of $oPO4$, this function returns the value of $PO4$ according to the discovered linear relation (try issuing "`fillPO4(6.5)`"). This function is then applied to all samples with unknown value on the variable $PO4$. This is done using the function `sapply()`, another example of a meta-function. This function has a vector as the first argument and a function as the second. The result is another vector with the same length, with the elements being the result of applying the function in the second argument to each element of the given vector. This means that the result of this call to `sapply()` will be a vector with the values to fill in the unknowns of the variable *PO4*. The last assignment is yet another example of the use of function composition. In effect, in a single instruction we are using the result of function `is.na()` to index the rows in the data frame, and then to the result of this data selection we are applying the function `fillPO4()` to each of its elements through function `sapply()`.

The study of the linear correlations enabled us to fill in some new unknown values. Still, there are several observations left with unknown values. We can try to explore the correlations between the variables with unknowns and the nominal variables of this problem. We can use conditioned histograms that are available through the `lattice` R package with this objective. For instance, Figure 2.7 shows an example of such a graph. This graph was produced as follows:

```
> histogram(~mxPH | season, data = algae)
```

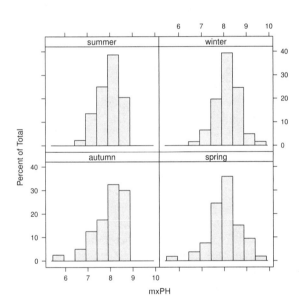

FIGURE 2.7: A histogram of variable *mxPH* conditioned by *season*.

This instruction obtains an histogram of the values of *mxPH* for the different values of *season*. Each histogram is built using only the subset of observations with a certain *season* value. You may have noticed that the ordering of the seasons in the graphs is a bit unnatural. If you wish the natural temporal ordering of the seasons, you have to change the ordering of the labels that form the factor *season* in the data frame. This could be done by

```
> algae$season <- factor(algae$season, levels = c("spring",
+     "summer", "autumn", "winter"))
```

By default, when we factor a set of nominal variable values, the levels parameter assumes the alphabetical ordering of these values. In this case we want a different ordering (the temporal order of the seasons), so we need to specify it to the factor function. Try executing this instruction and afterward obtain again the histogram to see the difference.

Notice that the histograms in Figure 2.7 are rather similar, thus leading us to conclude that the values of *mxPH* are not seriously influenced by the season of the year when the samples were collected. If we try the same using the size of the river, with `histogram(~ mxPH | size,data=algae)`, we can observe a tendency for smaller rivers to show lower values of *mxPH*. We can extend our study of these dependencies using several nominal variables. For instance,

```
> histogram(~mxPH | size * speed, data = algae)
```

shows the variation of *mxPH* for all combinations of size and speed of the rivers. It is curious to note that there is no information regarding small rivers with low speed.[21] The single sample that has these properties is exactly sample 48, the one for which we do not know the value of *mxPH*!

Another alternative to obtain similar information but now with the concrete values of the variable is

```
> stripplot(size ~ mxPH | speed, data = algae, jitter = T)
```

The result of this instruction is shown in Figure 2.8. The `jitter=T` parameter setting is used to perform a small random permutation of the values in the Y-direction to avoid plotting observations with the same values over each other, thus losing some information on the concentration of observations with some particular value.

This type of analysis could be carried out for the other variables with unknown values. Still, this is a tedious process because there are too many combinations to analyze. Nevertheless, this is a method that can be applied in small datasets with few nominal variables.

2.5.4   Filling in the Unknown Values by Exploring Similarities between Cases

Instead of exploring the correlation between the columns (variables) of a dataset, we can try to use the similarities between the rows (observations) to fill in the unknown values. We will illustrate this method to fill in all unknowns with the exception of the two samples with too many NAs. Let us read in again the data to override the code of the previous sections (assuming you have tried it).

---

[21] Actually, if you have executed the instruction given before to fill in the value of *mxPH* with the mean value of this variable, this is not true anymore!

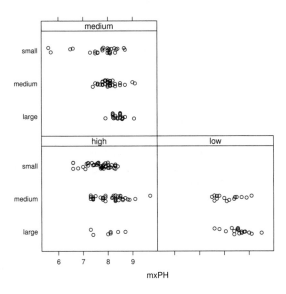

FIGURE 2.8: The values of variable *mxPH* by river size and speed.

```
> data(algae)
> algae <- algae[-manyNAs(algae), ]
```

The approach described in this section assumes that if two water samples are similar, and one of them has an unknown value in some variable, there is a high probability that this value is similar to the value of the other sample. In order to use this intuitively appealing method, we need to define the notion of similarity. This notion is usually defined using a metric over the multivariate space of the variables used to describe the observations. Many metrics exist in the literature, but a common choice is the Euclidean distance. This distance can be informally defined as the square root of the sum of the squared differences between the values of any two cases, that is,

$$d(\mathbf{x}, \mathbf{y}) = \sqrt{\sum_{i=1}^{p}(\mathbf{x}_i - \mathbf{y}_i)^2} \qquad (2.1)$$

The method we describe below will use this metric to find the ten most similar cases of any water sample with some unknown value in a variable, and then use their values to fill in the unknown. We will consider two ways of using their values. The first simply calculates the median of the values of the ten nearest neighbors to fill in the gaps. In case of unknown nominal variables (which do not occur in our `algae` dataset), we would use the most frequent value (the mode) among the neighbors. The second method uses a weighted average of the values of the neighbors. The weights decrease as the distance to the case of the neighbors increases. We use a Gaussian kernel function to obtain the weights from the distances. If one of the neighbors is at distance d from the case to fill in, its value will enter the weighted average with a weight given by

$$w(d) = e^{-d} \tag{2.2}$$

This idea is implemented in function `knnImputation()` available in the book package. The function uses a variant of the Euclidean distance to find the k nearest neighbors of any case. This variant allows the application of the function to datasets with both nominal and continuous variables. The used distance function is the following:

$$d(\mathbf{x}, \mathbf{y}) = \sqrt{\sum_{i=1}^{p} \delta_i(\mathbf{x}_i, \mathbf{y}_i)} \tag{2.3}$$

where $\delta_i()$ determines the distance between two values on variable i and is given by

$$\delta_i(v_1, v_2) = \begin{cases} 1 & \text{if } i \text{ is nominal and } v_1 \neq v_2 \\ 0 & \text{if } i \text{ is nominal and } v_1 = v_2 \\ (v_1 - v_2)^2 & \text{if } i \text{ is numeric} \end{cases} \tag{2.4}$$

These distances are calculated after normalizing the numeric values, that is,

$$\mathbf{y}_i = \frac{\mathbf{x}_i - \bar{\mathbf{x}}}{\sigma_{\mathbf{x}}} \tag{2.5}$$

Let us now see how to use the `knnImputation()` function:

```
> algae <- knnImputation(algae, k = 10)
```

In case you prefer to use the strategy of using the median values for filling in the unknowns, you could use the call

```
> algae <- knnImputation(algae, k = 10, meth = "median")
```

In summary, after these simple instructions we have the data frame free of NA values, and we are better prepared to take full advantage of several R functions.

In terms of deciding which of the methods for filling in unknowns that were described in the previous sections should be used, the answer is domain dependent most of the time. The method of exploring the similarities between cases seems more rational, although it suffers from some problems. These include the possible existence of irrelevant variables that may distort the notion of similarity, or even excessive computational complexity for extremely large datasets. Still, for these large problems we can always use random samples to calculate the similarities.

Further readings on handling unknown values

The book *Data Preparation for Data Mining* by Pyle (1999) is an extensive source of information on all issues of preparing data for data mining, and includes handling missing values. The book *Predictive Data Mining* by Weiss and Indurkhya (1999) is another good source of information on data preparation in general, and unknown values in particular.
Hong (1997) and Wilson and Martinez (1997) are good references on distance measures involving variables with different types. Further references can also be found in Torgo (1999a).

2.6   Obtaining Prediction Models

The main goal of this case study is to obtain predictions for the frequency values of the seven algae in a set of 140 water samples. Given that these frequencies are numbers, we are facing a regression task.[22] In simple words, this task consists of trying to obtain a model relating a numerical variable to a set of other explanatory variables. This model can be used either to predict the value of the target variable for future observations of the explanatory variables, or to provide a better understanding of the interactions among the variables in our problem.

In this section we will initially explore two different predictive models that could be applied to the algae domain: multiple linear regression and regression trees. Our choice was mainly guided by illustrative purposes in the context of this book, and not as a consequence of some formal model selection step. Still, these models are two good alternatives for regression problems as they are quite different in terms of their assumptions regarding the "shape" of the regression function being approximated and they are easy to interpret and fast to run on any computer. This does not mean that in a real data mining scenario we should not try other alternatives and then use some form of model selection (*see* Section 2.7) to select one or more of them for the final predictions on our 140 test samples.

The models we are going to try handle missing values in a different way. While the implementation of linear regression available in R is not able to use datasets with unknown values, the implementation of regression trees handles these values naturally. As such, we will follow a different path concerning the preparation of the data before model construction. For linear regression we will use one of the techniques described in Section 2.5 for pre-processing the

---

[22]Actually, as we want to predict seven values for each water sample, we can handle this problem as seven different regression problems.

data so that we can use these models. Regarding regression trees we will use the original 200 water samples.[23]

In the analysis we are going to carry out, we will assume that we do not know the true values of the target variables for the 140 test samples. As we have mentioned before, the book Web page also includes a file with these solutions. Still, they are given just for you to get a final opinion on the value of the models we are going to obtain.

2.6.1 Multiple Linear Regression

Multiple linear regression is among the most used statistical data analysis techniques. These models obtain an additive function relating a target variable to a set of predictor variables. This additive function is a sum of terms of the form $\beta_i \times X_i$, where X_i is a predictor variable and β_i is a number.

As mentioned before, there is no predefined way of handling missing values for this type of modeling technique. As such, we will use the data resulting from applying the method of exploring the similarities among the training cases to fill in the unknowns (*see* Section 2.5.4). Nevertheless, before we apply this method, we will remove water samples number 62 and 199 because, as mentioned before, they have six of the eleven predictor variables missing. The following code obtains a data frame without missing values:

```
> data(algae)
> algae <- algae[-manyNAs(algae), ]
> clean.algae <- knnImputation(algae, k = 10)
```

After executing this code we have a data frame, `clean.algae`, that has no missing variable values.

Let us start by learning how to obtain a linear regression model for predicting the frequency of one of the algae.

```
> lm.a1 <- lm(a1 ~ ., data = clean.algae[, 1:12])
```

The function `lm()` obtains a linear regression model. The first argument of this function[24] indicates the functional form of the model. In this example, it states that we want a model that predicts the variable *a1* using all other variables present in the data, which is the meaning of the dot character. For instance, if we wanted a model to predict *a1* as a function of the variables *mxPH* and *NH4*, we should have indicated the model as "`a1 ~ mxPH + NH4`". There are other variants of this model language, called formulas in R, that we will introduce as necessary. The `data` parameter sets the data sample to be used to obtain the model.[25]

The result of the function is an object that contains the linear model

---

[23] Actually, we will remove two of them because they have too many missing values.

[24] Actually, of most functions used to obtain models in R.

[25] We have indicated the 11 explanatory variables plus the column respecting algal *a1*.

information. We can obtain more details on the linear model with the following instruction:

```
> summary(lm.a1)

Call:
lm(formula = a1 ~ ., data = clean.algae[, 1:12])

Residuals:
    Min      1Q   Median      3Q     Max
-37.679 -11.893  -2.567   7.410  62.190

Coefficients:
              Estimate Std. Error t value Pr(>|t|)
(Intercept)  42.942055  24.010879   1.788  0.07537 .
seasonspring  3.726978   4.137741   0.901  0.36892
seasonsummer  0.747597   4.020711   0.186  0.85270
seasonwinter  3.692955   3.865391   0.955  0.34065
sizemedium    3.263728   3.802051   0.858  0.39179
sizesmall     9.682140   4.179971   2.316  0.02166 *
speedlow      3.922084   4.706315   0.833  0.40573
speedmedium   0.246764   3.241874   0.076  0.93941
mxPH         -3.589118   2.703528  -1.328  0.18598
mnO2          1.052636   0.705018   1.493  0.13715
Cl           -0.040172   0.033661  -1.193  0.23426
NO3          -1.511235   0.551339  -2.741  0.00674 **
NH4           0.001634   0.001003   1.628  0.10516
oPO4         -0.005435   0.039884  -0.136  0.89177
PO4          -0.052241   0.030755  -1.699  0.09109 .
Chla         -0.088022   0.079998  -1.100  0.27265
---
Signif. codes:  0 '***' 0.001 '**' 0.01 '*' 0.05 '.' 0.1 ' ' 1

Residual standard error: 17.65 on 182 degrees of freedom
Multiple R-squared: 0.3731,        Adjusted R-squared: 0.3215
F-statistic: 7.223 on 15 and 182 DF,  p-value: 2.444e-12
```

Before we analyze the information provided by the function `summary()` when applied to linear models, let us say something about how R handled the three nominal variables. When using them as shown above, R will create a set of auxiliary variables.[26] Namely, for each factor variable with k levels, R will create $k-1$ auxiliary variables. These variables have the values 0 or 1. A value of 1 means that the associated value of the factor is "present", and that will also mean that the other auxiliary variables will have the value 0. If all $k-1$ variables are 0, then it means that the factor variable has the remaining kth value. Looking at the summary presented above, we can see that R has created three auxiliary variables for the factor *season* (`seasonspring`, `seasonsummer`,

---

[26] Often called *dummy* variables.

and `seasonwinter`). This means that if we have a water sample with the value "autumn" in the variable *season*, all three auxiliary variables will be set to zero.

The application of the function `summary()` to a linear model gives some diagnostic information concerning the obtained model. First of all, we have information concerning the residuals (i.e., the errors) of the fit of the linear model to the used data. These residuals should have a mean zero and should have a normal distribution (and obviously be as small as possible!).

For each coefficient (variable) of the multiple regression equation, R will show its value and also its standard error (an estimate of the variability of these coefficients). In order to check the importance of each coefficient, we can test the hypothesis that each of them is null, that is, $H0 : \beta_i = 0$. To test this hypothesis, the *t*-test is normally used. R calculates a *t* value, which is defined as the ratio between the coefficient value and its standard error, that is, $\frac{\beta_i}{s_{\beta_i}}$. R will show us a column (`Pr(>|t|)`) associated with each coefficient with the level at which the hypothesis that the coefficient is null is rejected. Thus a value of 0.0001 has the meaning that we are 99.99% confident that the coefficient is not null. R marks each test with a symbol corresponding to a set of common confidence levels used for these tests. In summary, only for the coefficients that have some symbol in front of them can we reject the hypothesis that they may be null with at least 90% confidence.

Another piece of relevant diagnostics information outputted by R are the R^2 coefficients (multiple and adjusted). These indicate the degree of fit of the model to the data, that is, the proportion of variance in the data that is explained by the model. Values near 1 are better (almost 100% explained variance) — while the smaller the values, the larger the lack of fit. The adjusted coefficient is more demanding as it takes into account the number of parameters of the regression model.

Finally, we can also test the null hypothesis that there is no dependence of the target variable on any of the explanatory variables, that is, $H0 : \beta_1 = \beta_2 = \ldots = \beta_m = 0$. The *F*-statistic can be used for this purpose by comparing it to a critical value. R provides the confidence level at which we are sure to reject this null hypothesis. Thus a *p*-level of 0.0001 means that we are 99.99% confident that the null hypothesis is not true. Usually, if the model fails this test (e.g., with a *p* value that is considered too high, for example, higher than 0.1), it makes no sense to look at the *t*-tests on the individual coefficients.

Some diagnostics may also be checked by plotting a linear model. In effect, we can issue a command like `plot(lm.a1)` to obtain a series of successive plots that help in understanding the performance of the model. One of the graphs simply plots each fitted target variable value against the respective residual (error) of the model. Larger errors are usually marked by adding the corresponding row number to the dot in the graph, so that you can inspect the observations if you wish. Another graph shown by R is a normal Q-Q plot of the errors that helps you check if they follow a normal distribution[27] as they should.

The proportion of variance explained by this model is not very impressive (around 32.0%). Still, we can reject the hypothesis that the target variable does not depend on the predictors (the p value of the F test is very small). Looking at the significance of some of the coefficients, we may question the inclusion of some of them in the model. There are several methods for simplifying regression models. In this section we will explore a method usually known as *backward elimination*.

We will start our study of simplifying the linear model using the `anova()` function. When applied to a single linear model, this function will give us a sequential analysis of variance of the model fit. That is, the reductions in the residual sum of squares (the total error of the model) as each term of the formula is added in turn. The result of this analysis for the model obtained above is shown below.

```
> anova(lm.a1)
```

```
Analysis of Variance Table
```

```
Response: a1
            Df Sum Sq Mean Sq F value    Pr(>F)
season       3     85   28.2   0.0905 0.9651944
size         2  11401 5700.7  18.3088 5.69e-08 ***
speed        2   3934 1967.2   6.3179 0.0022244 **
mxPH         1   1329 1328.8   4.2677 0.0402613 *
mnO2         1   2287 2286.8   7.3444 0.0073705 **
Cl           1   4304 4304.3  13.8239 0.0002671 ***
NO3          1   3418 3418.5  10.9789 0.0011118 **
NH4          1    404  403.6   1.2963 0.2563847
oPO4         1   4788 4788.0  15.3774 0.0001246 ***
PO4          1   1406 1405.6   4.5142 0.0349635 *
Chla         1    377  377.0   1.2107 0.2726544
Residuals  182  56668  311.4
---
Signif. codes:  0 '***' 0.001 '**' 0.01 '*' 0.05 '.' 0.1 ' ' 1
```

These results indicate that the variable *season* is the variable that least contributes to the reduction of the fitting error of the model. Let us remove it from the model:

```
> lm2.a1 <- update(lm.a1, . ~ . - season)
```

The `update()` function can be used to perform small changes to an existing linear model. In this case we use it to obtain a new model by removing the variable *season* from the `lm.a1` model. The summary information for this new model is given below:

---

[27] Ideally, all errors would be in a straight line in this graph.

```
> summary(lm2.a1)

Call:
lm(formula = a1 ~ size + speed + mxPH + mnO2 + Cl + NO3 + NH4 +
    oPO4 + PO4 + Chla, data = clean.algae[, 1:12])

Residuals:
    Min      1Q  Median      3Q     Max
-36.460 -11.953  -3.044   7.444  63.730

Coefficients:
               Estimate Std. Error t value Pr(>|t|)
(Intercept) 44.9532874 23.2378377   1.934  0.05458 .
sizemedium   3.3092102  3.7825221   0.875  0.38278
sizesmall   10.2730961  4.1223163   2.492  0.01358 *
speedlow     3.0546270  4.6108069   0.662  0.50848
speedmedium -0.2976867  3.1818585  -0.094  0.92556
mxPH        -3.2684281  2.6576592  -1.230  0.22033
mnO2         0.8011759  0.6589644   1.216  0.22561
Cl          -0.0381881  0.0333791  -1.144  0.25407
NO3         -1.5334300  0.5476550  -2.800  0.00565 **
NH4          0.0015777  0.0009951   1.586  0.11456
oPO4        -0.0062392  0.0395086  -0.158  0.87469
PO4         -0.0509543  0.0305189  -1.670  0.09669 .
Chla        -0.0841371  0.0794459  -1.059  0.29096
---
Signif. codes:  0 '***' 0.001 '**' 0.01 '*' 0.05 '.' 0.1 ' ' 1

Residual standard error: 17.57 on 185 degrees of freedom
Multiple R-squared: 0.3682,        Adjusted R-squared: 0.3272
F-statistic: 8.984 on 12 and 185 DF,  p-value: 1.762e-13
```

The fit has improved a bit (32.8%) but it is still not too impressive. We can carry out a more formal comparison between the two models by using again the anova() function, but this time with both models as arguments:

```
> anova(lm.a1,lm2.a1)

Analysis of Variance Table

Model 1: a1 ~ season + size + speed + mxPH + mnO2 + Cl + NO3 + NH4 +
    oPO4 + PO4 + Chla
Model 2: a1 ~ size + speed + mxPH + mnO2 + Cl + NO3 + NH4 + oPO4 +
    PO4 + Chla
  Res.Df   RSS Df Sum of Sq      F Pr(>F)
1    182 56668
2    185 57116 -3      -448 0.4792 0.6971
```

This function performs an analysis of variance of the two models using an F-test to assess the significance of the differences. In this case, although the sum of the squared errors has decreased (-448), the comparison shows that the differences are not significant (a value of 0.6971 tells us that with only around 30% confidence we can say they are different). Still, we should recall that this new model is simpler. In order to check if we can remove more coefficients, we would again use the anova() function, applied to the lm2.a1 model. This process would continue until we have no candidate coefficients for removal. However, to simplify our backward elimination process, R has a function that performs all process for us.

The following code creates a linear model that results from applying the backward elimination method to the initial model we have obtained (lm.a1):[28]

```
> final.lm <- step(lm.a1)

Start:  AIC= 1151.85
  a1 ~ season + size + speed + mxPH + mnO2 + Cl + NO3 + NH4 + oPO4 +
      PO4 + Chla
```

	Df	Sum of Sq	RSS	AIC
- season	3	425	57043	1147
- speed	2	270	56887	1149
- oPO4	1	5	56623	1150
- Chla	1	401	57018	1151
- Cl	1	498	57115	1152
- mxPH	1	542	57159	1152
<none>			56617	1152
- mnO2	1	650	57267	1152
- NH4	1	799	57417	1153
- PO4	1	899	57516	1153
- size	2	1871	58488	1154
- NO3	1	2286	58903	1158

```
Step:  AIC= 1147.33
  a1 ~ size + speed + mxPH + mnO2 + Cl + NO3 + NH4 + oPO4 + PO4 +
      Chla
```

	Df	Sum of Sq	RSS	AIC
- speed	2	213	57256	1144
- oPO4	1	8	57050	1145
- Chla	1	378	57421	1147
- mnO2	1	427	57470	1147
- mxPH	1	457	57500	1147
- Cl	1	464	57506	1147
<none>			57043	1147
- NH4	1	751	57794	1148
- PO4	1	859	57902	1148
- size	2	2184	59227	1151
- NO3	1	2353	59396	1153

---

[28]We have omitted some of the output of the step() function for space reasons.

```
...
...

Step:  AIC= 1140.09
  a1 ~ size + mxPH + Cl + NO3 + PO4

          Df Sum of Sq   RSS   AIC
<none>                 58432  1140
- mxPH   1        801  59233  1141
- Cl     1        906  59338  1141
- NO3    1       1974  60405  1145
- size   2       2652  61084  1145
- PO4    1       8514  66946  1165
```

The function `step()` uses the Akaike Information Criterion to perform model search. The search uses backward elimination by default, but with the parameter `direction` you may use other algorithms (check the help of this function for further details).

We can obtain the information on the final model by

```
> summary(final.lm)
```

```
Call:
lm(formula = a1 ~ size + mxPH + Cl + NO3 + PO4, data = clean.algae[,
    1:12])

Residuals:
    Min      1Q  Median      3Q     Max
-28.874 -12.732  -3.741   8.424  62.926

Coefficients:
            Estimate Std. Error t value Pr(>|t|)
(Intercept) 57.28555   20.96132   2.733  0.00687 **
sizemedium   2.80050    3.40190   0.823  0.41141
sizesmall   10.40636    3.82243   2.722  0.00708 **
mxPH        -3.97076    2.48204  -1.600  0.11130
Cl          -0.05227    0.03165  -1.651  0.10028
NO3         -0.89529    0.35148  -2.547  0.01165 *
PO4         -0.05911    0.01117  -5.291 3.32e-07 ***
---
Signif. codes:  0 '***' 0.001 '**' 0.01 '*' 0.05 '.' 0.1 ' ' 1

Residual standard error: 17.5 on 191 degrees of freedom
Multiple R-squared: 0.3527,      Adjusted R-squared: 0.3324
F-statistic: 17.35 on 6 and 191 DF,  p-value: 5.554e-16
```

The proportion of variance explained by this model is still not very interesting. This kind of proportion is usually considered a sign that the linearity assumptions of this model are inadequate for the domain.

Further readings on multiple linear regression models

Linear regression is one of the most used statistics techniques. As such, most statistics books will include a chapter on this subject. Still, specialized books should be used for deeper analysis. Two extensive books are the ones by Drapper and Smith (1981) and Myers (1990). These books should cover most of the topics you will ever want to know about linear regression.

2.6.2   Regression Trees

Let us now look at a different kind of regression model available in R. Namely, we will learn how to obtain a regression tree (e.g., Breiman et al., 1984) to predict the value of the frequencies of algal *a1*. As these models handle datasets with missing values, we only need to remove samples 62 and 199 for the reasons mentioned before.

The necessary instructions to obtain a regression tree are presented below:

```
> library(rpart)
> data(algae)
> algae <- algae[-manyNAs(algae), ]
> rt.a1 <- rpart(a1 ~ ., data = algae[, 1:12])
```

The first instruction loads the **rpart** (Therneau and Atkinson, 2010) package that implements regression trees in R.[29] The last instruction obtains the tree. Note that this function uses the same schema as the `lm()` function to describe the functional form of the model. The second argument of `rpart()` indicates which data to use to obtain the tree.

The content of the object `rt.a1` object is the following:

```
> rt.a1

n= 198

node), split, n, deviance, yval
      * denotes terminal node

  1) root 198 90401.290 16.996460
    2) PO4>=43.818 147 31279.120   8.979592
      4) Cl>=7.8065 140 21622.830   7.492857
        8) oPO4>=51.118 84   3441.149   3.846429 *
        9) oPO4< 51.118 56 15389.430 12.962500
         18) mnO2>=10.05 24   1248.673   6.716667 *
         19) mnO2< 10.05 32 12502.320 17.646870
           38) NO3>=3.1875 9    257.080   7.866667 *
           39) NO3< 3.1875 23 11047.500 21.473910
             78) mnO2< 8 13   2919.549 13.807690 *
             79) mnO2>=8 10   6370.704 31.440000 *
```

---

[29] Actually, there are other packages implementing this type of model, but we will use only the package **rpart** in our illustration.

```
    5) Cl< 7.8065 7   3157.769 38.714290 *
  3) PO4< 43.818 51 22442.760 40.103920
    6) mxPH< 7.87 28 11452.770 33.450000
     12) mxPH>=7.045 18  5146.169 26.394440 *
     13) mxPH< 7.045 10  3797.645 46.150000 *
    7) mxPH>=7.87 23  8241.110 48.204350
     14) PO4>=15.177 12  3047.517 38.183330 *
     15) PO4< 15.177 11  2673.945 59.136360 *
```

A regression tree is a hierarchy of logical tests on some of the explanatory variables. Tree-based models automatically select the more relevant variables; thus, not all variables need to appear in the tree. A tree is read from the *root node* that is marked by R with the number 1. R provides some information of the data in this node. Namely, we can observe that we have 198 samples (the overall training data used to obtain the tree) at this node, that these 198 samples have an average value for the frequency of algal *a1* of 16.99, and that the deviance[30] from this average is 90401.29. Each node of a tree has two branches. These are related to the outcome of a test on one of the predictor variables. For instance, from the root node we have a branch (tagged by R with "2)") for the cases where the test "$PO4 \geq 43.818$" is true (147 samples); and also a branch for the 51 remaining cases not satisfying this test (marked by R with "3)"). From node 2 we have two other branches leading to nodes 4 and 5, depending on the outcome of a test on *Cl*. This testing goes on until a *leaf node* is reached. These nodes are marked with asterisks by R. At these leaves we have the predictions of the tree. This means that if we want to use a tree to obtain a prediction for a particular water sample, we only need to follow a branch from the root node until a leaf, according to the outcome of the tests for this sample. The average target variable value found at the leaf we have reached is the prediction of the tree.

We can also obtain a graphical representation of the tree. This can be done by successively applying the functions `plot()` and `text()` to the tree. These functions have several parameters to control the visualization of the tree. To facilitate obtaining such graphs with nice setups, we have included in the book package the function `prettyTree()`. Applying it to the obtained tree, we obtain the result shown in Figure 2.9.

```
> prettyTree(rt.a1)
```

The `summary()` function can also be applied to tree objects. This will produce a lot of information concerning the tests on the tree, the alternative tests that could be considered, and also the surrogate splits. These last splits are part of the strategy used in R regression trees to handle unknown values.

Trees are usually obtained in two steps. Initially, a large tree is grown, and then this tree is pruned by deleting bottom nodes through a process of statistical estimation. This process has the goal of avoiding overfitting. This has

---

[30]The sum of squared differences from the average.

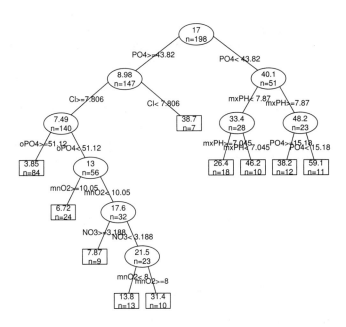

FIGURE 2.9: A regression tree for predicting algal *a1*.

to do with the fact that an overly large tree will fit the training data almost perfectly, but will be capturing spurious relationships of the given dataset (overfitting it), and thus will perform badly when faced with a new data sample for which predictions are required. The overfitting problem occurs in many modeling techniques, particularly when the assumptions regarding the function to approximate are more relaxed. These models, although having a wider application range (due to these relaxed criteria), suffer from this over-fitting problem, thus requiring a posterior, statistically based estimation step to preclude this effect.

The function `rpart()` that we have used to obtain our tree only grows the tree, stopping when certain criteria are met. Namely, the tree stops growing whenever (1) the decrease in the deviance goes below a certain threshold; when (2) the number of samples in the node is less than another threshold; or when (3) the tree depth exceeds another value. These thresholds are controlled by the parameters `cp`, `minsplit`, and `maxdepth`, respectively. Their default values are 0.01, 20, and 30, respectively. If we want to avoid the overfitting problem we should always check the validity of these default criteria. This can be carried out through a process of post-pruning the obtained tree.

The `rpart` package implements a pruning method called *cost complexity* pruning (Breiman et al., 1984). This method uses the values of the parameter `cp` that R calculates for each node of the tree. The pruning method tries to estimate the value of `cp` that ensures the best compromise between predictive accuracy and tree size. Given a tree obtained with the `rpart()` function, R can produce a set of sub-trees of this tree and estimate their predictive performance. This information can be obtained using the function `printcp()`:[31]

```
> printcp(rt.a1)

Regression tree:
rpart(formula = a1 ~ ., data = algae[, 1:12])

Variables actually used in tree construction:
[1] Cl    mnO2 mxPH NO3  oPO4 PO4

Root node error: 90401/198 = 456.57

n= 198
```

	CP	nsplit	rel error	xerror	xstd
1	0.405740	0	1.00000	1.00932	0.12986
2	0.071885	1	0.59426	0.73358	0.11884
3	0.030887	2	0.52237	0.71855	0.11518
4	0.030408	3	0.49149	0.70161	0.11585
5	0.027872	4	0.46108	0.70635	0.11403
6	0.027754	5	0.43321	0.69618	0.11438

---

[31] You can obtain similar information in graphical form using `plotcp(rt.a1)`.

```
7 0.018124      6    0.40545 0.69270 0.11389
8 0.016344      7    0.38733 0.67733 0.10892
9 0.010000      9    0.35464 0.70241 0.11523
```

The tree produced by the `rpart()` function is the last tree of this list (tree 9). This tree has a `cp` value of 0.01 (the default value of this parameter), includes nine tests and has a relative error (compared to the root node) of 0.354. However, R estimates, using an internal process of ten-fold cross-validation, that this tree will have an average relative error[32] of 0.70241 ± 0.11523. Using the information provided by these more reliable estimates of performance, which avoid the overfitting problem, we can observe that we would theoretically be better off with the tree number 8, which has a lower estimated relative error (0.67733). An alternative selection rule is to choose the best tree according to the 1-SE rule. This consists of looking at the cross-validation error estimates ("xerror" columns) and their standard deviations ("xstd" column). In this case the 1-SE tree is the smallest tree with error less than $0.67733 + 0.10892 = 0.78625$, which in this case is the tree number 2 with 1 test and an estimated error of 0.73358. If we prefer this tree to the one suggested by R, we can obtain it using the respective `cp` value:[33]

```
> rt2.a1 <- prune(rt.a1, cp = 0.08)
> rt2.a1

n= 198

node), split, n, deviance, yval
      * denotes terminal node

1) root 198 90401.29 16.996460
  2) PO4>=43.818 147 31279.12  8.979592 *
  3) PO4< 43.818 51 22442.76 40.103920 *
```

In the book package we provide the function `rpartXse()` that automates this process and takes as argument the `se` value, defaulting to 1:

```
> (rt.a1 <- rpartXse(a1 ~ ., data = algae[, 1:12]))

n= 198

node), split, n, deviance, yval
      * denotes terminal node

1) root 198 90401.29 16.996460
  2) PO4>=43.818 147 31279.12  8.979592 *
  3) PO4< 43.818 51 22442.76 40.103920 *
```

---

[32] It is important to note that you may have obtained different numbers on the columns 'xerror' and 'xstd'. The cross-validation estimates are obtained using a random sampling process, meaning that your samples will probably be different and thus the results will also differ.

[33] Actually, any value that is between its `cp` value and the one of the tree above it.

R also allows a kind of interactive pruning of a tree through the function
snip.rpart(). This function can be used to generate a pruned tree in two
ways. The first consists of indicating the number of the nodes (you can obtain
these numbers by printing a tree object) at which you want to prune the tree:

```
> first.tree <- rpart(a1 ~ ., data = algae[, 1:12])
> snip.rpart(first.tree, c(4, 7))

n= 198

node), split, n, deviance, yval
      * denotes terminal node

 1) root 198 90401.290 16.996460
   2) PO4>=43.818 147 31279.120  8.979592
     4) Cl>=7.8065 140 21622.830  7.492857 *
     5) Cl< 7.8065 7  3157.769 38.714290 *
   3) PO4< 43.818 51 22442.760 40.103920
     6) mxPH< 7.87 28 11452.770 33.450000
       12) mxPH>=7.045 18  5146.169 26.394440 *
       13) mxPH< 7.045 10  3797.645 46.150000 *
     7) mxPH>=7.87 23  8241.110 48.204350 *
```

Note that the function returns a tree object like the one returned by the
rpart() function, which means that you can store your pruned tree using
something like my.tree <- snip.rpart(first.tree,c(4,7)).

Alternatively, you can use snip.rpart() in a graphical way. First, you
plot the tree, and then you call the function without the second argument. If
you click the mouse at some node, R prints on its console some information
about the node. If you click again on that node, R prunes the tree at that
node.[34] You can go on pruning nodes in this graphical way. You finish the
interaction by clicking the right mouse button. The result of the call is again
a tree object:

```
> prettyTree(first.tree)
> snip.rpart(first.tree)

node number: 2  n= 147
    response= 8.979592
    Error (dev) =  31279.12
node number: 6  n= 28
    response= 33.45
    Error (dev) =  11452.77
n= 198

node), split, n, deviance, yval
```

---

[34]Note that the plot of the tree is not updated, so you will not see the pruning being
carried out in the graphics window.

```
* denotes terminal node

1) root 198 90401.290 16.996460
    2) PO4>=43.818 147 31279.120  8.979592 *
    3) PO4< 43.818 51 22442.760 40.103920
      6) mxPH< 7.87 28 11452.770 33.450000 *
      7) mxPH>=7.87 23  8241.110 48.204350
       14) PO4>=15.177 12  3047.517 38.183330 *
       15) PO4< 15.177 11  2673.945 59.136360 *
```

In this example, I have clicked and pruned nodes 2 and 6.

Further readings on regression trees

A more complete study of regression trees is probably the book by Breiman et al. (1984). This is the standard reference on both classification and regression trees. It provides an in-depth study of these two types of models. The approach can be seen as a bit formal (at least in some chapters) for some readers. Nevertheless, it is definitely a good reference, although slightly biased toward statistical literature. The book on the system C4.5 by Quinlan (1993) is a good reference on classification trees from the machine learning community perspective. My Ph.D. thesis (Torgo, 1999a), which you can freely download from my home page, should provide a good introduction, references, and advanced topics on regression trees. It will also introduce you to other types of tree-based models that have the goal of improving the accuracy of regression trees using more sophisticated models at the leaves (see also Torgo, 2000).

2.7 Model Evaluation and Selection

In Section 2.6 we saw two examples of prediction models that could be used in this case study. The obvious question is which one we should use for obtaining the predictions for the seven algae of the 140 test samples. To answer this question, one needs to specify some preference criteria over the space of possible models; that is, we need to specify how we will evaluate the performance of the models.

Several criteria exist for evaluating (and thus comparing) models. Among the most popular are criteria that calculate the predictive performance of the models. Still, other criteria exist such as the model interpretability, or even the model computational efficiency, that can be important for very large data mining problems.

The predictive performance of regression models is obtained by comparing the predictions of the models with the real values of the target variables, and calculating some average error measure from this comparison. One such measure is the mean absolute error (MAE). Let us see how to obtain this measure for our two models (linear regression and regression trees). The first step is to obtain the model predictions for the set of cases where we want to evaluate it. To obtain the predictions of any model in R, one uses the function `predict()`. This general function receives a model and a test dataset and retrieves the correspondent model predictions:

```
> lm.predictions.a1 <- predict(final.lm, clean.algae)
> rt.predictions.a1 <- predict(rt.a1, algae)
```

These two statements collect the predictions of the models obtained in Section 2.6 for alga *a1*. Note that we have used the `clean.algae` data frame with linear models, because of the missing values.

Having the predictions of the models, we can calculate their mean absolute error as follows:

```
> (mae.a1.lm <- mean(abs(lm.predictions.a1 - algae[, "a1"])))
```

`[1] 13.10681`

```
> (mae.a1.rt <- mean(abs(rt.predictions.a1 - algae[, "a1"])))
```

`[1] 11.61717`

Another popular error measure is the mean squared error (MSE). This measure can be obtained as follows:

```
> (mse.a1.lm <- mean((lm.predictions.a1 - algae[, "a1"])^2))
```

`[1] 295.5407`

```
> (mse.a1.rt <- mean((rt.predictions.a1 - algae[, "a1"])^2))
```

`[1] 271.3226`

This latter statistic has the disadvantage of not being measured in the same units as the target variable, and thus being less interpretable from the user perspective. Even if we use the MAE statistic, we can ask ourselves the question whether the scores obtained by the models are good or bad. An alternative statistic that provides a reasonable answer to this question is the normalized mean squared error (NMSE). This statistic calculates a ratio between the performance of our models and that of a baseline predictor, usually taken as the mean value of the target variable:

```
> (nmse.a1.lm <- mean((lm.predictions.a1-algae[,'a1'])^2)/
+                mean((mean(algae[,'a1'])-algae[,'a1'])^2))
```

`[1] 0.6473034`

```
> (nmse.a1.rt <- mean((rt.predictions.a1-algae[,'a1'])^2)/
+                mean((mean(algae[,'a1'])-algae[,'a1'])^2))
```

`[1] 0.5942601`

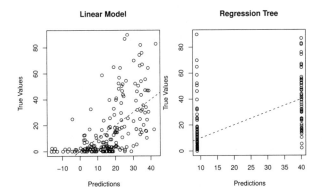

FIGURE 2.10: Errors scatter plot.

The NMSE is a unit-less error measure with values usually ranging from 0 to 1. If your model is performing better than this very simple baseline predictor, then the NMSE should be clearly less than 1. The smaller the NMSE, the better. Values grater than 1 mean that your model is performing worse than simply predicting always the average for all cases!

In the book package you can find the function `regr.eval()` that calculates the value of a set of regression evaluation metrics. Below you can find an example use of this function. Check its help to see different uses of this function.

```
> regr.eval(algae[, "a1"], rt.predictions.a1, train.y = algae[,
+     "a1"])

        mae         mse        rmse        nmse        nmae
11.6171709 271.3226161  16.4718735   0.5942601   0.6953711
```

It is also interesting to have some kind of visual inspection of the predictions of the models. A possibility is to use a scatter plot of the errors. Figure 2.10 shows an example of this type of analysis for the predictions of our two models, and it was produced with the following code:

```
> old.par <- par(mfrow = c(1, 2))
> plot(lm.predictions.a1, algae[, "a1"], main = "Linear Model",
+     xlab = "Predictions", ylab = "True Values")
> abline(0, 1, lty = 2)
> plot(rt.predictions.a1, algae[, "a1"], main = "Regression Tree",
+     xlab = "Predictions", ylab = "True Values")
> abline(0, 1, lty = 2)
> par(old.par)
```

Looking at Figure 2.10 we can observe that the models have rather poor performance in several cases. In the ideal scenario that they make correct predictions for all cases, all the circles in the plots should lie on the dashed lines, which were obtained with the `abline(0,1,lty=2)` calls. These lines cross the origin of the plots and represent the points where the X-coordinate is equal to the Y-coordinate. Given that each circle in the plots obtains its coordinates from the predicted and truth values of the target variable, if these values were equal, the circles would all be placed on this ideal line. As we observe, that is not the case at all! We can check which is the sample number where a particularly bad prediction is made with the function `identify()`, which we have seen can be used to let the user interactively click on the dots in a graph:

```
> plot(lm.predictions.a1,algae[,'a1'],main="Linear Model",
+      xlab="Predictions",ylab="True Values")
> abline(0,1,lty=2)
> algae[identify(lm.predictions.a1,algae[,'a1']),]
```

Using this code and after finishing the interaction with the graphics window by right-clicking on the graph, you should see the rows of the `algae` data frame corresponding to the clicked circles — because we are using the vector returned by the `identify()` function to index the `algae` data frame.

Looking at Figure 2.10 (left) with the predictions of the linear model, we can see that this model predicts negative algae frequencies for some cases. In this application domain, it makes no sense to say that the occurrence of an alga in a water sample is negative (at most, it can be zero). As such, we can take advantage of this domain knowledge and use this minimum value as a form of improving the linear model performance:

```
> sensible.lm.predictions.a1 <- ifelse(lm.predictions.a1 <
+     0, 0, lm.predictions.a1)
> regr.eval(algae[, "a1"], lm.predictions.a1, stats = c("mae",
+     "mse"))

      mae       mse
 13.10681  295.54069

> regr.eval(algae[, "a1"], sensible.lm.predictions.a1, stats = c("mae",
+     "mse"))

      mae       mse
 12.48276  286.28541
```

We have used the function `ifelse()` to achieve this effect. This function has three arguments. The first is a logical condition, the second is the result of the function call when the condition is true, while the third argument is the result when the condition is false. Notice how this small detail has increased the performance of our model.

According to the performance measures calculated previously, one should prefer the regression tree to obtain the predictions for the 140 test samples as it obtained a lower NMSE. However, there is a trap on this reasoning. Our goal is to choose the best model for obtaining the predictions on the 140 test samples. As we do not know the target variables values for those samples, we have to estimate which of our models will perform better on these test samples. The key issue here is to obtain a reliable estimate of a model performance on data for which we do not know the true target value. Calculating the performance metrics using the training data (as we did before) is unreliable because the obtained estimates are biased. In effect, there are models that can easily obtain zero prediction error on the training data. However, this performance will hardly generalize over new samples for which the target variable value is unknown. This phenomenon is usually known as *overfitting* the training data, as mentioned previously. Thus, to select a model, one needs to obtain more reliable estimates of the models performance on unseen data. k-fold cross-validation (k-fold CV) is among the most frequently used methods for obtaining these reliable estimates for small datasets like our case study. This method can be briefly described as follows. Obtain k equally sized and random subsets of the training data. For each of these k subsets, build a model using the remaining $k-1$ sets and evaluate this model on the kth subset. Store the performance of the model and repeat this process for all remaining subsets. In the end, we have k performance measures, all obtained by testing a model on data not used for its construction, and that is the key issue. The k-fold cross-validation estimate is the average of these k measures. A common choice for k is 10. Sometimes we even repeat the overall k-fold CV process several times to get even more reliable estimates.

In general, we can say that when facing a predictive task, we have to make the following decisions:

- Select the alternative models to consider (the models can actually be alternative settings of the same algorithm) for the predictive task(s) we want to address.

- Select the evaluation metrics that will be used to compare the models.

- Choose the experimental methodology for obtaining reliable estimates of these metrics.

In the book package we provide the function `experimentalComparison()`, which is designed to help in this model selection/comparison tasks. It can be used with different estimation methods, including cross-validation. The function has three parameters: (1) the data sets to use for the comparison, (2) the alternative models, and (3) the experimental process parameters. We will illustrate its use by comparing a linear model with several variants of regression trees, on the algae dataset.

The `experimentalComparison()` function is generic in the sense that it can be used for any model(s) and any dataset(s). The user supplies a set of functions implementing the models to be compared. Each of these functions should implement a full train+test+evaluate cycle for the given training and test datasets. The functions will be called from the experimental routines on each iteration of the estimation process. These functions should return a vector with the values of whatever evaluation metrics the user wants to estimate by cross-validation. Let us construct such functions for our two target models:

```
> cv.rpart <- function(form,train,test,...) {
+    m <- rpartXse(form,train,...)
+    p <- predict(m,test)
+    mse <- mean((p-resp(form,test))^2)
+    c(nmse=mse/mean((mean(resp(form,train))-resp(form,test))^2))
+ }
> cv.lm <- function(form,train,test,...) {
+    m <- lm(form,train,...)
+    p <- predict(m,test)
+    p <- ifelse(p < 0,0,p)
+    mse <- mean((p-resp(form,test))^2)
+    c(nmse=mse/mean((mean(resp(form,train))-resp(form,test))^2))
+ }
```

In this illustrative example, we have assumed that we want to use the NMSE as evaluation metric of our regression trees and linear models. All of these user-defined functions should have as the first three parameters a formula, the training data, and the test data. The remaining parameters that may be included in the call by the experimental routines are parameters of the learner being evaluated. Both functions carry out the same train+test+evaluate cycle although using obviously a different learning algorithm. Both return as result a named vector with the score in terms of NMSE. The functions definitions also include a special parameter, "...". This parameter can be used when creating any R function. It allows the specification of functions with a variable number of parameters. The "..." construct is in effect a list that captures all arguments eventually passed in the function call after the first three that are specified by name. This facility is used to pass eventual extra learning parameters to the actual learning function (in one case the `rpartXse()` function and in the other the `lm()` function). Another particularity of these functions is the use of the `resp()` function, available in our book package, to obtain the target variable values of a data set given a formula.

Having defined the functions that will carry out the learning and testing phase of our models, we can carry out the cross-validation comparison as follows:

```
> res <- experimentalComparison(
+            c(dataset(a1 ~ .,clean.algae[,1:12],'a1')),
+            c(variants('cv.lm'),
+              variants('cv.rpart',se=c(0,0.5,1))),
+            cvSettings(3,10,1234))
```

```
#####  CROSS VALIDATION  EXPERIMENTAL COMPARISON #####

** DATASET :: a1

++ LEARNER :: cv.lm  variant -> cv.lm.defaults
Repetition  1
Fold:  1  2  3  4  5  6  7  8  9  10
Repetition  2
Fold:  1  2  3  4  5  6  7  8  9  10
Repetition  3
Fold:  1  2  3  4  5  6  7  8  9  10


++ LEARNER :: cv.rpart  variant -> cv.rpart.v1
Repetition  1
Fold:  1  2  3  4  5  6  7  8  9  10
Repetition  2
Fold:  1  2  3  4  5  6  7  8  9  10
Repetition  3
Fold:  1  2  3  4  5  6  7  8  9  10


++ LEARNER :: cv.rpart  variant -> cv.rpart.v2
Repetition  1
Fold:  1  2  3  4  5  6  7  8  9  10
Repetition  2
Fold:  1  2  3  4  5  6  7  8  9  10
Repetition  3
Fold:  1  2  3  4  5  6  7  8  9  10


++ LEARNER :: cv.rpart  variant -> cv.rpart.v3
Repetition  1
Fold:  1  2  3  4  5  6  7  8  9  10
Repetition  2
Fold:  1  2  3  4  5  6  7  8  9  10
Repetition  3
Fold:  1  2  3  4  5  6  7  8  9  10
```

As mentioned previously, the first argument should be a vector with the datasets to be used in the experimental comparison. Each dataset is specified as dataset(<formula>,<data frame>,<label>). The second argument of experimentalComparison() contains a vector of learning systems variants. Each variant is specified using the function variant(). Its first argument is the name of the user-defined function that will carry out the learn+test+evaluate cycle. Any remaining and optional arguments will specify sets of alternative values of the parameters of the learning function. The variants() function generates a set of alternative models resulting from all possible combinations of the parameters values. In this example call, we are using the "cv.lm" only with its default parameters, and for the "cv.rpart" we are specifying different alternative values for the parameter se. This means that the experiment includes three variants of regression trees, as you can confirm on the output generated by the previous call. The third parameter of the `experimentalComparison()` function specifies the settings of the cross-validation experiment, namely how many repetitions of the k-folds cross-validation process are to be carried out (in this case, 3), what is the value of k (10), and what is the seed for the random number generator. This last parameter is to ensure the possibility of replicating the experiments if required (for instance, with other learning systems).

The result of this call is a complex object containing all information concerning the experimental comparison. In our package we provide several utility functions to explore this information. For instance, the following provides a summary of the results of the comparison:

```
> summary(res)

== Summary of a  Cross Validation  Experiment ==

 3 x 10 - Fold Cross Validation run with seed =  1234

* Datasets ::  a1
* Learners  ::  cv.lm.defaults, cv.rpart.v1, cv.rpart.v2, cv.rpart.v3

* Summary of Experiment Results:


-> Datataset:  a1

            *Learner: cv.lm.defaults
                nmse
avg        0.7196105
std        0.1833064
min        0.4678248
max        1.2218455
invalid 0.0000000

            *Learner: cv.rpart.v1
                nmse
avg        0.6440843
std        0.2521952
min        0.2146359
max        1.1712674
invalid 0.0000000

            *Learner: cv.rpart.v2
                nmse
avg        0.6873747
std        0.2669942
```

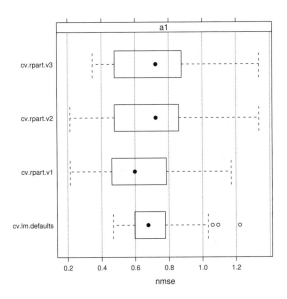

FIGURE 2.11: Visualization of the cross-validation results.

```
min      0.2146359
max      1.3356744
invalid  0.0000000

         *Learner: cv.rpart.v3
             nmse
avg      0.7167122
std      0.2579089
min      0.3476446
max      1.3356744
invalid  0.0000000
```

As it can be seen, one of the variants of the regression tree achieves the best average NMSE score. Whether the difference is statistically significant with respect to the other alternatives is a question we will address later in this section. We can also obtain a visualization (Figure 2.11) of these results as follows:

```
> plot(res)
```

The `experimentalComparison()` function assigns a label to each model variant. In case you want to know the specific parameter settings corresponding to any label, you can proceed as follows:

```
> getVariant("cv.rpart.v1", res)
```

```
Learner::  "cv.rpart"

Parameter values
        se  =  0
```

We can carry out a similar comparative experiment for all seven prediction tasks we are facing at the same time. The following code implements that idea:

```
> DSs <- sapply(names(clean.algae)[12:18],
+           function(x,names.attrs) {
+             f <- as.formula(paste(x,"~ ."))
+             dataset(f,clean.algae[,c(names.attrs,x)],x)
+           },
+           names(clean.algae)[1:11])
> res.all <- experimentalComparison(
+                 DSs,
+                 c(variants('cv.lm'),
+                   variants('cv.rpart',se=c(0,0.5,1))
+                 ),
+                 cvSettings(5,10,1234))
```

For space reasons we have omitted the output of the above commands. This code starts by creating the vector of datasets to use in the comparisons, that is, the seven prediction tasks. For this we need to create a formula for each problem. We have obtained this formula creating a string by concatenating the name of the column of each target variable with the string "~ .". This string is then transformed into an R formula using the function as.formula(). Having created the vector of datasets we have used the function experimentalComparison() as before, with the single difference that this time we have carried out five repetitions of the tenfold cross-validation process for increased statistical significance of the results. Depending on the power of your computer, this code may take a while to run.

In Figure 2.12 we show the results of the models for the different algae on the CV process. The figure was obtained with

```
> plot(res.all)
```

As we can observe, there are several very bad results; that is, NMSE scores clearly above 1, which is the baseline of being as competitive as predicting always the average target variable value for all test cases! If we want to check which is the best model for each problem, we can use the function bestScores() from our package:

```
> bestScores(res.all)

$a1
          system    score
nmse cv.rpart.v1 0.64231
```

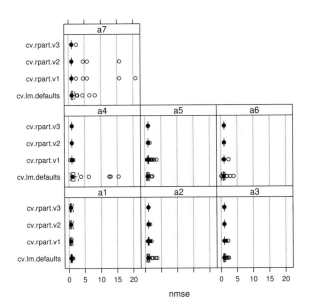

FIGURE 2.12: Visualization of the cross-validation results on all algae.

```
$a2
          system score
nmse cv.rpart.v3       1

$a3
          system score
nmse cv.rpart.v2       1

$a4
          system score
nmse cv.rpart.v2       1

$a5
            system        score
nmse cv.lm.defaults 0.9316803

$a6
            system        score
nmse cv.lm.defaults 0.9359697

$a7
```

```
       system      score
nmse cv.rpart.v3 1.029505
```

The output of this function confirms that, with the exception of alga 1, the results are rather disappointing. The variability of the results (see Figure 2.12) provides good indications that this might be a good candidate for an ensemble approach. Ensembles are model construction methods that basically try to overcome some limitations of individual models by generating a large set of alternative models and then combining their predictions. There are many approaches to obtain ensembles that differ not only in the way the diversity of models is obtained (e.g., different training samples, different variables, different modeling techniques, etc.), but also in how the ensemble prediction is reached (e.g., voting, averaging, etc.). Random forests (Breiman, 2001) are regarded as one of the more competitive examples of ensembles. They are formed by a large set of tree-based models (regression or classification trees). Each tree is fully grown (no post-pruning); and at each step of the tree growing process, the best split for each node is chosen from a random subset of attributes. Predictions for regression tasks are obtained by averaging the predictions of the trees in the ensemble. The R package `randomForest` (Liaw and Wiener, 2002) implements these ideas on function `randomForest()`. The following code repeats the previous cross-validation experiment, this time including three variants of random forests, each with a different number of trees in the ensemble. We have again omitted the output for space reasons.

```
> library(randomForest)
> cv.rf <- function(form,train,test,...) {
+    m <- randomForest(form,train,...)
+    p <- predict(m,test)
+    mse <- mean((p-resp(form,test))^2)
+    c(nmse=mse/mean((mean(resp(form,train))-resp(form,test))^2))
+ }
> res.all <- experimentalComparison(
+              DSs,
+              c(variants('cv.lm'),
+                variants('cv.rpart',se=c(0,0.5,1)),
+                variants('cv.rf',ntree=c(200,500,700))
+                ),
+              cvSettings(5,10,1234))
```

Using the function `bestScores()` we can confirm the advantages of the ensemble approach:

```
> bestScores(res.all)

$a1
        system      score
nmse cv.rf.v3 0.5447361
```

```
$a2
        system     score
nmse cv.rf.v3 0.7777851

$a3
        system     score
nmse cv.rf.v2 0.9946093

$a4
        system     score
nmse cv.rf.v3 0.9591182

$a5
        system     score
nmse cv.rf.v1 0.7907947

$a6
        system     score
nmse cv.rf.v3 0.9126477

$a7
           system     score
nmse cv.rpart.v3 1.029505
```

In effect, for all problems except alga 7, the best score is obtained by some variant of a random forest. Still, the results are not always very good, in particular for alga 7. The output of the function bestScores() does not tell us whether the difference between the scores of these best models and the remaining alternatives is statistically significant; that is, what is the confidence that with another random sample of data we get a similar outcome? The function compAnalysis() in our package provides this information. It carries out a set of paired *Wilcoxon* tests, between a model and the other alternatives. Let us see some examples of its use.

The model "cv.rf.v3" is the best for algae 1, 2, 4, and 6. The following checks the statistical significance of this statement:

```
> compAnalysis(res.all,against='cv.rf.v3',
              datasets=c('a1','a2','a4','a6'))


== Statistical Significance Analysis of Comparison Results ==

Baseline Learner::          cv.rf.v3  (Learn.1)

** Evaluation Metric::           nmse

- Dataset: a1
      Learn.1   Learn.2 sig.2   Learn.3 sig.3   Learn.4 sig.4
AVG 0.5447361 0.7077282    ++  0.6423100     +  0.6569726    ++
```

```
STD 0.1736676 0.1639373        0.2399321           0.2397636
      Learn.5 sig.5  Learn.6 sig.6   Learn.7 sig.7
AVG 0.6875212     ++  0.5490511       0.5454724
STD 0.2348946         0.1746944       0.1766636

- Dataset: a2
      Learn.1   Learn.2 sig.2   Learn.3 sig.3    Learn.4 sig.4
AVG 0.7777851 1.0449317     ++ 1.0426327     ++ 1.01626123    ++
STD 0.1443868 0.6276144        0.2005522        0.07435826
        Learn.5 sig.5   Learn.6 sig.6   Learn.7 sig.7
AVG 1.000000e+00     ++ 0.7829394       0.7797307
STD 2.389599e-16        0.1433550       0.1476815

- Dataset: a4
      Learn.1  Learn.2 sig.2   Learn.3 sig.3       Learn.4 sig.4
AVG 0.9591182 2.111976        1.0073953     +  1.000000e+00    +
STD 0.3566023 3.118196        0.1065607        2.774424e-16
        Learn.5 sig.5   Learn.6 sig.6   Learn.7 sig.7
AVG 1.000000e+00     +  0.9833399       0.9765730
STD 2.774424e-16        0.3824403       0.3804456

- Dataset: a6
      Learn.1   Learn.2 sig.2   Learn.3 sig.3       Learn.4 sig.4
AVG 0.9126477 0.9359697     ++ 1.0191041       1.000000e+00
STD 0.3466902 0.6045963        0.1991436        2.451947e-16
        Learn.5 sig.5   Learn.6 sig.6   Learn.7 sig.7
AVG 1.000000e+00        0.9253011       0.9200022
STD 2.451947e-16        0.3615926       0.3509093

Legends:
Learners -> Learn.1 = cv.rf.v3 ; Learn.2 = cv.lm.defaults ;
Learn.3 = cv.rpart.v1 ; Learn.4 = cv.rpart.v2 ; Learn.5 = cv.rpart.v3 ;
Learn.6 = cv.rf.v1 ; Learn.7 = cv.rf.v2 ;
Signif. Codes -> 0 '++' or '--' 0.001 '+' or '-' 0.05 ' ' 1
```

The columns "sig.X" provide the information we are seeking. Absence of a symbol means that our confidence in the observed difference between the respective model and the "cv.rf.v3" being statistically significant is lower than 95% (check the legend to understand the meaning of the symbols). Plus signals mean that the average evaluation metric of the model is significantly higher than the one of "cv.rf.v3", which is bad as best NMSE scores are the lower ones. Minus signals represent the opposite.

As you can confirm, the difference between this variant of random forests and the other variants is usually not statistically significant. With respect to the other models, there is in most cases a significant advantage to this variant of random forests.

We could carry out a similar analysis for the other models that have best scores for the other algae by simply using different values in the `against` and `datasets` parameters of the function `compAnalysis()`.

Further readings on model selection and model ensembles

Comparing/selecting among different models has been the subject of much research. Among these we can suggest the works by Dietterich (1998), Provost et al. (1998), Nemenyi (1969) and Demsar (2006).

With respect to ensemble learning, there is again a huge amount of work among which we can highlight the works on *bagging* (Breiman, 1996) and *boosting* (Freund and Shapire, 1996; Shapire, 1990). A good overview of research on these topics can be found in Dietterich (2000).

2.8 Predictions for the Seven Algae

In this section we will see how to obtain the predictions for the seven algae on the 140 test samples. Section 2.7 described how to proceed to choose the best models to obtain these predictions. The used procedure consisted of obtaining unbiased estimates of the NMSE for a set of models on all seven predictive tasks, by means of a cross-validation experimental process.

The main goal in this data mining problem is to obtain seven predictions for each of the 140 test samples. Each of these seven predictions will be obtained using the model that our cross-validation process has indicated as being the "best" for that task. This will be one of either the models shown by our call to the `bestScores()` function in the previous section. Namely, it will be one of either "cv.rf.v3", "cv.rf.v2", "cv.rf.v1", or "cv.rpart.v3".

Let us start by obtaining these models using all the available training data so that we can apply them to the test set. Notice that, for simplicity, we will grow the regression tree using the `clean.algae` data frame that had the NA values substituted by a k nearest neighbor imputation process. This can be avoided for regression trees as they incorporate their own method for handling unknown values. Random forests, on the contrary, do not include such a method so they will need to be learned using the `clean.algae` data frame.

The following code obtains all seven models:

```
> bestModelsNames <- sapply(bestScores(res.all),
+                           function(x) x['nmse','system'])
> learners <- c(rf='randomForest',rpart='rpartXse')
> funcs <- learners[sapply(strsplit(bestModelsNames,'\\.'),
+                          function(x) x[2])]
> parSetts <- lapply(bestModelsNames,
+                     function(x) getVariant(x,res.all)@pars)
> bestModels <- list()
> for(a in 1:7) {
```

```
+    form <- as.formula(paste(names(clean.algae)[11+a],'~ .'))
+    bestModels[[a]] <- do.call(funcs[a],
+           c(list(form,clean.algae[,c(1:11,11+a)]),parSetts[[a]]))
+ }
```

We start by obtaining a vector with the names of the winning variants for each task. We then obtain the respective names of the R functions that learn these variants on the vector `funcs`. This is achieved by extracting a part of the name of the variant with the `strsplit()` function. As this step is a slightly more sophisticated example of function composition, you may find it useful to execute this code in separate parts to fully understand the role of the different function calls involved in the statement that obtains these function names. The list `parSetts` is assigned with the parameter settings for each of the winning variants. The `getVariant()` function gives the model corresponding to a variant name. The object returned by this function is of the class `learner`. These objects have different "slots", one of which is named `pars` and contains a list with the parameters of the variant. The slots of an object can be obtained in R by the operator "@". Finally, we obtain the models and collect them on the list `bestModels`. For each alga, we construct the formula as before and then call the respective R function using the proper parameter settings. This is achieved with the function `do.call()` that allows us to call any function by providing its name as a string on the first argument, and then including the arguments of the call as a list in the second argument. After the execution of this code, we have a list with seven models obtained for each algae and ready for making predictions for the test set.[35]

The data frame `test.algae`, available in our package, contains the 140 test samples. This dataset also includes unknown values; thus our first step will be to fill in these unknowns using the same methodology as before. The first temptation to carry out this task would be to apply the `knnImputation()` function to the `test.algae` data frame. This would carry out the task but it would be slightly against one of the golden rules of predictive modeling: do not use any information from your test sets to obtain the models. In effect, by applying the function directly to the test set, we would be using the other test cases to find the ten nearest neighbors that would be used to fill in each unknown. Although we would not use the information on the target variables, which would be really wrong, we still can avoid this process by using the training data for finding the neighbors instead. This will be more correct but also more realistic in the sense that if we were to apply the models on real problems, we would probably get the water samples sequentially, one at a time. The function `knnImputation()` has an extra argument that can be used for these situations of filling in unknowns on a test set. We can use it as follows:

```
> clean.test.algae <- knnImputation(test.algae, k = 10, distData = algae[,
+      1:11])
```

---

[35] A word of warning: trying to print the `bestModels` object may fill your screen!

The `distData` argument allows you to supply an extra set of data where the ten nearest neighbors are to be found for each case with unknowns in the `test.algae` data frame. Notice that we have omitted the target variables from the `algae` dataset, as the test set does not include information on these variables.

We are now ready to obtain the matrix with the predictions for the entire test set:

```
> preds <- matrix(ncol=7,nrow=140)
> for(i in 1:nrow(clean.test.algae))
+   preds[i,] <- sapply(1:7,
+                       function(x)
+                         predict(bestModels[[x]],clean.test.algae[i,])
+                       )
```

With this simple code we obtain a matrix (`preds`) with the required 7×140 predictions. At this stage we can compare these predictions with the real values to obtain some feedback on the quality of our approach to this prediction problem. The true values of the test set are contained in the `algae.sols` data frame, available in our package. The following code calculates the NMSE scores of our models:

```
> avg.preds <- apply(algae[,12:18],2,mean)
> apply( ((algae.sols-preds)^2),           2,mean) /
+ apply( (scale(algae.sols,avg.preds,F)^2),2,mean)
```

a1	a2	a3	a4	a5	a6	a7
0.4650380	0.8743948	0.7798143	0.7329075	0.7308526	0.8281238	1.0000000

We first obtain the predictions of the baseline model used to calculate the NMSE, which in our case consists of predicting the average value of the target variable. Then we proceed to calculate the NMSEs for the seven models/algae. This is done on a single statement that may seem a bit complex at first but as soon as you understand it, we are sure you will be amazed by its simplicity and compactness. The `scale()` function can be used to normalize a dataset. It works by subtracting the second argument from the first and then dividing the result by the third, unless this argument is FALSE, as is the case above. In this example we are thus using it to subtract a vector (the average target value of all seven algae) from each line of a matrix.

The results that we obtained are in accordance with the cross-validation estimates obtained previously. They confirm the difficulty in obtaining good scores for alga 7, while for the other problems the results are more competitive, in particular for alga 1.

In summary, with a proper model selection phase, we were able to obtain interesting scores for these prediction problems.

2.9   Summary

The main goal of this first case study was to familiarize the reader with R. For this purpose we used a small problem — at least by data mining standards. We described how to perform some of the most basic data analysis tasks in R.

If you are interested in knowing more about the international data analysis competition that was behind the data used in this chapter, you can browse through the competition Web page,[36] or read some of the papers of the winning solutions (Bontempi et al., 1999; Chan, 1999; Devogelaere et al., 1999; Torgo, 1999b) to compare the data analysis strategies followed by these authors.

In terms of data mining, this case study has provided information on

- Data visualization

- Descriptive statistics

- Strategies to handle unknown variable values

- Regression tasks

- Evaluation metrics for regression tasks

- Multiple linear regression

- Regression trees

- Model selection/comparison through k-fold cross-validation

- Model ensembles and random forests

We hope that by now you are more acquainted with the interaction with R, and also familiarized with some of its features. Namely, you should have learned some techniques for

- Loading data from text files

- How to obtain descriptive statistics of datasets

- Basic visualization of data

- Handling datasets with unknown values

- How to obtain some regression models

- How to use the obtained models to obtain predictions for a test set

Further cases studies will give you more details on these and other data mining techniques.

---

[36]http://www.erudit.de/erudit/competitions/ic-99/.

Chapter 3

Predicting Stock Market Returns

This second case study tries to move a bit further in terms of the use of data mining techniques. We will address some of the difficulties of incorporating data mining tools and techniques into a concrete business problem. The specific domain used to illustrate these problems is that of automatic stock trading systems. We will address the task of building a stock trading system based on prediction models obtained with daily stock quotes data. Several models will be tried with the goal of predicting the future returns of the S&P 500 market index. These predictions will be used together with a trading strategy to reach a decision regarding the market orders to generate. This chapter addresses several new data mining issues, among which are (1) how to use R to analyze data stored in a database, (2) how to handle prediction problems with a time ordering among data observations (also known as time series), and (3) an example of the difficulties of translating model predictions into decisions and actions in real-world applications.

3.1 Problem Description and Objectives

Stock market trading is an application domain with a large potential for data mining. In effect, the existence of an enormous amount of historical data suggests that data mining can provide a competitive advantage over human inspection of these data. On the other hand, there are researchers claiming that the markets adapt so rapidly in terms of price adjustments that there is no space to obtain profits in a consistent way. This is usually known as the *efficient markets hypothesis*. This theory has been successively replaced by more relaxed versions that leave some space for trading opportunities due to temporary market inefficiencies.

The general goal of stock trading is to maintain a portfolio of assets based on buy and sell orders. The long-term objective is to achieve as much profit as possible from these trading actions. In the context of this chapter we will constrain a bit more this general scenario. Namely, we will only "trade" a single security, actually a market index. Given this security and an initial capital, we will try to maximize our profit over a future testing period by means of trading actions (Buy, Sell, Hold). Our trading strategy will use as a basis for decision making the indications provided by the result of a data mining process. This process will consist of trying to predict the future evolution of the index based on a model obtained with historical quotes data. Thus our prediction model will be incorporated in a trading system that generates its decisions based on the predictions of the model. Our overall evaluation criteria will be the performance of this trading system, that is, the profit/loss resulting from the actions of the system as well as some other statistics that are of interest to investors. This means that our main evaluation criteria will be the operational results of applying the knowledge discovered by our data mining process and not the predictive accuracy of the models developed during this process.

3.2   The Available Data

In our case study we will concentrate on trading the S&P 500 market index. Daily data concerning the quotes of this security are freely available in many places, for example, the Yahoo finance site.[1]

The data we will use is available in the book package. Once again we will explore other means of getting the data as a form of illustrating some of the capabilities of R. Moreover, some of these other alternatives will allow you to apply the concepts learned in this chapter to more recent data than the one packaged at the time of writing this book.

In order to get the data through the book R package, it is enough to issue

```
> library(DMwR)
> data(GSPC)
```

The first statement is only required if you have not issued it before in your R session. The second instruction will load an object, GSPC,[2] of class xts. We will describe this class of objects in Section 3.2.1, but for now you can manipulate it as if it were a matrix or a data frame (try, for example, head(GSPC)).

At the book Web site,[3] you can find these data in two alternative formats. The first is a comma separated values (CSV) file that can be read into R in the same way as the data used in Chapter 2. The other format is a MySQL database dump file that we can use to create a database with the S&P 500 quotes in MySQL. We will illustrate how to load these data into R for these two alternative formats. It is up to you to decide which alternative you will download, or if you prefer the easy path of loading it from the book package. The remainder of the chapter (i.e., the analysis after reading the data) is independent of the storage schema you decide to use.

---

[1]http://finance.yahoo.com.

[2]^GSPC is the ticker ID of S&P 500 at Yahoo finance from where the quotes were obtained.

[3]http://www.liaad.up.pt/~ltorgo/DataMiningWithR.

For the sake of completeness we will also mention yet another way of getting this data into R, which consists of downloading it directly from the Web. If you choose to follow this path, you should remember that you will probably be using a larger dataset than the one used in the analysis carried out in this book.

Whichever source you choose to use, the daily stock quotes data includes information regarding the following properties:

- Date of the stock exchange session

- Open price at the beginning of the session

- Highest price during the session

- Lowest price

- Closing price of the session

- Volume of transactions

- Adjusted close price[4]

3.2.1 Handling Time-Dependent Data in R

The data available for this case study depends on time. This means that each observation of our dataset has a time tag attached to it. This type of data is frequently known as time series data. The main distinguishing feature of this kind of data is that order between cases matters, due to their attached time tags. Generally speaking, a time series is a set of ordered observations of a variable Y:

$$y_1, y_2, \ldots, y_{t-1}, y_t, y_{t+1}, \ldots, y_n \qquad (3.1)$$

where y_t is the value of the series variable Y at time t.

The main goal of time series analysis is to obtain a model based on past observations of the variable, $y_1, y_2, \ldots, y_{t-1}, y_t$, which allows us to make predictions regarding future observations of the variable, $y_{t+1}, \ldots, y_n$.

In the case of our stocks data, we have what is usually known as a multivariate time series, because we measure several variables at the same time tags, namely the *Open, High, Low, Close, Volume*, and *AdjClose*.[5]

R has several packages devoted to the analysis of this type of data, and in effect it has special classes of objects that are used to store type-dependent

---

[4]This is basically the closing price adjusted for stock splits, dividends/distributions, and rights offerings.

[5]Actually, if we wanted to be more precise, we would have to say that we have only two time series (*Price* and *Volume*) because all quotes are actually the same variable (*Price*) sampled at different times of the day.

data. Moreover, R has many functions tuned for this type of objects, like special plotting functions, etc.

Among the most flexible R packages for handling time-dependent data are zoo (Zeileis and Grothendieck, 2005) and xts (Ryan and Ulrich, 2010). Both offer similar power, although xts provides a set of extra facilities (e.g., in terms of sub-setting using ISO 8601 time strings) to handle this type of data. In technical terms the class xts extends the class zoo, which means that any xts object is also a zoo object, and thus we can apply any method designed for zoo objects to xts objects. We will base our analysis in this chapter primarily on xts objects. We start with a few illustrative examples of the creation and use of this type of object. Please note that both zoo and xts are extra packages (i.e., that do not come with a base installation of R), and that you need to download and install in R (see Section 1.2.1, page 3).

The following examples illustrate how to create objects of class xts.

```
> library(xts)
> x1 <- xts(rnorm(100), seq(as.POSIXct("2000-01-01"), len = 100,
+       by = "day"))
> x1[1:5]

                 [,1]
2000-01-01   0.82029230
2000-01-02   0.99165376
2000-01-03   0.05829894
2000-01-04  -0.01566194
2000-01-05   2.02990349

> x2 <- xts(rnorm(100), seq(as.POSIXct("2000-01-01 13:00"),
+       len = 100, by = "min"))
> x2[1:4]

                         [,1]
2000-01-01 13:00:00 1.5638390
2000-01-01 13:01:00 0.7876171
2000-01-01 13:02:00 1.0860185
2000-01-01 13:03:00 1.2332406

> x3 <- xts(rnorm(3), as.Date(c("2005-01-01", "2005-01-10",
+       "2005-01-12")))
> x3

                 [,1]
2005-01-01  -0.6733936
2005-01-10  -0.7392344
2005-01-12  -1.2165554
```

The function xts() receives the time series data in the first argument. This can either be a vector, or a matrix if we have a multivariate time series.[6]

---

[6]Note that this means that we cannot have xts with mix-mode data, such as in a data frame.

In the latter case each column of the matrix is interpreted as a variable being sampled at each time tag (i.e., each row). The time tags are provided in the second argument. This needs to be a set of time tags in any of the existing time classes in R. In the examples above we have used two of the most common classes to represent time information in R: the POSIXct/POSIXlt classes and the Date class. There are many functions associated with these objects for manipulating dates information, which you may want to check using the help facilities of R. One such example is the seq() function. We have used this function before to generate sequences of numbers. Here we are using it[7] to generate time-based sequences as you see in the example.

As you might observe in the above small examples, the objects may be indexed as if they were "normal" objects without time tags (in this case we see a standard vector sub-setting). Still, we will frequently want to subset these time series objects based on time-related conditions. This can be achieved in several ways with xts objects, as the following small examples try to illustrate:

```
> x1[as.POSIXct("2000-01-04")]

                [,1]
2000-01-04 -0.01566194

> x1["2000-01-05"]

                [,1]
2000-01-05 2.029903

> x1["20000105"]

                [,1]
2000-01-05 2.029903

> x1["2000-04"]

                        [,1]
2000-04-01 01:00:00   0.2379293
2000-04-02 01:00:00  -0.1005608
2000-04-03 01:00:00   1.2982820
2000-04-04 01:00:00  -0.1454789
2000-04-05 01:00:00   1.0436033
2000-04-06 01:00:00  -0.3782062
2000-04-07 01:00:00  -1.4501869
2000-04-08 01:00:00  -1.4123785
2000-04-09 01:00:00   0.7864352

> x1["2000-03-27/"]
```

---

[7]Actually, it is a specific method of the generic function seq() applicable to objects of class POSIXt. You may know more about this typing "? seq.POSIXt".

```
                            [,1]
2000-03-27 01:00:00   0.10430346
2000-03-28 01:00:00  -0.53476341
2000-03-29 01:00:00   0.96020129
2000-03-30 01:00:00   0.01450541
2000-03-31 01:00:00  -0.29507179
2000-04-01 01:00:00   0.23792935
2000-04-02 01:00:00  -0.10056077
2000-04-03 01:00:00   1.29828201
2000-04-04 01:00:00  -0.14547894
2000-04-05 01:00:00   1.04360327
2000-04-06 01:00:00  -0.37820617
2000-04-07 01:00:00  -1.45018695
2000-04-08 01:00:00  -1.41237847
2000-04-09 01:00:00   0.78643516
```

```
> x1["2000-02-26/2000-03-03"]
```

```
                  [,1]
2000-02-26   1.77472194
2000-02-27  -0.49498043
2000-02-28   0.78994304
2000-02-29   0.21743473
2000-03-01   0.54130752
2000-03-02  -0.02972957
2000-03-03   0.49330270
```

```
> x1["/20000103"]
```

```
               [,1]
2000-01-01 0.82029230
2000-01-02 0.99165376
2000-01-03 0.05829894
```

The first statement uses a concrete value of the same class as the object given in the second argument at the time of creation of the **x1** object. The other examples illustrate a powerful indexing schema introduced by the xts package, which is one of its advantages over other time series packages in R. This schema implements time tags as strings with the CCYY-MM-DD HH:MM:SS[.s] general format. As you can confirm in the examples, separators can be omitted and parts of the time specification left out to include sets of time tags. Moreover, the "/" symbol can be used to specify time intervals that can unspecified on both ends, with the meaning of start or final time tag.

Multiple time series can be created in a similar fashion as illustrated below:

```
> mts.vals <- matrix(round(rnorm(25),2),5,5)
> colnames(mts.vals) <- paste('ts',1:5,sep='')
> mts <- xts(mts.vals,as.POSIXct(c('2003-01-01','2003-01-04',
+                      '2003-01-05','2003-01-06','2003-02-16')))
> mts
```

```
              ts1    ts2    ts3    ts4    ts5
2003-01-01  0.96  -0.16  -1.03   0.17   0.62
2003-01-04  0.10   1.64  -0.83  -0.55   0.49
2003-01-05  0.38   0.03  -0.09  -0.64   1.37
2003-01-06  0.73   0.98  -0.66   0.09  -0.89
2003-02-16  2.68   0.10   1.44   1.37  -1.37

> mts["2003-01",c("ts2","ts5")]

              ts2    ts5
2003-01-01  -0.16   0.62
2003-01-04   1.64   0.49
2003-01-05   0.03   1.37
2003-01-06   0.98  -0.89
```

The functions `index()` and `time()` can be used to "extract" the time tags information of any `xts` object, while the `coredata()` function obtains the data values of the time series:

```
> index(mts)

[1] "2003-01-01 WET" "2003-01-04 WET" "2003-01-05 WET" "2003-01-06 WET"
[5] "2003-02-16 WET"

> coredata(mts)

        ts1    ts2    ts3    ts4    ts5
[1,]  0.96  -0.16  -1.03   0.17   0.62
[2,]  0.10   1.64  -0.83  -0.55   0.49
[3,]  0.38   0.03  -0.09  -0.64   1.37
[4,]  0.73   0.98  -0.66   0.09  -0.89
[5,]  2.68   0.10   1.44   1.37  -1.37
```

In summary, `xts` objects are adequate to store stock quotes data, as they allow to store multiple time series with irregular time tags, and provide powerful indexing schemes.

3.2.2 Reading the Data from the CSV File

As we have mentioned before, at the book Web site you can find different sources containing the data to use in this case study. If you decide to use the CSV file, you will download a file whose first lines look like this:

```
"Index"     "Open"  "High" "Low"  "Close" "Volume"   "AdjClose"
1970-01-02 92.06   93.54  91.79  93      8050000    93
1970-01-05 93      94.25  92.53  93.46   11490000   93.46
1970-01-06 93.46   93.81  92.13  92.82   11460000   92.82
1970-01-07 92.82   93.38  91.93  92.63   10010000   92.63
1970-01-08 92.63   93.47  91.99  92.68   10670000   92.68
1970-01-09 92.68   93.25  91.82  92.4    9380000    92.4
1970-01-12 92.4    92.67  91.2   91.7    8900000    91.7
```

Assuming you have downloaded the file and have saved it with the name "sp500.csv" on the current working directory of your R session, you can load it into R and create an `xts` object with the data, as follows:

```
> GSPC <- as.xts(read.zoo("sp500.csv", header = T))
```

The function `read.zoo()` of package `zoo`[8] reads a CSV file and transforms the data into a `zoo` object assuming that the first column contains the time tags. The function `as.xts()` coerces the resulting object into an object of class `xts`.

3.2.3   Getting the Data from the Web

Another alternative way of getting the S&P 500 quotes is to use the free service provided by Yahoo finance, which allows you to download a CSV file with the quotes you want. The `tseries` (Trapletti and Hornik, 2009) R package[9] includes the function `get.hist.quote()` that can be used to download the quotes into a `zoo` object. The following is an example of the use of this function to get the quotes of S&P 500:

```
> library(tseries)
> GSPC <- as.xts(get.hist.quote("^GSPC",start="1970-01-02",
          quote=c("Open", "High", "Low", "Close","Volume","AdjClose")))

...
...

> head(GSPC)
```

	Open	High	Low	Close	Volume	AdjClose
1970-01-02	92.06	93.54	91.79	93.00	8050000	93.00
1970-01-05	93.00	94.25	92.53	93.46	11490000	93.46
1970-01-06	93.46	93.81	92.13	92.82	11460000	92.82
1970-01-07	92.82	93.38	91.93	92.63	10010000	92.63
1970-01-08	92.63	93.47	91.99	92.68	10670000	92.68
1970-01-09	92.68	93.25	91.82	92.40	9380000	92.40

As the function `get.hist.quote()` returns an object of class `zoo`, we have again used the function `as.xts()` to coerce it to `xts`. We should remark that if you issue these commands, you will get more data than what is provided with the object in the book package. If you want to ensure that you get the same results in future commands in this chapter, you should instead use the command

---

[8] You may wonder why we did not load the package `zoo` with a call to the `library()` function. The reason is that this was already done when we loaded the package `xts` because it depends on package `zoo`.

[9] Another extra package that needs to be installed.

```
> GSPC <- as.xts(get.hist.quote("^GSPC",
        start="1970-01-02",end='2009-09-15',
        quote=c("Open", "High", "Low", "Close","Volume","AdjClose")))
```

where "2009-09-15" is the last day with quotes in our package GSPC object.

Another way of obtaining quotes data from the Web (but not the only, as we will see later), is to use the function getSymbols() from package quantmod (Ryan, 2009). Again this is an extra package that you should install before using it. It provides several facilities related to financial data analysis that we will use throughout this chapter. Function getSymbols() in conjunction with other functions of this package provide a rather simple but powerful way of getting quotes data from different data sources. Let us see some examples of its use:

```
> library(quantmod)
> getSymbols("^GSPC")
```

The function getSymbols() receives on the first argument a set of symbol names and will fetch the quotes of these symbols from different Web sources or even local databases, returning by default an xts object with the same name as the symbol,[10] which will silently be created in the working environment. The function has many parameters that allow more control over some of these issues. As you can verify, the returned object does not cover the same period as the data coming with our book package, and it has slightly different column names. This can be easily worked around as follows:

```
> getSymbols("^GSPC", from = "1970-01-01", to = "2009-09-15")
> colnames(GSPC) <- c("Open", "High", "Low", "Close", "Volume",
+        "AdjClose")
```

With the framework provided by package quantmod you may actually have several symbols with different associated sources of data, each with its own parameters. All these settings can be specified at the start of your R session with the setSymbolLookup() function, as you may see in the following simple example:

```
> setSymbolLookup(IBM=list(name='IBM',src='yahoo'),
+                 USDEUR=list(name='USD/EUR',src='oanda))
> getSymbols(c('IBM','USDEUR'))
```

```
> head(IBM)
```

	IBM.Open	IBM.High	IBM.Low	IBM.Close	IBM.Volume	IBM.Adjusted
2007-01-03	97.18	98.40	96.26	97.27	9196800	92.01
2007-01-04	97.25	98.79	96.88	98.31	10524500	93.00
2007-01-05	97.60	97.95	96.91	97.42	7221300	92.16
2007-01-08	98.50	99.50	98.35	98.90	10340000	93.56
2007-01-09	99.08	100.33	99.07	100.07	11108200	94.66
2007-01-10	98.50	99.05	97.93	98.89	8744800	93.55

[10]Eventually pruned from invalid characters for R object names.

```
> head(USDEUR)

            USDEUR
2009-01-01 0.7123
2009-01-02 0.7159
2009-01-03 0.7183
2009-01-04 0.7187
2009-01-05 0.7188
2009-01-06 0.7271
```

In this code we have specified several settings for getting the quotes from the Web of two different symbols: IBM from Yahoo! finance; and US Dollar—Euro exchange rate from Oanda.[11] This is done through function setSymbolLookup(), which ensures any subsequent use of the getSymbols() function in the current R session with the identifiers specified in the call, will use the settings we want. In this context, the second statement will fetch the quotes of the two symbols using the information we have specified. Functions saveSymbolLookup() and loadSymbolLookup() can be used to save and load these settings across different R sessions. Check the help of these functions for further examples and more thorough explanations of the workings behind these handy functions.

3.2.4   Reading the Data from a **MySQL** Database

Another alternative form of storing the data used in this case study is in a MySQL database. At the book Web site there is a file containing SQL statements that can be downloaded and executed within MySQL to upload S&P 500 quotes into a database table. Information on the use and creation of MySQL databases can be found in Section 1.3 (page 35).

After creating a database to store the stock quotes, we are ready to execute the SQL statements of the file downloaded from the book site. Assuming that this file is in the same directory from where you have entered MySQL, and that the database you have created is named Quotes, you can log in to MySQL and then type

```
mysql> use Quotes;
mysql> source sp500.sql;
```

The SQL statements contained in the file "sp500.sql" (the file downloaded from the book Web site) will create a table named "gspc" and insert several records in this table containing the data available for this case study. You can confirm that everything is OK by executing the following statements at the MySQL prompt:

```
mysql> show tables;
```

---
[11]http://www.oanda.com.

```
+-------------------+
| Tables_in_Quotes  |
+-------------------+
| gspc              |
+-------------------+
1 row in set (0.00 sec)
```

```
mysql> select * from gspc;
```

The last SQL statement should print a large set of records, namely the quotes of S&P 500. If you want to limit this output, simply add `limit 10` at the end of the statement.

There are essentially two paths to communicate with databases in R. One based on the ODBC protocol and the other is based on the general interface provided by package `DBI` (R Special Interest Group on Databases, 2009) together with specific packages for each database management system (DBMS).

If you decide to use the ODBC protocol, you need to ensure that you are able to communicate with your DBMS using this protocol. This may involve installing some drivers on the DBMS side. From the side of R, you only need to install package `RODBC`.

Package `DBI` implements a series of database interface functions. These functions are independent of the database server that is actually used to store the data. The user only needs to indicate which communication interface he will use at the first step when he establishes a connection to the database. This means that if you change your DBMS, you will only need to change a single instruction (the one that specifies the DBMS you wish to communicate with). In order to achieve this independence the user also needs to install other packages that take care of the communication details for each different DBMS. R has many DBMS-specific packages for major DBMSs. Specifically, for communication with a MySQL database stored in some server, you have the package `RMySQL` (James and DebRoy, 2009).

3.2.4.1 Loading the Data into R Running on Windows

If you are running R on Windows, independently of whether the MySQL database server resides on that same PC or in another computer (eventually running other operating system), the simplest way to connect to the database from R is through the ODBC protocol. In order to use this protocol in R, you need to install the `RODBC` package.

Before you are able to connect to any MySQL database for the first time using the ODBC protocol, a few extra steps are necessary. Namely, you need also to install the MySQL ODBC driver on your Windows system, which is called "`myodbc`" and can be downloaded from the MySQL site. This only needs to be done the first time you use ODBC to connect to MySQL. After installing this driver, you can create ODBC connections to MySQL databases residing on your computer or any other system to which you have access through your local network. According to the ODBC protocol, every database connection you create has a name (the *Data Source Name*, or DSN according to ODBC jargon). This name will be used to access the MySQL database from R. To create an ODBC connection on a Windows PC, you must use a program called "ODBC data sources", available at the Windows control panel. After running this program you have to create a new User Data Source using the MySQL ODBC driver (`myodbc`) that you are supposed to have previously installed. During this creation process, you will be asked several things, such as the MySQL server address (`localhost` if it is your own computer, or e.g., `myserver.xpto.pt` if it is a remote server), the name of the database to which you want to establish a connection (`Quotes` in our previous example), and the name you wish to give to this connection (the DSN). Once you have completed this process, which you only have to do for the first time, you are ready to connect to this MySQL database from R.

The following R code establishes a connection to the `Quotes` database from R, and loads the S&P 500 quotes data into a data frame,

```
> library(RODBC)
> ch <- odbcConnect("QuotesDSN",uid="myusername",pwd="mypassword")
> allQuotes <- sqlFetch(ch,"gspc")
> GSPC <- xts(allQuotes[,-1],order.by=as.Date(allQuotes[,1]))
> head(GSPC)
```

```
             Open   High    Low Close   Volume AdjClose
1970-01-02 92.06 93.54 91.79 93.00  8050000    93.00
1970-01-05 93.00 94.25 92.53 93.46 11490000    93.46
1970-01-06 93.46 93.81 92.13 92.82 11460000    92.82
1970-01-07 92.82 93.38 91.93 92.63 10010000    92.63
1970-01-08 92.63 93.47 91.99 92.68 10670000    92.68
1970-01-09 92.68 93.25 91.82 92.40  9380000    92.40
```

```
> odbcClose(ch)
```

After loading the RODBC package, we establish a connection with our database using the previously created DSN,[12] using the function `odbcConnect()`. We then use one of the functions available to query a table, in this case the `sqlFetch()` function, which obtains all rows of a table and returns them as a data frame object. The next step is to create an `xts` object from this data frame using the date information and the quotes. Finally, we close the connection to the database with the `odbcClose()` function.

A brief note on working with extremely large databases: If your query generates a result too large to fit in your computer main memory, then you have to use some other strategy. If that is feasible for your analysis, you can try to handle the data in chunks, and this can be achieved with the parameter `max` of the functions `sqlFecth()` and `sqlFecthMore()`. Other alternatives/approaches

---

[12]Here you should substitute whichever DSN name you have used when creating the data source in the Windows control panel, and also your MySQL username and password.

can be found in the High-Performance and Parallel Computing task view,[13] for instance, through the package ff (Adler et al., 2010).

3.2.4.2   Loading the Data into R Running on Linux

In case you are running R from a Unix-type box the easiest way to communicate to your MySQL database is probably through the package DBI in conjunction with the package RMySQL. Still, the ODBC protocol is also available for these operating systems. With the RMySQL package you do not need any preparatory stages as with RODBC. After installing the package you can start using it as shown by the following example.

```
> library(DBI)
> library(RMySQL)
> drv <- dbDriver("MySQL")
> ch <- dbConnect(drv,dbname="Quotes","myusername","mypassword")
> allQuotes <- dbGetQuery(ch,"select * from gspc")
> GSPC <- xts(allQuotes[,-1],order.by=as.Date(allQuotes[,1]))
> head(GSPC)

             Open  High   Low Close   Volume AdjClose
1970-01-02 92.06 93.54 91.79 93.00  8050000    93.00
1970-01-05 93.00 94.25 92.53 93.46 11490000    93.46
1970-01-06 93.46 93.81 92.13 92.82 11460000    92.82
1970-01-07 92.82 93.38 91.93 92.63 10010000    92.63
1970-01-08 92.63 93.47 91.99 92.68 10670000    92.68
1970-01-09 92.68 93.25 91.82 92.40  9380000    92.40

> dbDisconnect(ch)

[1] TRUE

> dbUnloadDriver(drv)
```

After loading the packages, we open the connection with the database using the functions dbDriver() and dbConnect(), with obvious semantics. The function dbGetQuery() allows us to send an SQL query to the database and receive the result as a data frame. After the usual conversion to an xts object, we close the database connection using the dbDisconnect() and dbUnloadDriver(). Further functions, including functions to obtain partial chunks of queries, also exist in the package DBI and may be consulted in the package documentation.

Another possibility regarding the use of data in a MySQL database is to use the infrastructure provided by the quantmod package that we described in Section 3.2.3. In effect, the function getSymbols() can use as source a MySQL database. The following is a simple illustration of its use assuming a database as the one described above:

---

[13]http://cran.at.r-project.org/web/views/HighPerformanceComputing.html.

```
> setSymbolLookup(GSPC=list(name='gspc',src='mysql',
+    db.fields=c('Index','Open','High','Low','Close','Volume','AdjClose'),
+    user='xpto',password='ypto',dbname='Quotes'))
> getSymbols('GSPC')

[1] "GSPC"
```

3.3   Defining the Prediction Tasks

Generally speaking, our goal is to have good forecasts of the future price of the S&P 500 index so that profitable orders can be placed on time. This general goal should allow us to easily define what to predict with our models—it should resort to forecast the future values of the price time series. However, it is easy to see that even with this simple task we immediately face several questions, namely, (1) which of the daily quotes? or (2) for which time in the future? Answering these questions may not be easy and usually depends on how the predictions will be used for generating trading orders.

3.3.1   What to Predict?

The trading strategies we will describe in Section 3.5 assume that we obtain a prediction of the tendency of the market in the next few days. Based on this prediction, we will place orders that will be profitable if the tendency is confirmed in the future.

Let us assume that if the prices vary more than $p\%$, we consider this worthwhile in terms of trading (e.g., covering transaction costs). In this context, we want our prediction models to forecast whether this margin is attainable in the next k days.[14] Please note that within these k days we can actually observe prices both above and below this percentage. This means that predicting a particular quote for a specific future time $t + k$ might not be the best idea. In effect, what we want is to have a prediction of the overall dynamics of the price in the next k days, and this is not captured by a particular price at a specific time. For instance, the closing price at time $t + k$ may represent a variation much lower than $p\%$, but it could have been preceded by a period of prices representing variations much higher than $p\%$ within the window $t \cdots t + k$. So, what we want in effect is to have a good prediction of the overall tendency of the prices in the next k days.

We will describe a variable, calculated with the quotes data, that can be seen as an indicator (a value) of the tendency in the next k days. The value of this indicator should be related to the confidence we have that the target margin p will be attainable in the next k days. At this stage it is important

---

[14]We obviously do not want to be waiting years to obtain the profit margin.

to note that when we mention a variation in $p\%$, we mean above or below the current price. The idea is that positive variations will lead us to buy, while negative variations will trigger sell actions. The indicator we are proposing resumes the tendency as a single value, positive for upward tendencies, and negative for downward price tendencies.

Let the daily average price be approximated by

$$\bar{P}_i = \frac{C_i + H_i + L_i}{3} \tag{3.2}$$

where C_i, H_i and L_i are the close, high, and low quotes for day i, respectively.

Let V_i be the set of k percentage variations of today's close to the following k days average prices (often called arithmetic returns):

$$V_i = \left\{ \frac{\bar{P}_{i+j} - C_i}{C_i} \right\}_{j=1}^{k} \tag{3.3}$$

Our indicator variable is the total sum of the variations whose absolute value is above our target margin $p\%$:

$$T_i = \sum_v \{ v \in V_i : v > p\% \vee v < -p\% \} \tag{3.4}$$

The general idea of the variable T is to signal k-days periods that have several days with average daily prices clearly above the target variation. High positive values of T mean that there are several average daily prices that are $p\%$ higher than today's close. Such situations are good indications of potential opportunities to issue a buy order, as we have good expectations that the prices will rise. On the other hand, highly negative values of T suggest sell actions, given the prices will probably decline. Values around zero can be caused by periods with "flat" prices or by conflicting positive and negative variations that cancel each other.

The following function implements this simple indicator:

```
> T.ind <- function(quotes, tgt.margin = 0.025, n.days = 10) {
+       v <- apply(HLC(quotes), 1, mean)
+       r <- matrix(NA, ncol = n.days, nrow = NROW(quotes))
+       for (x in 1:n.days) r[, x] <- Next(Delt(v, k = x), x)
+       x <- apply(r, 1, function(x) sum(x[x > tgt.margin | x <
+           -tgt.margin]))
+       if (is.xts(quotes))
+           xts(x, time(quotes))
+       else x
+ }
```

The function starts by obtaining the average price calculated according to Equation 3.2. The function HLC() extracts the High, Low, and Close quotes from a quotes object. We then obtain the returns of the next n.days days with respect to the current close price. The Next() function allows one to

shift the values of a time series in time (both forward or backward). The
Delt() function can be used to calculate percentage or log returns of a series
of prices. Finally, the T.ind() function sums up the large absolute returns,
that is, returns above the target variation margin, which we have set by default
to 2.5%.

We can get a better idea of the behavior of this indicator in Figure 3.1,
which was produced with the following code:

```
> candleChart(last(GSPC, "3 months"), theme = "white", TA = NULL)
> avgPrice <- function(p) apply(HLC(p), 1, mean)
> addAvgPrice <- newTA(FUN = avgPrice, col = 1, legend = "AvgPrice")
> addT.ind <- newTA(FUN = T.ind, col = "red", legend = "tgtRet")
> addAvgPrice(on = 1)
> addT.ind()
```

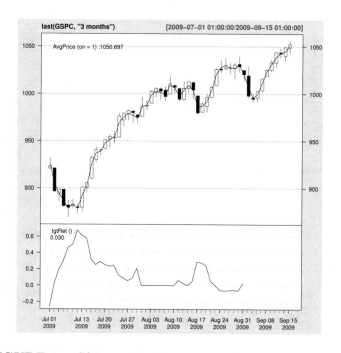

FIGURE 3.1: S&P500 on the last 3 months and our indicator.

The function candleChart() draws candlestick graphs of stock quotes.
These graphs represent the daily quotes by a colored box and a vertical bar.
The bar represents the High and Low prices of the day, while the box represents
the Open-Close amplitude. The color of the box indicates if the top of the
box is the Open or the Close price, that is, if the prices declined (black in
Figure 3.1, orange in an interactive R session) or rose (white in our graphs,
green in R sessions) across the daily session. We have added to the candlestick
graph two indicators: the average price (on the same graph as the candlesticks)

and our T indicator (below). The function `newTA()` can be used to create new plotting functions for indicators that we wish to include in candlestick graphs. The return value of this function is a plotting function![15] This means that the objects `addT.ind` and `addAvgPrice` can be called like any other R function. This is done on the last two instructions. Each of them adds an indicator to the initial graph produced by the `candleChart()` function. The function `addAvgPrice()` was called with the parameter set to 1, which means that the indicator will be plotted on the first graph window; that is, the graph where the candlesticks are. The function `addT.ind()` was not called with this argument, leading to a new graph below the candlesticks. This is what makes sense in the case of our indicator, given the completely different scale of values.

As you can observe in Figure 3.1, the T indicator achieves the highest values when there is a subsequent period of positive variations. Obviously, to obtain the value of the indicator for time i, we need to have the quotes for the following 10 days, so we are not saying that T anticipates these movements. This is not the goal of the indicator. Its goal is to summarize the observed future behavior of the prices into a single value and not to predict this behavior!

In our approach to this problem we will assume that the correct trading action at time t is related to what our expectations are concerning the evolution of prices in the next k days. Moreover, we will describe this future evolution of the prices by our indicator T. The correct trading signal at time t will be "buy" if the T score is higher than a certain threshold, and will be "sell" if the score is below another threshold. In all other cases, the correct signal will be do nothing (i.e., "hold"). In summary, we want to be able to predict the correct signal for time t. On historical data we will fill in the correct signal for each day by calculating the respective T scores and using the thresholding method just outlined above.

3.3.2 Which Predictors?

We have defined an indicator (T) that summarizes the behavior of the price time series in the next k days. Our data mining goal will be to predict this behavior. The main assumption behind trying to forecast the future behavior of financial markets is that it is possible to do so by observing the past behavior of the market. More precisely, we are assuming that if in the past a certain behavior p was followed by another behavior f, and if that causal chain happened frequently, then it is plausible to assume that this will occur again in the future; and thus if we observe p now, we predict that we will observe f next. We are approximating the future behavior (f), by our indicator T. We now have to decide on how we will describe the recent prices pattern (p in the description above). Instead of using again a single indicator to de-

---

[15]You can confirm that by issuing `class(addT.ind)` or by typing the name of the object to obtain its contents.

scribe these recent dynamics, we will use several indicators, trying to capture different properties of the price time series to facilitate the forecasting task.

The simplest type of information we can use to describe the past are the recent observed prices. Informally, that is the type of approach followed in several standard time series modeling approaches. These approaches develop models that describe the relationship between future values of a time series and a window of past q observations of this time series. We will try to enrich our description of the current dynamics of the time series by adding further features to this window of recent prices.

Technical indicators are numeric summaries that reflect some properties of the price time series. Despite their debatable use as tools for deciding when to trade, they can nevertheless provide interesting summaries of the dynamics of a price time series. The amount of technical indicators available can be overwhelming. In R we can find a very good sample of them, thanks to package TTR (Ulrich, 2009).

The indicators usually try to capture some properties of the prices series, such as if they are varying too much, or following some specific trend, etc. In our approach to this problem, we will not carry out an exhaustive search for the indicators that are most adequate to our task. Still, this is a relevant research question, and not only for this particular application. It is usually known as the feature selection problem, and can informally be defined as the task of finding the most adequate subset of available input variables for a modeling task. The existing approaches to this problem can usually be cast in two groups: (1) feature filters and (2) feature wrappers. The former are independent of the modeling tool that will be used after the feature selection phase. They basically try to use some statistical properties of the features (e.g., correlation) to select the final set of features. The wrapper approaches include the modeling tool in the selection process. They carry out an iterative search process where at each step a candidate set of features is tried with the modeling tool and the respective results are recorded. Based on these results, new tentative sets are generated using some search operators, and the process is repeated until some convergence criteria are met that will define the final set.

We will use a simple approach to select the features to include in our model. The idea is to illustrate this process with a concrete example and not to find the best possible solution to this problem, which would require other time and computational resources. We will define an initial set of features and then use a technique to estimate the importance of each of these features. Based on these estimates we will select the most relevant features.

We will center our analysis on the Close quote, as our buy/sell decisions will be made at the end of each daily session. The initial set of features will be formed by several past returns on the Close price. The h-days (arithmetic) returns,[16] or percentage variations, can be calculated as

---

[16]Log returns are defined as $\log(C_i/C_{i-h})$.

$$R_{i-h} = \frac{C_i - C_{i-h}}{C_{i-h}} \tag{3.5}$$

where C_i is the Close price at session i.

We have included in the set of candidate features ten of these returns by varying h from 1 to 10. Next, we have selected a representative set of technical indicators, from those available in package TTR—namely, the Average True Range (ATR), which is an indicator of the volatility of the series; the Stochastic Momentum Index (SMI), which is a momentum indicator; the Welles Wilder's Directional Movement Index (ADX); the Aroon indicator that tries to identify starting trends; the Bollinger Bands that compare the volatility over a period of time; the Chaikin Volatility; the Close Location Value (CLV) that relates the session Close to its trading range; the Arms' Ease of Movement Value (EMV); the MACD oscillator; the Money Flow Index (MFI); the Parabolic Stop-and-Reverse; and the Volatility indicator. More details and references on these and other indicators can be found in the respective help pages of the functions implementing them in package TTR. Most of these indicators produce several values that together are used for making trading decisions. As mentioned before, we do not plan to use these indicators for trading. As such, we have carried out some post-processing of the output of the TTR functions to obtain a single value for each one. The following functions implement this process:

```
> myATR <- function(x) ATR(HLC(x))[, "atr"]
> mySMI <- function(x) SMI(HLC(x))[, "SMI"]
> myADX <- function(x) ADX(HLC(x))[, "ADX"]
> myAroon <- function(x) aroon(x[, c("High", "Low")])$oscillator
> myBB <- function(x) BBands(HLC(x))[, "pctB"]
> myChaikinVol <- function(x) Delt(chaikinVolatility(x[, c("High",
+     "Low")]))[, 1]
> myCLV <- function(x) EMA(CLV(HLC(x)))[, 1]
> myEMV <- function(x) EMV(x[, c("High", "Low")], x[, "Volume"])[,
+     2]
> myMACD <- function(x) MACD(Cl(x))[, 2]
> myMFI <- function(x) MFI(x[, c("High", "Low", "Close")],
+     x[, "Volume"])
> mySAR <- function(x) SAR(x[, c("High", "Close")])[, 1]
> myVolat <- function(x) volatility(OHLC(x), calc = "garman")[,
+     1]
```

The variables we have just described form our initial set of predictors for the task of forecasting the future value of the T indicator. We will try to reduce this set of 22 variables using a feature selection method. Random forests (Breiman, 2001) were used in Section 2.7 to obtain predictions of algae occurrences. Random forests can also be used to estimate the importance of the variables involved in a prediction task. Informally, this importance can be estimated by calculating the percentage increase in the error of the random forest if we remove each variable in turn. In a certain way this resembles the idea of wrapper filters as it includes a modeling tool in the process of selecting the features. However, this is not an iterative search process and moreover, we will use other predictive models to forecast T, which means that the set of variables selected by this process is not optimized for these other models, and in this sense this method is used more like a filter approach.

In our approach to this application, we will split the available data into two separate sets: (1) one used for constructing the trading system; and (2) other to test it. The first set will be formed by the first 30 years of quotes of S&P 500. We will leave the remaining data (around 9 years) for the final test of our trading system. In this context, we must leave this final test set out of this feature selection process to ensure unbiased results.

We first build a random forest using the data available for training:

```
> data(GSPC)
> library(randomForest)
> data.model <- specifyModel(T.ind(GSPC) ~ Delt(Cl(GSPC),k=1:10) +
+         myATR(GSPC) + mySMI(GSPC) + myADX(GSPC) + myAroon(GSPC) +
+         myBB(GSPC)  + myChaikinVol(GSPC) + myCLV(GSPC) +
+         CMO(Cl(GSPC)) + EMA(Delt(Cl(GSPC))) + myEMV(GSPC) +
+         myVolat(GSPC)  + myMACD(GSPC) + myMFI(GSPC) + RSI(Cl(GSPC)) +
+         mySAR(GSPC) + runMean(Cl(GSPC)) + runSD(Cl(GSPC)))
> set.seed(1234)
> rf <- buildModel(data.model,method='randomForest',
+              training.per=c(start(GSPC),index(GSPC["1999-12-31"])),
+              ntree=50, importance=T)
```

The code given above starts by specifying and obtaining the data to be used for modeling using the function `specifyModel()`. This function creates a `quantmod` object that contains the specification of a certain abstract model (described by a formula). This specification may refer to data coming from different types of sources, some of which may even not be currently in the memory of the computer. The function will take care of these cases using `getSymbols()` to obtain the necessary data. This results in a very handy form of specifying and getting the data necessary for your subsequent modeling stages. Moreover, for symbols whose source is the Web, you can later use the obtained object (`data.model` in our case) as an argument to the function `getModelData()`, to obtain a refresh of the object including any new quotes that may be available at that time. Again, this is quite convenient if you want to maintain a trading system that should be updated with new quotes information.

The function `buildModel()` uses the resulting model specification and obtains a model with the corresponding data. Through, parameter `training.per`, you can specify the data that should be used to obtain the model (we are using the first 30 years). This function currently contains wrappers for several modeling tools,[17] among which are random forests. In case you wish to use a model not contemplated by buildModel(), you may obtain the data using the function modelData(), and use it with your favorite modeling function, as shown in the following illustrative example:

```
> ex.model <- specifyModel(T.ind(IBM) ~ Delt(Cl(IBM), k = 1:3))
> data <- modelData(ex.model, data.window = c("2009-01-01",
+     "2009-08-10"))
```

The obtained data object is a standard zoo object, which can be easily cast into a matrix or data frame, for use as a parameter of any modeling function, as the following artificial[18] example illustrates:

```
> m <- myFavouriteModellingTool(ex.model@model.formula,
+                               as.data.frame(data))
```

Notice how we have indicated the model formula. The "real" formula is not exactly the same as the one provided in the argument of function specifyModel(). This latter formula is used to fetch the data, but the "real" formula should use whichever columns and respective names the specifyModel() call has generated. This information is contained in the slot model.formula of the quantmod object generated by the function.

Notice that on this small artificial example we have mentioned a ticker (IBM) for which we currently had no data in memory. The specifyModel() function takes care of that by silently fetching the quotes data from the Web using the getSymbols() function. All this is done in a transparent way to the user and you may even include symbols in your model specification that are obtained from different sources (see, for instance, the examples in Section 3.2.3 with the function setSymbolLookup()).

Returning to our feature selection problem, notice that we have included the parameter importance=TRUE so that the random forest estimates the variable importance. For regression problems, the R implementation of random forests estimates variable importance with two alternative scores. The first is the percentage increase in the error of the forest if we remove each variable in turn. This is measured by calculating the increase in the mean squared error of each tree on an out-of-bag sample when each variable is removed. This increase is averaged over all trees in the forest and normalized with the standard error. The second score has to do with the decrease in node impurity that is accountable with each variable, again averaged over all trees. We will use the first score as it is the one mentioned in the original paper on random forests (Breiman, 2001). After obtaining the model, we can check the importance of the variables as follows:

```
> varImpPlot(rf@fitted.model, type = 1)
```

---

[17]Check its help page to know which ones.
[18]Do not run it as this is a "fake" modeling tool.

The result of this function call is given in Figure 3.2. The arguments to the `varImpPlot()` function are the random forest and the score we wish to plot (if ommited both arc plotted). The generic function `buildModel()` returns the obtained model as a slot (`fitted.model`) of the `quantmod` object it produces as a result.

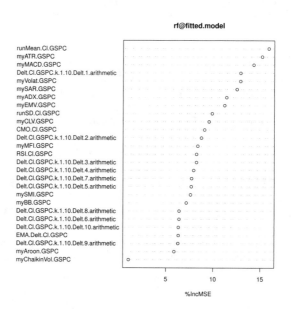

FIGURE 3.2: Variable importance according to the random forest.

At this stage we need to decide on a threshold on the importance score to select only a subset of the features. Looking at the results on the figure and given that this is a simple illustration of the concept of using random forests for selecting features, we will use the value of 10 as the threshold:

```
> imp <- importance(rf@fitted.model, type = 1)
> rownames(imp)[which(imp > 10)]
```

```
[1] "Delt.Cl.GSPC.k.1.10.Delt.1.arithmetic"
[2] "myATR.GSPC"
[3] "myADX.GSPC"
[4] "myEMV.GSPC"
[5] "myVolat.GSPC"
[6] "myMACD.GSPC"
[7] "mySAR.GSPC"
[8] "runMean.Cl.GSPC"
```

The function `importance()` obtains the concrete scores (in this case the first score) for each variable, which we then filter with our threshold to obtain the names of the variables that we will use in our modeling attempts. Using this information we can obtain our final data set as follows:

```
> data.model <- specifyModel(T.ind(GSPC) ~ Delt(Cl(GSPC), k = 1) +
+        myATR(GSPC) + myADX(GSPC) + myEMV(GSPC) + myVolat(GSPC) +
+        myMACD(GSPC) + mySAR(GSPC) + runMean(Cl(GSPC)))
```

3.3.3 The Prediction Tasks

In the previous section we have obtained a quantmod object (data.model) containing the data we plan to use with our predictive models. This data has as a target the value of the T indicator and as predictors a series of other variables that resulted from a feature selection process. We have seen in Section 3.3.1 that our real goal is to predict the correct trading signal at any time t. How can we do that, given the data we have generated in the previous section? We will explore two paths to obtain predictions for the correct trading signal.

The first alternative is to use the T value as the target variable and try to obtain models that forecast this value using the predictors information. This is a multiple regression task similar to the ones we considered in the previous chapter. If we follow this path, we will then have to "translate" our model predictions into trading signals. This means to decide upon the thresholds on the predicted T values that will lead to either of the three possible trading actions. We will carry out this transformation using the following values:

$$signal = \begin{cases} sell & \text{if } T < -0.1 \\ hold & \text{if } -0.1 \leq T \leq 0.1 \\ buy & \text{if } T > 0.1 \end{cases} \quad (3.6)$$

The selection of the values 0.1 and −0.1 is purely heuristic and we can also use other thresholds. Still, these values mean that during the 10 day-period used to generate the T values, there were at least four average daily prices that are 2.5% above the current close ($4 \times 0.025 = 0.1$). If you decide to use other values, you should consider that too high absolute values will originate fewer signals, while too small values may lead us to trade on too small variations of the market, thus incurring a larger risk. Function trading.signals(), available in the book package, can carry out this transformation of the numeric T values into a factor with three possible values: "s", "h", and "b", for sell, hold and buy actions, respectively.

The second alternative prediction task we consider consists of predicting the signals directly. This means to use as a target variable the "correct" signal for day d. How do we obtain these correct signals? Again using the T indicator and the same thresholds used in Equation 3.6. For the available historical data, we obtain the signal of each day by calculating the T value using the following 10 days and using the thresholds in Equation 3.6 to decide on the signal. The target variable in this second task is nominal. This type of prediction problem is known as a classification task.[19] The main distinction between classification and regression tasks is thus the type of the target variable. Regression tasks have a numeric target variable (e.g., our T indicator), while classification tasks use a nominal target variable, that is, with a finite set of possible values. Different approaches and techniques are used for these two types of problems.

The `xts` package infrastructure is geared toward numeric data. The data slots of `xts` objects must be either vectors or matrices, thus single mode data. This means it is not possible to have one of the columns of our training data as a nominal variable (a factor in R), together with all the numeric predictors. We will overcome this difficulty by carrying out all modeling steps outside the `xts` framework. This is easy and not limiting, as we will see. The infrastructure provided by `xts` is mostly used for data sub-setting and plotting, but the modeling stages do not need these facilities.

The following code creates all the data structures that we will use in the subsequent sections for obtaining predictive models for the two tasks.

```
> Tdata.train <- as.data.frame(modelData(data.model,
+                      data.window=c('1970-01-02','1999-12-31')))
> Tdata.eval <- na.omit(as.data.frame(modelData(data.model,
+                      data.window=c('2000-01-01','2009-09-15'))))
> Tform <- as.formula('T.ind.GSPC ~ .')
```

The `Tdata.train` and `Tdata.eval` are data frames with the data to be used for the training and evaluation periods, respectively. We have used data frames as the basic data structures to allow for mixed mode data that will be required in the classification tasks. For these tasks we will replace the target value column with the corresponding signals that will be generated using the `trading.signals()` function. The `Tdata.eval` data frame will be left out of all model selection and comparison processes we carry out. It will be used in the final evaluation of the "best" models we select. The call to `na.omit()` is necessary to avoid NAs at the end of the data frame caused by lack of future data to calculate the T indicator.

3.3.4 Evaluation Criteria

The prediction tasks described in the previous section can be used to obtain models that will output some form of indication regarding the future market direction. This indication will be a number in the case of the regression tasks (the predicted value of T), or a direct signal in the case of classification tasks. Even in the case of regression tasks, we have seen that we will cast this number into a signal by a thresholding mechanism. In Section 3.5 we will describe several trading strategies that use these predicted signals to act on the market.

In this section we will address the question of how to evaluate the signal predictions of our models. We will not consider the evaluation of the numeric

---

[19]Some statistics schools prefer the term "discrimination tasks".

predictions of the T indicator. Due to the way we are using these numeric predictions, this evaluation is a bit irrelevant. One might even question whether it makes sense to have these regression tasks, given that we are only interested in the trading signals. We have decided to maintain these numeric tasks because different trading strategies could take advantage of the numeric predictions, for instance, to decide which amount of money to invest when opening a position. For example, T values much higher than our thresholds for acting ($T > 0.1$ for buying and $T < -0.1$ for selling) could lead to stronger investments.

The evaluation of the signal predictions could be carried out by measuring the error rate, defined as

$$error.rate = \frac{1}{N} \sum_{i=1}^{N} L_{0/1}(y_i, \hat{y}_i) \qquad (3.7)$$

where $\hat{y}_i$ is the prediction of the model for test case i, which has true class label y_i, and $L_{0/1}$ is known as the 0/1 loss function:

$$L_{0/1}(y_i, \hat{y}_i) = \begin{cases} 1 & \text{if } \hat{y}_i \neq y_i \\ 0 & \text{if } \hat{y}_i = y_i \end{cases} \qquad (3.8)$$

One often uses the complement of this measure, known as *accuracy*, given by $1 - error.rate$.

These two statistics basically compare the model predictions to what really happened to the markets in the k future days.

The problem with accuracy (or error rate) is that it turns out not to be a good measure for this type of problem. In effect, there will be a very strong imbalance between the three possible outcomes, with a strong prevalence of hold signals over the other two, as big movements in prices are rare phenomena in financial markets.[20] This means that the accuracy scores will be dominated by the performance of the models on the most frequent outcome that is *hold*. This is not very interesting for trading. We want to have models that are accurate at the rare signals (*buy* and *sell*). These are the ones that lead to market actions and thus potential profit—the final goal of this application.

Financial markets forecasting is an example of an application driven by rare events. Event-based prediction tasks are usually evaluated by the precision and recall metrics that focus the evaluation on the events, disregarding the performance of the common situations (in our case, the hold signals). *Precision* can be informally defined as the proportion of event signals produced by the models that are correct. *Recall* is defined as the proportion of events occurring in the domain that is signaled as such by the models. These metrics can be easily calculated with the help of confusion matrices that sum up the results of a model in terms of the comparison between its predictions and the true values for a particular test set. Table 3.1 shows an example of a confusion matrix for our domain.

---

[20]This obviously depends on the target profit margin you establish; but to cover the trading costs, this margin should be large enough, and this rarity will be a fact.

TABLE 3.1: A Confusion Matrix for the Prediction of Trading Signals

		Predictions			
		sell	hold	buy	
True	sell	$n_{s,s}$	$n_{s,h}$	$n_{s,b}$	$N_{s,.}$
Values	hold	$n_{h,s}$	$n_{h,h}$	$n_{h,b}$	$N_{h,.}$
	buy	$n_{b,s}$	$n_{b,h}$	$n_{b,b}$	$N_{b,.}$
		$N_{.,s}$	$N_{.,h}$	$N_{.,b}$	N

With the help of Table 3.1 we can formalize the notions of precision and recall for this problem, as follows:

$$Prec = \frac{n_{s,s} + n_{b,b}}{N_{.,s} + N_{.,b}} \tag{3.9}$$

$$Rec = \frac{n_{s,s} + n_{b,b}}{N_{s,.} + N_{b,.}} \tag{3.10}$$

We can also calculate these statistics for particular signals by obtaining the precision and recall for sell and buy signals, independently; for example,

$$Prec_b = \frac{n_{b,b}}{N_{.,b}} \tag{3.11}$$

$$Rec_b = \frac{n_{b,b}}{N_{b,.}} \tag{3.12}$$

Precision and recall are often "merged" into a single statistic, called the $F - measure$ (Rijsbergen, 1979), given by

$$F = \frac{(\beta^2 + 1) \cdot Prec \cdot Rec}{\beta^2 \cdot Prec + Rec} \tag{3.13}$$

where $0 \leq \beta \leq 1$, controls the relative importance of recall to precision.

3.4   The Prediction Models

In this section we will explore some models that can be used to address the prediction tasks defined in the previous section. The selection of models was mainly guided by the fact that these techniques are well known by their ability to handle highly nonlinear regression problems. That is the case in our problem. Still, many other methods could have been applied to this problem. Any thorough approach to this domain would necessarily require a larger comparison of more alternatives. In the context of this book, such exploration does not make sense due to its costs in terms of space and computation power required.

3.4.1   How Will the Training Data Be Used?

Complex time series problems frequently exhibit different regimes, such as periods with strong variability followed by more "stable" periods, or periods with some form of systematic tendency. These types of phenomena are often called non-stationarities and can cause serious problems to several modeling techniques due to their underlying assumptions. It is reasonably easy to see, for instance by plotting the price time series, that this is the case for our data. There are several strategies we can follow to try to overcome the negative impact of these effects. For instance, several transformation techniques can be applied to the original time series to eliminate some of the effects. The use of percentage variations (returns) instead of the original absolute price values is such an example. Other approaches include using the available data in a more selective way. Let us suppose we are given the task of obtaining a model using a certain period of training data and then testing it in a subsequent period. The standard approach would use the training data to develop the model that would then be applied to obtain predictions for the testing period. If we have strong reason to believe that there are regime shifts, using the same model on all testing periods may not be the best idea, particularly if during this period there is some regime change that can seriously damage the performance of the model. In these cases it is often better to change or adapt the model using more recent data that better captures the current regime of the data.

In time series problems there is an implicit (time) ordering among the test cases. In this context, it makes sense to assume that when we are obtaining a prediction for time i, all test cases with time tag $k < i$ already belong to the past. This means that it is safe to assume that we already know the true value of the target variable of these past test cases and, moreover, that we can safely use this information. So, if at some time m of the testing period we are confident that there is a regime shift in the time series, then we can incorporate the information of all test cases occurring before m into the initial training data, and with this refreshed training set that contains observations of the "new" regime, somehow update our predictive model to improve the performance on future test cases. One form of updating the model could be to change it in order to take into account the new training cases. These approaches are usually known as incremental learners as they adapt the current model to new evidence instead of starting from scratch. There are not so many modeling techniques that can be used in this way, particularly in R. In this context, we will follow the other approach to the updating problem, which consists of re-learning a new model with the new updated training set. This is obviously more expensive in computational terms and may even be inadequate for applications where the data arrives at a very fast pace and for which models and decisions are required almost in real-time. This is rather frequent in applications addressed in a research area usually known as data streams. In our application, we are making decisions on a daily basis after the market closes, so speed is not a key issue.[21] Assuming that we will use a re-learn approach, we have essentially two forms of incorporating the new cases into our training set. The growing window approach simply adds them to the current training set, thus constantly increasing the size of this set. The eventual problem of this approach lies in the fact that as we are assuming that more recent data is going to be helpful in producing better models, we may also consider whether the oldest part of our training data may already be too outdated and in effect, contributing to decreasing the accuracy of the models. Based on these considerations, the sliding window approach deletes the oldest data of the training set at the same time it incorporates the fresher observations, thus maintaining a training set of constant size.

Both the growing and the sliding window approaches involve a key decision: when to change or adapt the model by incorporating fresher data. There are essentially two ways of answering this question. The first involves estimating this time by checking if the performance of our current model is starting to degrade. If we observe a sudden decrease in this performance, then we can take this as a good indication of some form of regime shift. The main challenge of these approaches lies in developing proper estimates of these changes in performance. We want to detect the change as soon as possible but we do not want to overreact to some spurious test case that our model missed. Another simpler approach consists of updating the model on a regular time basis, that is, every w test case, we obtain a new model with fresher data. In this case study we follow this simpler method.

Summarizing, for each model that we will consider, we will apply it using three different approaches: (1) single model for all test period, (2) growing window with a fixed updating step of w days, and (3) sliding window with the same updating step w. Figure 3.3 illustrates the three approaches.

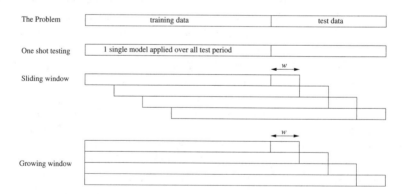

FIGURE 3.3: Three forms of obtaining predictions for a test period.

---

[21]It could be if we were trading in real-time, that is, intra-day trading.

Further readings on regime changes

The problem of detecting changes of regime in time series data is a subject studied for a long time in an area known as statistic process control (e.g., Oakland, 2007), which use techniques like control charts to detect break points in the data. This subject has been witnessing an increased interest with the impact of data streams (e.g., Gama and Gaber, 2007) in the data mining field. Several works (e.g., Gama et al., 2004; Kifer et al., 2004; Klinkenberg, 2004) have addressed the issues of how to detect the changes of regime and also how to learn models in the presence of these changes.

3.4.2   The Modeling Tools

In this section we briefly describe the modeling techniques we will use to address our prediction tasks and illustrate how to use them in R.

3.4.2.1   Artificial Neural Networks

Artificial neural networks (ANNs) are frequently used in financial forecasting (e.g., Deboeck, 1994) because of their ability to deal with highly nonlinear problems. The package nnet implements feed-forward neural nets in R. This type of neural networks is among the most used and also what we will be applying.

ANNs are formed by a set of computing units (the neurons) linked to each other. Each neuron executes two consecutive calculations: a linear combination of its inputs, followed by a nonlinear computation of the result to obtain its output value that is then fed to other neurons in the network. Each of the neuron connections has an associated weight. Constructing an artificial neural network consists of establishing an architecture for the network and then using an algorithm to find the weights of the connections between the neurons.

Feed-forward artificial neural networks have their neurons organized in layers. The first layer contains the input neurons of the network. The training observations of the problem are presented to the network through these input neurons. The final layer contains the predictions of the neural network for any case presented at its input neurons. In between, we usually have one or more "hidden" layers of neurons. The weight updating algorithms, such as the back-propagation method, try to obtain the connection weights that optimize a certain error criterion, that is, trying to ensure that the network outputs are in accordance with the cases presented to the model. This is accomplished by an iterative process of presenting several times the training cases at the input nodes of the network, and after obtaining the prediction of the network at the output nodes and calculating the respective prediction error, updating the weights in the network to try to improve its prediction error. This iterative process is repeated until some convergence criterion is met.

Feed-forward ANNs with one hidden layer can be easily obtained in R using a function of the package nnet (Venables and Ripley, 2002). The networks obtained by this function can be used for both classification and regression problems and thus are applicable to both our prediction tasks (see Section 3.3.3).

ANNs are known to be sensitive to different scales of the variables used in a prediction problem. In this context, it makes sense to transform the data before giving them to the network, in order to avoid eventual negative impacts on the performance. In our case we will normalize the data with the goal of making all variables have a mean value of zero and a standard deviation of one. This can be easily accomplished by the following transformation applied to each column of our data set:

$$y_i = \frac{x_i - \bar{x}}{\sigma_x} \qquad (3.14)$$

where $\bar{x}$ is the mean value of the original variable X, and σ_x its standard deviation.

The function `scale()` can be used to carry out this transformation for our data. In the book package you can also find the function `unscale()` that inverts the normalization process putting the values back on the original scale. Below you can find a very simple illustration of how to obtain and use this type of ANN in R:

```
> set.seed(1234)
> library(nnet)
> norm.data <- scale(Tdata.train)
> nn <- nnet(Tform, norm.data[1:1000, ], size = 10, decay = 0.01,
+      maxit = 1000, linout = T, trace = F)
> norm.preds <- predict(nn, norm.data[1001:2000, ])
> preds <- unscale(norm.preds, norm.data)
```

By default, the function `nnet()` sets the initial weights of the links between nodes with random values in the interval $[-0.5 \cdots 0.5]$. This means that two successive runs of the function with exactly the same arguments can actually lead to different solutions. To ensure you get the same results as we present below, we have added a call to the function `set.seed()` that initializes the random number generator to some seed number. This ensures that you will get exactly the same ANN as the one we report here. In this illustrative example we have used the first 1,000 cases to obtain the network and tested the model on the following 1,000. After normalizing our training data, we call the function `nnet()` to obtain the model. The first two parameters are the usual of any modeling function in R: the functional form of the model specified by a formula, and the training sample used to obtain the model. We have also used some of the parameters of the `nnet()` function. Namely, the parameter `size` allows us to specify how many nodes the hidden layer will have. There is no magic recipe on which value to use here. One usually tries several values to observe the network behavior. Still, it is reasonable to assume it should be smaller than the number of predictors of the problem. The parameter `decay` controls the weight updating rate of the back-propagation algorithm. Again, trial and error is your best friend here. Finally, the parameter `maxit` controls the maximum number of iterations the weight convergence process is allowed to use, while the `linout=T` setting tells the function that we are handling a regression problem. The `trace=F` is used to avoid some of the output of the function regarding the optimization process.

The function `predict()` can be used to obtain the predictions of the neural network for a set of test data. After obtaining these predictions, we convert them back to the original scale using the function `unscale()` provided by our package. This function receives in the first argument the values, and on the second argument the object with the normalized data. This latter object is necessary because it is within that object that the averages and standard deviations that were used to normalize the data are stored,[22] and these are required to invert the normalization.

Let us evaluate the results of the ANN for predicting the correct signals for the test set. We do this by transforming the numeric predictions into signals and then evaluate them using the statistics presented in Section 3.3.4.

```
> sigs.nn <- trading.signals(preds, 0.1, -0.1)
> true.sigs <- trading.signals(Tdata.train[1001:2000, "T.ind.GSPC"],
+       0.1, -0.1)
> sigs.PR(sigs.nn, true.sigs)

    precision    recall
s   0.2101911 0.1885714
b   0.2919255 0.5911950
s+b 0.2651357 0.3802395
```

Function `trading.signals()` transforms numeric predictions into signals, given the buy and sell thresholds, respectively. The function `sigs.PR()` obtains a matrix with the precision and recall scores of the two types of events, and overall. These scores show that the performance of the ANN is not brilliant. In effect, you get rather low precision scores, and also not so interesting recall values. The latter are not so serious as they basically mean lost opportunities and not costs. On the contrary, low precision scores mean that the model gave wrong signals rather frequently. If these signals are used for trading, this may lead to serious losses of money.

ANNs can also be used for classification tasks. For these problems the main difference in terms of network topology is that instead of a single output unit, we will have as many output units as there are values of the target variable (sometimes known as the class variable). Each of these output units will produce a probability estimate of the respective class value. This means that for each test case, an ANN can produce a set of probability values, one for each possible class value.

The use of the `nnet()` function for these tasks is very similar to its use for regression problems. The following code illustrates this, using our training data:

---

[22] As object attributes.

```
> set.seed(1234)
> library(nnet)
> signals <- trading.signals(Tdata.train[, "T.ind.GSPC"], 0.1,
+     -0.1)
> norm.data <- data.frame(signals = signals, scale(Tdata.train[,
+     -1]))
> nn <- nnet(signals ~ ., norm.data[1:1000, ], size = 10, decay = 0.01,
+     maxit = 1000, trace = F)
> preds <- predict(nn, norm.data[1001:2000, ], type = "class")
```

The `type="class"` argument is used to obtain a single class label for each test case instead of a set of probability estimates. With the network predictions we can calculate the model precision and recall as follows:

```
> sigs.PR(preds, norm.data[1001:2000, 1])
```

```
      precision    recall
s     0.2838710  0.2514286
b     0.3333333  0.2264151
s+b   0.2775665  0.2185629
```

Both the precision and recall scores are higher than the ones obtained in the regression task, although still low values.

Further readings on neural networks

The book by Rojas (1996) is a reasonable general reference on neural networks. For more financially oriented readings, the book by Zirilli (1997) is a good and easy reading book. The collection of papers entitled "Artificial Neural Networks Forecasting Time Series" (Rogers and Vemuri, 1994) is another example of a good source of references. Part I of the book by Deboeck (1994) provides several chapters devoted to the application of neural networks to trading. The work of McCulloch and Pitts (1943) presents the first model of an artificial neuron. This work was generalized by Ronsenblatt (1958) and Minsky and Papert (1969). The back-propagation algorithm, the most frequently used weight updating method, although frequently attributed to Rumelhart et al. (1986), was, according to Rojas (1996), invented by Werbos (1974, 1996).

3.4.2.2 Support Vector Machines

Support vector machines (SMVs)[23] are modeling tools that, as ANNs, can be applied to both regression and classification tasks. SVMs have been witnessing increased attention from different research communities based on their successful application to several domains and also their strong theoretical background. Vapnik (1995, 1998) and Shawe-Taylor and Cristianini (2000) are two of the essential references for SVMs. Smola and Schölkopf (2004, 1998) published an excellent tutorial giving an overview of the basic ideas underlying SVMs for regression. In R we have several implementations of SMVs available, among which we can refer to the package `kernlab` by Karatzoglou

---

[23]Extensive information on this class of models can be obtained at http://www.kernel-machines.org.

et al. (2004) with several functionalities available, and also the function `svm()` on package `e1071` by Dimitriadou et al. (2009).

The basic idea behind SVMs is that of mapping the original data into a new, high-dimensional space, where it is possible to apply linear models to obtain a separating hyper plane, for example, separating the classes of the problem, in the case of classification tasks. The mapping of the original data into this new space is carried out with the help of the so-called kernel functions. SMVs are linear machines operating on this dual representation induced by kernel functions.

The hyper plane separation in the new dual representation is frequently done by maximizing a separation margin between cases belonging to different classes; see Figure 3.4. This is an optimization problem often solved with quadratic programming methods. Soft margin methods allow for a small proportion of cases to be on the "wrong" side of the margin, each of these leading to a certain "cost".

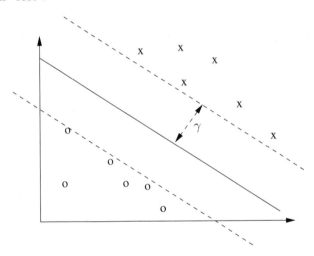

FIGURE 3.4: The margin maximization in SVMs.

In support of vector regression, the process is similar, with the main difference being on the form the errors and associated costs are calculated. This resorts usually to the use of the so-called *ε-insensitive* loss function $| \xi |_\epsilon$ given by

$$| \xi |_\epsilon = \begin{cases} 0 & \text{if } | \xi | \leq \epsilon \\ | \xi | - \epsilon & \text{otherwise} \end{cases} \tag{3.15}$$

We will now provide very simple examples of the use of this type of models in R. We start with the regression task for which we will use the function provided in the package `e1071`:

```
> library(e1071)
```

```
> sv <- svm(Tform, Tdata.train[1:1000, ], gamma = 0.001, cost = 100)
> s.preds <- predict(sv, Tdata.train[1001:2000, ])
> sigs.svm <- trading.signals(s.preds, 0.1, -0.1)
> true.sigs <- trading.signals(Tdata.train[1001:2000, "T.ind.GSPC"],
+         0.1, -0.1)
> sigs.PR(sigs.svm, true.sigs)

      precision      recall
s     0.4285714 0.03428571
b     0.3333333 0.01257862
s+b 0.4000000 0.02395210
```

In this example we have used the `svm()` function with most of its default parameters with the exception of the parameters `gamma` and `cost`. In this context, the function uses a radial basis kernel function

$$K(\mathbf{x}, \mathbf{y}) = \exp\left(-\gamma \times \|\mathbf{x} - \mathbf{y}\|^2\right) \tag{3.16}$$

where γ is a user parameter that in our call we have set to 0.001 (function `svm()` uses as default `1/ncol(data)`).

The parameter `cost` indicates the cost of the violations of the margin. You may wish to explore the help page of the function to learn more details on these and other parameters.

As we can observe, the SVM model achieves a considerably better score than the ANN in terms of precision, although with a much lower recall.

Next, we consider the classification task, this time using the `kernlab` package:

```
> library(kernlab)
> data <- cbind(signals = signals, Tdata.train[, -1])
> ksv <- ksvm(signals ~ ., data[1:1000, ], C = 10)

Using automatic sigma estimation (sigest) for RBF or laplace kernel

> ks.preds <- predict(ksv, data[1001:2000, ])
> sigs.PR(ks.preds, data[1001:2000, 1])

      precision      recall
s     0.1935484 0.2742857
b     0.2688172 0.1572327
s+b 0.2140762 0.2185629
```

We have used the C parameter of the `ksvm()` function of package `kernlab`, to specify a different cost of constraints violations, which by default is 1. Apart from this we have used the default parameter values, which for classification involves, for instance, using the radial basis kernel. Once again, more details can be obtained in the help pages of the `ksvm()` function.

The results of this SVM are not as interesting as the SVM obtained with the regression data. We should remark that by no means do we want to claim that these are the best scores we can obtain with these techniques. These are just simple illustrative examples of how to use these modeling techniques in R.

3.4.2.3 Multivariate Adaptive Regression Splines

Multivariate adaptive regression splines (Friedman, 1991) are an example of an additive regression model (Hastie and Tibshirani, 1990). A MARS model has the following general form:

$$mars\,(\mathbf{x}) = c_0 + \sum_{i=1}^{k} c_i B_i(\mathbf{x}) \qquad (3.17)$$

where the c_is are constants and the B_is are basis functions.

The basis functions can take several forms, from simple constants to functions modeling the interaction between two or more variables. Still, the most common basis functions are the so-called *hinge* functions that have the form

$$H[-(x_i - t)] = \max(0, t - x_i) \qquad H[+(x_i - t)] = \max(0, x_i - t)$$

where x_i is a predictor and t a threshold value on this predictor. Figure 3.5 shows an example of two of these functions.

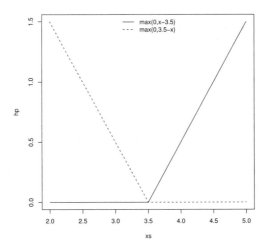

FIGURE 3.5: An example of two hinge functions with the same threshold.

MARS models have been implemented in at least two packages within R. Package `mda` (Leisch et al., 2009) contains the function `mars()` that implements this method. Package `earth` (Milborrow, 2009) has the function `earth()` that also implements this methodology. This latter function has the advantage of following a more standard R schema in terms of modeling functions, by providing a formula-based interface. It also implements several other facilities not present in the other package and thus it will be our selection.

The following code applies the function `earth()` to the regression task

```
> library(earth)
> e <- earth(Tform, Tdata.train[1:1000, ])
> e.preds <- predict(e, Tdata.train[1001:2000, ])
> sigs.e <- trading.signals(e.preds, 0.1, -0.1)
> true.sigs <- trading.signals(Tdata.train[1001:2000, "T.ind.GSPC"],
+        0.1, -0.1)
> sigs.PR(sigs.e, true.sigs)

      precision     recall
s     0.2785714 0.2228571
b     0.4029851 0.1698113
s+b 0.3188406 0.1976048
```

The results are comparable to the ones obtained with SVMs for classification, with precision scores around 30%, although with lower recall.

MARS is only applicable to regression problems so we do not show any example for the classification task.

Further readings on multivariate adaptive regression splines

The definitive reference on MARS is the original journal article by Friedman (1991). This is a very well-written article providing all details concerning the motivation for the development of MARS as well as the techniques used in the system. The article also includes quite an interesting discussion section by other scientists that provides other views of this work.

3.5   From Predictions into Actions

This section will address the issue of how will we use the signal predictions obtained with the modeling techniques described previously. Given a set of signals output by some model there are many ways we can use them to act on the market.

3.5.1   How Will the Predictions Be Used?

In our case study we will assume we will be trading in future markets. These markets are based on contracts to buy or sell a commodity on a certain date in the future at the price determined by the market at that future time. The technical details of these contracts are beyond the scope of this manuscript. Still, in objective terms, this means that our trading system will be able to open two types of trading positions: long and short. Long positions are opened by buying a commodity at time t and price p, and selling it at a later time $t + x$. It makes sense for the trader to open such positions when he has the expectation that the price will rise in the future, thus allowing him to make some profit with that transaction. On short positions, the trader sells the security at time t with price p with the obligation of buying it in the future. This is possible thanks to a borrowing schema whose details you can find in appropriate documents (e.g., Wikipedia). These types of positions allows the trader to make profit when the prices decline as he/she will buy the security at a time later than t. Informally, we can say that we will open short positions when we believe the prices are going down, and open long positions when we believe the prices are going up.

Given a set of signals, there are many ways we can use them to trade in future markets. We will describe a few plausible trading strategies that we will be using and comparing in our experiments with the models. Due to space and time constraints, it is not possible to explore this important issue further. Still, the reader is left with some plausible strategies and with the means to develop and try other possibilities.

The mechanics of the first trading strategy we are going to use are the following. First, all decisions will be taken at the end of the day, that is, after knowing all daily quotes of the current session. Suppose that at the end of day t, our models provide evidence that the prices are going down, that is, predicting a low value of T or a sell signal. If we already have a position opened, the indication of the model will be ignored. If we currently do not hold any opened position, we will open a short position by issuing a sell order. When this order is carried out by the market at a price pr sometime in the future, we will immediately post two other orders. The first is a buy limit order with a limit price of $pr - p\%$, where $p\%$ is a target profit margin. This type of order is carried out only if the market price reaches the target limit price or below. This order expresses what our target profit is for the short position just opened. We will wait 10 days for this target to be reached. If the order is not carried out by this deadline, we will buy at the closing price of the 10th day. The second order is a buy stop order with a price limit $pr + l\%$. This order is placed with the goal of limiting our eventual losses with this position. The order will be executed if the market reaches the price $pr + l\%$, thus limiting our possible losses to $l\%$.

If our models provide indications that the prices will rise in the near future, with high predicted T values or buy signals, we will consider opening a long position. This position will only be opened if we are currently out of the market. With this purpose we will post a buy order that will be accomplished at a time t and price pr. As before, we will immediately post two new orders. The first will be a sell limit order with a target price of $pr + p\%$, which will only be executed if the market reaches a price of $pr + p\%$ or above. This sell limit order will have a deadline of 10 days, as before.The second order is a sell stop order with price $pr - l\%$, which will again limit our eventual losses to $l\%$.

This first strategy can be seen as a bit conservative as it will only have a single position opened at any time. Moreover, after 10 days of waiting for the target profit, the positions are immediately closed. We will also consider a more "risky" trading strategy. This other strategy is similar to the previous one, with the exception that we will always open new positions if there are signals with that indication, and if we have sufficient money for that. Moreover, we will wait forever for the positions to reach either the target profit or the maximum allowed loss.

We will only consider these two main trading strategies with slight variations on the used parameters (e.g., holding time, expected profit margin, or amount of money invested on each position). As mentioned, these are simply chosen for illustrative purposes.

3.5.2   Trading-Related Evaluation Criteria

The metrics described in Section 3.3.4 do not translate directly to the overall goal of this application, which has to do with economic performance. Factors like the economic results and the risk exposure of some financial instrument or tool are of key importance in this context. This is an area that alone could easily fill this chapter. The R package `PerformanceAnalytics` (Carl and Peterson, 2009) implements many of the existing financial metrics for analyzing the returns of some trading algorithm as the one we are proposing in this chapter. We will use some of the functions provided by this package to collect information on the economic performance of our proposals. Our evaluation will be focused on the overall results of the methods, on their risk exposure, and on the average results of each position hold by the models. In the final evaluation of our proposed system to be described in Section 3.7, we will carry out a more in-depth analysis of its performance using tools provided by this package.

With respect to the overall results, we will use (1) the simple net balance between the initial capital and the capital at the end of the testing period (sometimes called the profit/loss), (2) the percentage return that this net balance represents, and (3) the excess return over the buy and hold strategy. This strategy consists of opening a long position at the beginning of the testing period and waiting until the end to close it. The return over the buy and hold measures the difference between the return of our trading strategy and this simple strategy.

Regarding risk-related measures, we will use the Sharpe ratio coefficient, which measures the return per unit of risk, the latter being measured as the standard deviation of the returns. We will also calculate the maximum drawdown, which measures the maximum cumulative successive loss of a model. This is an important risk measure for traders, as any system that goes over a serious draw-down is probably doomed to be without money to run, as investors will most surely be scared by these successive losses and redraw their money.

Finally, the performance of the positions hold during the test period will be evaluated by their number, the average return per position, and the percentage of profitable positions, as well as other less relevant metrics.

3.5.3   Putting Everything Together: A Simulated Trader

This section describes how to implement the ideas we have sketched regarding trading with the signals of our models. Our book package provides the function `trading.simulator()`, which can be used to put all these ideas together by carrying out a trading simulation with the signals of any model. The main parameters of this function are the market quotes for the simulation period and the model signals for this period. Two other parameters are the name of the user-defined trading policy function and its list of parameters. Finally, we can also specify the cost of each transaction and the initial capital available for the trader. The simulator will call the user-provided trading policy function at the end of each daily section, and the function should return the orders that it wants the simulator to carry out. The simulator carries out these orders on the market and records all activity on several data structures. The result of the simulator is an object of class `tradeRecord` containing the information of this simulation. This object can then be used in other functions to obtain economic evaluation metrics or graphs of the trading activity, as we will see.

Before proceeding with an example of this type of simulation, we need to provide further details on the trading policy functions that the user needs to supply to the simulator. These functions should be written using a certain protocol, that is, they should be aware of how the simulator will call them, and should return the information this simulator is expecting.

At the end of each daily session d, the simulator calls the trading policy function with four main arguments plus any other parameters the user has provided in the call to the simulator. These four arguments are (1) a vector with the predicted signals until day d, (2) the market quotes (up to d), (3) the currently opened positions, and (4) the money currently available to the trader. The current position is a matrix with as many rows as there are open positions at the end of day d. This matrix has four columns: "pos.type" that can be 1 for a long position or -1 for a short position; "N.stocks", which is the number of stocks of the position; "Odate", which is the day on which the position was opened (a number between 1 and d); and "Oprice", which is the price at which the position was opened. The row names of this matrix contain the IDs of the positions that are relevant when we want to indicate the simulator that a certain position is to be closed.

All this information is provided by the simulator to ensure the user can define a broad set of trading policy functions. The user-defined functions should return a data frame with a set of orders that the simulator should carry out. This data frame should include the following information (columns): "order", which should be 1 for buy orders and -1 for sell orders; "order.type", which should be 1 for market orders that are to be carried out immediately (actually at next day open price), 2 for limit orders or 3 for stop orders; "val", which should be the quantity of stocks to trade for opening market orders, NA for closing market orders, or a target price for limit and stop orders; "action", which should be "open" for orders that are opening a new position or "close" for orders closing an existing position; and finally, "posID", which should contain the ID of the position that is being closed, if applicable.

The following is an illustration of a user-defined trading policy function:

```
> policy.1 <- function(signals,market,opened.pos,money,
+                       bet=0.2,hold.time=10,
+                       exp.prof=0.025, max.loss= 0.05
+                      )
+    {
+       d <- NROW(market) # this is the ID of today
+       orders <- NULL
+       nOs <- NROW(opened.pos)
+       # nothing to do!
+       if (!nOs && signals[d] == 'h') return(orders)
+
+       # First lets check if we can open new positions
+       # i) long positions
+       if (signals[d] == 'b' && !nOs) {
+         quant <- round(bet*money/market[d,'Close'],0)
+         if (quant > 0)
+           orders <- rbind(orders,
+                 data.frame(order=c(1,-1,-1),order.type=c(1,2,3),
+                       val = c(quant,
+                                 market[d,'Close']*(1+exp.prof),
+                                 market[d,'Close']*(1-max.loss)
+                                ),
+                       action = c('open','close','close'),
+                       posID = c(NA,NA,NA)
+                      )
+                     )
+
+       # ii) short positions
+       } else if (signals[d] == 's' && !nOs) {
+         # this is the nr of stocks we already need to buy
+         # because of currently opened short positions
+         need2buy <- sum(opened.pos[opened.pos[,'pos.type']==-1,
+                             "N.stocks"])*market[d,'Close']
+         quant <- round(bet*(money-need2buy)/market[d,'Close'],0)
+         if (quant > 0)
+           orders <- rbind(orders,
+                 data.frame(order=c(-1,1,1),order.type=c(1,2,3),
+                       val = c(quant,
+                                 market[d,'Close']*(1-exp.prof),
+                                 market[d,'Close']*(1+max.loss)
+                                ),
```

```
+                              action = c('open','close','close'),
+                              posID = c(NA,NA,NA)
+                              )
+                     )
+    }
+
+    # Now lets check if we need to close positions
+    # because their holding time is over
+    if (nOs)
+      for(i in 1:nOs) {
+        if (d - opened.pos[i,'Odate'] >= hold.time)
+          orders <- rbind(orders,
+               data.frame(order=-opened.pos[i,'pos.type'],
+                          order.type=1,
+                          val = NA,
+                          action = 'close',
+                          posID = rownames(opened.pos)[i]
+                          )
+                     )
+      }
+
+    orders
+  }
```

This `policy.1()` function implements the first trading strategy we described in Section 3.5.1. The function has four parameters that we can use to tune this strategy. These are the `bet` parameter, which specifies the percentage of our current money, that we will invest each time we open a new position; the `exp.prof` parameter, which indicates the profit margin we wish for our positions and is used when posting the limit orders; the `max.loss`, which indicates the maximum loss we are willing to admit before we close the position, and is used in stop orders; and the `hold.time` parameter, which indicates the number of days we are willing to wait to reach the profit margin. If the holding time is reached without achieving the wanted margin, the positions are closed.

Notice that whenever we open a new position, we send three orders back to the simulator: a market order to open the position, a limit order to specify our target profit margin, and a stop order to limit our losses.

Equivalently, the following function implements our second trading strategy:

```
> policy.2 <- function(signals,market,opened.pos,money,
+                       bet=0.2,exp.prof=0.025, max.loss= 0.05
+                      )
+    {
+      d <- NROW(market) # this is the ID of today
+      orders <- NULL
+      nOs <- NROW(opened.pos)
```

```
+       # nothing to do!
+       if (!nOs && signals[d] == 'h') return(orders)
+
+       # First lets check if we can open new positions
+       # i) long positions
+       if (signals[d] == 'b') {
+         quant <- round(bet*money/market[d,'Close'],0)
+         if (quant > 0)
+           orders <- rbind(orders,
+                 data.frame(order=c(1,-1,-1),order.type=c(1,2,3),
+                         val = c(quant,
+                                 market[d,'Close']*(1+exp.prof),
+                                 market[d,'Close']*(1-max.loss)
+                                 ),
+                         action = c('open','close','close'),
+                         posID = c(NA,NA,NA)
+                         )
+                         )
+
+       # ii) short positions
+       } else if (signals[d] == 's') {
+         # this is the money already committed to buy stocks
+         # because of currently opened short positions
+         need2buy <- sum(opened.pos[opened.pos[,'pos.type']==-1,
+                                 "N.stocks"])*market[d,'Close']
+         quant <- round(bet*(money-need2buy)/market[d,'Close'],0)
+         if (quant > 0)
+           orders <- rbind(orders,
+                 data.frame(order=c(-1,1,1),order.type=c(1,2,3),
+                         val = c(quant,
+                                 market[d,'Close']*(1-exp.prof),
+                                 market[d,'Close']*(1+max.loss)
+                                 ),
+                         action = c('open','close','close'),
+                         posID = c(NA,NA,NA)
+                         )
+                         )
+       }
+
+       orders
+   }
```

This function is very similar to the previous one. The main difference lies in the fact that in this trading policy we allow for more than one position to be opened at the same time, and also there is no aging limit for closing the positions.

Having defined the trading policy functions, we are ready to try our trading simulator. For illustration purposes we will select a small sample of our data to obtain an SVM, which is then used to obtain predictions for a subsequent period. We call our trading simulator with these predictions to obtain the results of trading using the signals of the SVM in the context of a certain trading policy.

```
> # Train and test periods
> start <- 1
> len.tr <- 1000
> len.ts <- 500
> tr <- start:(start+len.tr-1)
> ts <- (start+len.tr):(start+len.tr+len.ts-1)
> # getting the quotes for the testing period
> data(GSPC)
> date <- rownames(Tdata.train[start+len.tr,])
> market <- GSPC[paste(date,'/',sep='')][1:len.ts]
> # learning the model and obtaining its signal predictions
> library(e1071)
> s <- svm(Tform,Tdata.train[tr,],cost=10,gamma=0.01)
> p <- predict(s,Tdata.train[ts,])
> sig <- trading.signals(p,0.1,-0.1)
> # now using the simulated trader
> t1 <- trading.simulator(market,sig,
+                 'policy.1',list(exp.prof=0.05,bet=0.2,hold.time=30))
```

Please note that for this code to work, you have to previously create the objects with the data for modeling, using the instructions given in Section 3.3.3.

In our call to the trading simulator we have selected the first trading policy and have provided some different values for some of its parameters. We have used the default values for transaction costs (five monetary units) and for the initial capital (1 million monetary units). The result of the call is an object of class `tradeRecord`. We can check its contents as follows:

```
> t1

Object of class tradeRecord with slots:

        trading: <xts object with a numeric  500 x 5  matrix>
        positions: <numeric  16 x 7  matrix>
        init.cap :   1e+06
        trans.cost :  5
        policy.func :  policy.1
        policy.pars :  <list with  3  elements>

> summary(t1)

== Summary of a Trading Simulation with  500  days ==

Trading policy function :  policy.1
Policy function parameters:
        exp.prof  =  0.05
```

```
      bet  =  0.2
      hold.time  =  30

Transaction costs :   5
Initial Equity    :   1e+06
Final Equity      :   997211.9   Return :   -0.28 %
Number of trading positions:   16
```

Use function "tradingEvaluation()" for further stats on this simulation.

The function `tradingEvaluation()` can be used to obtain a series of economic indicators of the performance during this simulation period:

```
> tradingEvaluation(t1)
```

NTrades	NProf	PercProf	PL	Ret	RetOverBH
16.00	8.00	50.00	-2788.09	-0.28	-7.13
MaxDD	SharpeRatio	AvgProf	AvgLoss	AvgPL	MaxProf
59693.15	0.00	4.97	-4.91	0.03	5.26
MaxLoss					
-5.00					

We can also obtain a graphical overview of the performance of the trader using the function `plot()` as follows:

```
> plot(t1, market, theme = "white", name = "SP500")
```

The result of this command is shown on Figure 3.6.

The results of this trader are bad, with a negative return. Would the scenario be different if we used the second trading policy? Let us see:

```
> t2 <- trading.simulator(market, sig, "policy.2", list(exp.prof = 0.05,
+      bet = 0.3))
> summary(t2)

== Summary of a Trading Simulation with  500  days ==

Trading policy function :  policy.2
Policy function parameters:
      exp.prof  =  0.05
      bet  =  0.3

Transaction costs :   5
Initial Equity    :   1e+06
Final Equity      :   961552.5   Return :   -3.84 %
Number of trading positions:   29
```

Use function "tradingEvaluation()" for further stats on this simulation.

```
> tradingEvaluation(t2)
```

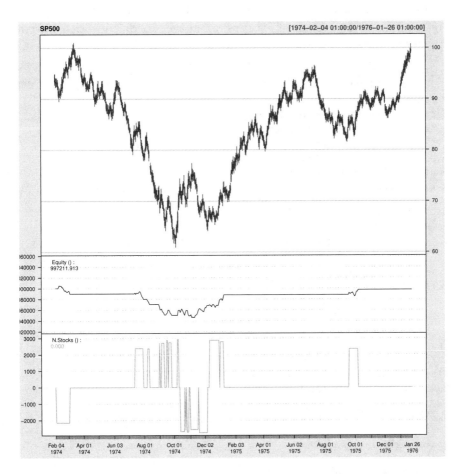

FIGURE 3.6: The results of trading using Policy 1 based on the signals of an SVM.

NTrades	NProf	PercProf	PL	Ret	RetOverBH
29.00	14.00	48.28	-38447.49	-3.84	-10.69
MaxDD	SharpeRatio	AvgProf	AvgLoss	AvgPL	MaxProf
156535.05	-0.02	4.99	-4.84	-0.10	5.26
MaxLoss					
-5.00					

Using the same signals but with a different trading policy the return decreased from -0.27% to -2.86%. Let us repeat the experiment with a different training and testing period:

```
> start <- 2000
> len.tr <- 1000
> len.ts <- 500
> tr <- start:(start + len.tr - 1)
> ts <- (start + len.tr):(start + len.tr + len.ts - 1)
> s <- svm(Tform, Tdata.train[tr, ], cost = 10, gamma = 0.01)
> p <- predict(s, Tdata.train[ts, ])
> sig <- trading.signals(p, 0.1, -0.1)
> t2 <- trading.simulator(market, sig, "policy.2", list(exp.prof = 0.05,
+     bet = 0.3))
> summary(t2)

== Summary of a Trading Simulation with  500  days ==

Trading policy function :  policy.2
Policy function parameters:
        exp.prof  =  0.05
        bet  =  0.3

Transaction costs :  5
Initial Equity    :  1e+06
Final Equity      :  107376.3   Return :  -89.26 %
Number of trading positions:  229

Use function "tradingEvaluation()" for further stats on this simulation.

> tradingEvaluation(t2)
```

NTrades	NProf	PercProf	PL	Ret	RetOverBH
229.00	67.00	29.26	-892623.73	-89.26	-96.11
MaxDD	SharpeRatio	AvgProf	AvgLoss	AvgPL	MaxProf
959624.80	-0.08	5.26	-4.50	-1.65	5.26
MaxLoss					
-5.90					

This trader, obtained by the same modeling technique and using the same trading strategy, obtained a considerable worse result. The major lesson to be learned here is: reliable statistical estimates. Do not be fooled by a few repetitions of some experiments, even if it includes a 2-year testing period.

We need more repetitions under different conditions to ensure some statistical reliability of our results. This is particularly true for time series models that have to handle different regimes (e.g., periods with rather different volatility or trend). This is the topic of the next section.

3.6   Model Evaluation and Selection

In this section we will consider how to obtain reliable estimates of the selected evaluation criteria. These estimates will allow us to properly compare and select among different alternative trading systems.

3.6.1   Monte Carlo Estimates

Time series problems like the one we are addressing bring new challenges in terms of obtaining reliable estimates of our evaluation metrics. This is caused by the fact that all data observations have an attached time tag that imposes an ordering among them. This ordering should be respected with the risk of obtaining estimates that are not reliable. In Chapter 2 we used the cross-validation method to obtain reliable estimates of evaluation statistics. This methodology includes a random re-sampling step that changes the original ordering of the observations. This means that cross-validation should not be applied to time series problems. Applying this method could mean to test models on observations that are older than the ones used to obtain them. This is not feasible in reality, and thus the estimates obtained by this process are unreliable and possibly overly optimistic, as it is easier to predict the past given the future than the opposite.

Any estimation process using time series data should ensure that the models are always tested on data that is more recent than the data used to obtain the models. This means no random re-sampling of the observations or any other process that changes the time ordering of the given data. However, any proper estimation process should include some random choices to ensure the statistical reliability of the obtained estimates. This involves repeating the estimation process several times under different conditions, preferably randomly selected. Given a time series dataset spanning from time t to time $t + N$, how can we ensure this? First, we have to choose the train+test setup for which we want to obtain estimates. This means deciding what is the size of both the train and test sets to be used in the estimation process. The sum of these two sizes should be smaller than N to ensure that we are able to randomly generate different experimental scenarios with the data that was provided to us. However, if we select a too small training size, we may seriously impair the performance of our models. Similarly, small test sets will also be less reliable, particularly if we suspect there are regime shifts in our problem and we wish to test the models under these circumstances.

Our dataset includes roughly 30 years of daily quotes. We will evaluate all alternatives by estimating their performance on a test set of 5 years of quotes, when given 10 years of training data. This ensures train and test sizes that are sufficiently large; and, moreover, it leaves space for different repetitions of this testing process as we have 30 years of data.

In terms of experimental methodology, we will use a Monte Carlo experiment to obtain reliable estimates of our evaluation metrics. Monte Carlo methods rely on random sampling to obtain their results. We are going to use this sampling process to choose a set of R points in our 30-year period of quotes. For each randomly selected time point r, we will use the previous 10 years of quotes to obtain the models and the subsequent 5 years to test them. At the end of these R iterations we will have R estimates for each of our evaluation metrics. Each of these estimates is obtained on a randomly selected window of 15 years of data, the first 10 years used for training and the remaining 5 years for testing. This ensures that our experiments always respect the time ordering of the time series data. Repeating the process R times will ensure sufficient variability on the train+test conditions, which increases the reliability of our estimates. Moreover, if we use the same set of R randomly selected points for evaluating different alternatives, we can carry out paired comparisons to obtain statistical confidence levels on the observed differences of mean performance. Figure 3.7 summarizes the Monte Carlo experimental method. Notice that as we have to ensure that for every random point r there are 10 years of data before and 5 years after, this eliminates some of the data from the random selection of the R points.

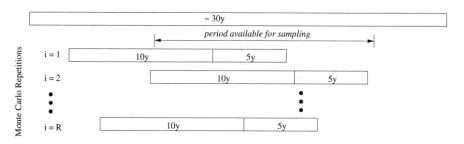

FIGURE 3.7: The Monte Carlo experimental process.

The function `experimentalComparison()`, which was used in Chapter 2 for carrying out k-fold cross-validation experiments, can also be used for Monte Carlo experiments. In the next section we will use it to obtain reliable estimates of the selected evaluation metrics for several alternative trading systems.

3.6.2 Experimental Comparisons

This section describes a set of Monte Carlo experiments designed to obtain reliable estimates of the evaluation criteria mentioned in Sections 3.3.4 and 3.5.2. The base data used in these experiments are the datasets created at the end of Section 3.3.3.

Each of the alternative predictive models considered on these experiments will be used in three different model updating setups. These were already described in Section 3.4.1 and consist of using a single model for all 5-year testing periods, using a sliding window or a growing window. The book package contains two functions that help in the use of any model with these windowing schemes. Functions `slidingWindow()` and `growingWindow()` have five main arguments. The first is an object of class `learner` that we have used before to hold all details on a learning system (function name and parameter values). The second argument is the formula describing the prediction task, while the third and fourth include the train and test datasets, respectively. The final argument is the re-learning step to use in the windowing schema. After the number of test cases is specified in this argument, the model is re-relearned, either by sliding or growing the training data used to obtain the previous model. Both functions return the predictions of the model for the provided test set using the respective windowing schema.

The following code creates a set of functions that will be used to carry out a full train+test+evaluate cycle of the different trading systems we will compare. These functions will be called from within the Monte Carlo routines for different train+test periods according to the schema described in Figure 3.7.

```
> MC.svmR <- function(form, train, test, b.t = 0.1, s.t = -0.1,
+        ...) {
+        require(e1071)
+        t <- svm(form, train, ...)
+        p <- predict(t, test)
+        trading.signals(p, b.t, s.t)
+ }
> MC.svmC <- function(form, train, test, b.t = 0.1, s.t = -0.1,
+        ...) {
+        require(e1071)
+        tgtName <- all.vars(form)[1]
+        train[, tgtName] <- trading.signals(train[, tgtName],
+            b.t, s.t)
+        t <- svm(form, train, ...)
+        p <- predict(t, test)
+        factor(p, levels = c("s", "h", "b"))
+ }
> MC.nnetR <- function(form, train, test, b.t = 0.1, s.t = -0.1,
+        ...) {
+        require(nnet)
+        t <- nnet(form, train, ...)
+        p <- predict(t, test)
```

```
+       trading.signals(p, b.t, s.t)
+ }
> MC.nnetC <- function(form, train, test, b.t = 0.1, s.t = -0.1,
+       ...) {
+       require(nnet)
+       tgtName <- all.vars(form)[1]
+       train[, tgtName] <- trading.signals(train[, tgtName],
+           b.t, s.t)
+       t <- nnet(form, train, ...)
+       p <- predict(t, test, type = "class")
+       factor(p, levels = c("s", "h", "b"))
+ }
> MC.earth <- function(form, train, test, b.t = 0.1, s.t = -0.1,
+       ...) {
+       require(earth)
+       t <- earth(form, train, ...)
+       p <- predict(t, test)
+       trading.signals(p, b.t, s.t)
+ }
> single <- function(form, train, test, learner, policy.func,
+       ...) {
+       p <- do.call(paste("MC", learner, sep = "."), list(form,
+           train, test, ...))
+       eval.stats(form, train, test, p, policy.func = policy.func)
+ }
> slide <- function(form, train, test, learner, relearn.step,
+       policy.func, ...) {
+       real.learner <- learner(paste("MC", learner, sep = "."),
+           pars = list(...))
+       p <- slidingWindowTest(real.learner, form, train, test,
+           relearn.step)
+       p <- factor(p, levels = 1:3, labels = c("s", "h", "b"))
+       eval.stats(form, train, test, p, policy.func = policy.func)
+ }
> grow <- function(form, train, test, learner, relearn.step,
+       policy.func, ...) {
+       real.learner <- learner(paste("MC", learner, sep = "."),
+           pars = list(...))
+       p <- growingWindowTest(real.learner, form, train, test,
+           relearn.step)
+       p <- factor(p, levels = 1:3, labels = c("s", "h", "b"))
+       eval.stats(form, train, test, p, policy.func = policy.func)
+ }
```

The functions MC.x() obtain different models using the provided formula and training set, and then test them on the given test set, returning the predictions. When appropriate, we have a version for the regression task (name ending in "R") and another for the classification tasks (name ending in "C"). Note that both these alternatives follow different pre- and post-processing steps to get to the final result that is a set of predicted signals. These functions are called from the `single()`, `slide()`, and `grow()` functions. These three functions obtain the predictions for the test set using the model specified in the parameter `learner`, using the respective model updating mechanism. After obtaining the predictions, these functions collect the evaluation statistics we want to estimate with a call to the function `eval.stats()` that is given below.

```
> eval.stats <- function(form,train,test,preds,b.t=0.1,s.t=-0.1,...) {
+    # Signals evaluation
+    tgtName <- all.vars(form)[1]
+    test[,tgtName] <- trading.signals(test[,tgtName],b.t,s.t)
+    st <- sigs.PR(preds,test[,tgtName])
+    dim(st) <- NULL
+    names(st) <- paste(rep(c('prec','rec'),each=3),
+                       c('s','b','sb'),sep='.')
+
+    # Trading evaluation
+    date <- rownames(test)[1]
+    market <- GSPC[paste(date,"/",sep="")][1:length(preds),]
+    trade.res <- trading.simulator(market,preds,...)
+
+    c(st,tradingEvaluation(trade.res))
+ }
```

The function `eval.stats()` uses two other functions to collect the precision and recall of the signals, and several economic evaluation metrics. Function `sigs.PR()` receives as arguments the predicted and true signals, and calculates precision and recall for the sell, buy, and sell+buy signals. The other function is `tradingEvaluation()`, which obtains the economic metrics of a given trading record. This trading record is obtained with the function `trading.simulator()`, which can be used to simulate acting on the market with the model signals. All these function were fully described and exemplified in Section 3.5.3.

The functions `single()`, `slide()`, and `grow()` are called from the Monte Carlo routines with the proper parameters filled in so that we obtain the models we want to compare. Below we describe how to set up a loop that goes over a set of alternative trading systems and calls these functions to obtain estimates of their performance. Each trading system is formed by some learning model with some specific learning parameters, plus a trading strategy that specifies how the model predictions are used for trading. With respect to trading policies, we will consider three variants that derive from the policies specified in Section 3.5.3 (functions `policy.1()` and `policy.2()`). The following functions implement these three variants:

```
> pol1 <- function(signals,market,op,money)
+    policy.1(signals,market,op,money,
+            bet=0.2,exp.prof=0.025,max.loss=0.05,hold.time=10)
```

```
> pol2 <- function(signals,market,op,money)
+   policy.1(signals,market,op,money,
+           bet=0.2,exp.prof=0.05,max.loss=0.05,hold.time=20)
> pol3 <- function(signals,market,op,money)
+   policy.2(signals,market,op,money,
+           bet=0.5,exp.prof=0.05,max.loss=0.05)
```

The following code runs the Monte Carlo experiments. We recommend that you think twice before running this code. Even on rather fast computers, it will take several days to complete. On the book Web page we provide the objects resulting from running the experiments so that you can replicate the result analysis that will follow, without having to run these experiments on your computer.

```
> # The list of learners we will use
> TODO <- c('svmR','svmC','earth','nnetR','nnetC')
> # The datasets used in the comparison
> DSs <- list(dataset(Tform,Tdata.train,'SP500'))
> # Monte Carlo (MC) settings used
> MCsetts <- mcSettings(20,      # 20 repetitions of the MC exps
+                       2540,    # ~ 10 years for training
+                       1270,    # ~ 5 years for testing
+                       1234)    # random number generator seed
> # Variants to try for all learners
> VARS <- list()
> VARS$svmR    <- list(cost=c(10,150),gamma=c(0.01,0.001),
+                      policy.func=c('pol1','pol2','pol3'))
> VARS$svmC    <- list(cost=c(10,150),gamma=c(0.01,0.001),
+                      policy.func=c('pol1','pol2','pol3'))
> VARS$earth <- list(nk=c(10,17),degree=c(1,2),thresh=c(0.01,0.001),
+                      policy.func=c('pol1','pol2','pol3'))
> VARS$nnetR  <- list(linout=T,maxit=750,size=c(5,10),
+                      decay=c(0.001,0.01),
+                      policy.func=c('pol1','pol2','pol3'))
> VARS$nnetC  <- list(maxit=750,size=c(5,10),decay=c(0.001,0.01),
+                      policy.func=c('pol1','pol2','pol3'))
> # main loop
> for(td in TODO) {
+   assign(td,
+          experimentalComparison(
+            DSs,
+            c(
+              do.call('variants',
+                      c(list('single',learner=td),VARS[[td]],
+                        varsRootName=paste('single',td,sep='.'))),
+              do.call('variants',
+                      c(list('slide',learner=td,
+                             relearn.step=c(60,120)),
+                        VARS[[td]],
```

```
+                        varsRootName=paste('slide',td,sep='.'))),
+              do.call('variants',
+                  c(list('grow',learner=td,
+                         relearn.step=c(60,120)),
+                    VARS[[td]],
+                    varsRootName=paste('single',td,sep='.')))
+          ),
+        MCsetts)
+      )
+
+    # save the results
+    save(list=td,file=paste(td,'Rdata',sep='.'))
+ }
```

The MCsetts object controls the general parameters of the experiment that specify the number of repetitions (20), the size of the training sets (2,540 $\sim$ 10 years), the size of the test sets (1,270 $\sim$ 5 years), and the random number generator seed to use.

The VARS list contains all parameter variants we want to try for each learner. The variants consist of all possible combinations of the values we indicate for the parameters in the list. Each of these variants will then be run in three different model updating "modes": single, sliding window, and growing window. Moreover, we will try for the two latter modes two re-learn steps: 60 and 120 days.

For the svm models we tried four learning parameter variants together with three different trading policies, that is, 12 variants. For earth we tried 24 variants and for nnet another 12. Each of these variants were tried in single mode and on the four windowing schemes (two strategies with two different re-learn steps). This obviously results in a lot of experiments being carried out. Namely, there will be 60 (= 12 + 24 + 24) svm variants, 120 (= 24 + 48 + 48) earth variants, and 60 nnet variants. Each of them will be executed 20 times with a training set of 10 years and a test set of 5 years. This is why we mentioned that it would take a long time to run the experiments. However, we should remark that this is a tiny sample of all possibilities of tuning that we have mentioned during the description of our approach to this problem. There were far too many "small" decisions where we could have followed other paths (e.g., the buy/sell thresholds, other learning systems, etc.). This means that any serious attempt at this domain of application will require massive computation resources to carry out a proper model selection. This is clearly outside the scope of this book. Our aim here is to provide the reader with proper methodological guidance and not to help find the best trading system for this particular data.

3.6.3   Results Analysis

The code provided in the previous section generates five data files with the objects containing the results of all variants involving the five learning systems we have tried. These data files are named "svmR.Rdata", "svmC.Rdata", "earth.Rdata", "nnetR.Rdata", and "nnetC.Rdata". Each of them contains an object with the same name as the file, except the extension. These objects are of class `compExp`, and our package contains several methods that can be used to explore the results they store.

Because you probably did not run the experiments yourself, you can find the files on the book Web page. Download them to your computer and then use the following commands to load the objects into R:

```
> load("svmR.Rdata")
> load("svmC.Rdata")
> load("earth.Rdata")
> load("nnetR.Rdata")
> load("nnetC.Rdata")
```

For each trading system variant, we have measured several statistics of performance. Some are related to the performance in terms of predicting the correct signals, while others are related to the economic performance when using these signals to trade. Deciding which are the best models according to our experiments involves a balance between all these scores. The selected model(s) may vary depending on which criteria we value the most.

Despite the diversity of evaluation scores we can still identify some of them as being more relevant. Among the signal prediction statistics, precision is clearly more important than recall for this application. In effect, precision has to do with the predicted signals, and these drive the trading activity as they are the causes for opening positions. Low precision scores are caused by wrong signals, which means opening positions at the wrong timings. This will most surely lead to high losses. Recall does not have this cost potential. Recall measures the ability of the models to capture trading opportunities. If this score is low, it means lost opportunities, but not high costs. In this context, we will be particularly interested in the scores of the models at the statistic "prec.sb", which measures the precision of the buy and sell signals.

In terms of trading performance, the return of the systems is important (statistic "Ret" in our experiments), as well as the return over the buy and hold strategy ("RetOverBH" in our experiments). Also important is the percentage of profitable trades, which should be clearly above 50% (statistic "PercProf"). In terms of risk analysis, it is relevant to look at both the value of the Sharpe ratio and the Maximum Draw-Down ("MaxDD").

The function `summary()` can be applied to our loaded `compExp` objects. However, given the number of variants and performance statistics, the output can be overwhelming in this case.

An alternative is to use the function `rankSystems()` provided by our package. With this function we can obtain a top chart for the evaluation statistics in which we are interested, indicating the best models and their scores:

```
> tgtStats <- c('prec.sb','Ret','PercProf',
+               'MaxDD','SharpeRatio')
> allSysRes <- join(subset(svmR,stats=tgtStats),
+                   subset(svmC,stats=tgtStats),
+                   subset(nnetR,stats=tgtStats),
+                   subset(nnetC,stats=tgtStats),
+                   subset(earth,stats=tgtStats),
+                   by = 'variants')
> rankSystems(allSysRes,5,maxs=c(T,T,T,F,T))

$SP500
$SP500$prec.sb
           system score
1  slide.svmC.v5      1
2  slide.svmC.v6      1
3 slide.svmC.v13      1
4 slide.svmC.v14      1
5 slide.svmC.v21      1


$SP500$Ret
             system   score
1 single.nnetR.v12 97.4240
2  single.svmR.v11  3.4960
3   slide.nnetR.v15  2.6230
4  single.svmC.v12  0.7875
5    single.svmR.v8  0.6115


$SP500$PercProf
           system   score
1 grow.nnetR.v5 60.4160
2 grow.nnetR.v6 60.3640
3 slide.svmR.v3 60.3615
4  grow.svmR.v3 59.8710
5 grow.nnetC.v1 59.8615


$SP500$MaxDD
           system     score
1  slide.svmC.v5 197.3945
2  slide.svmC.v6 197.3945
3   grow.svmC.v5 197.3945
4   grow.svmC.v6 197.3945
5 slide.svmC.v13 399.2800


$SP500$SharpeRatio
          system score
1  slide.svmC.v5  0.02
2  slide.svmC.v6  0.02
```

```
3 slide.svmC.v13  0.02
4 slide.svmC.v14  0.02
5 slide.svmC.v21  0.02
```

The function `subset()` can be applied to `compExps` objects to select a part of the information stored in these objects. In this case we are selecting only a subset of the estimated statistics. Then we put all trading variants together in a single `compExp` object, using the function `join()`. This function can join `compExp` objects along different dimensions. In this case it makes sense to join then by system variants, as all other experimental conditions are the same. Finally, we use the function `rankSystems()` to obtain the top five scores among all trading systems for the statistics we have selected. The notion of best score varies with each metric. Sometimes we want the largest values, while for others we want the lowest values. This can be set up by the parameter `maxs` of function `rankSystems()`, which lets you specify the statistics that are to be maximized.

The first thing we notice when looking at these top five results is that all of them involve either the `svm` or `nnet` algorithm. Another noticeable pattern is that almost all these variants use some windowing mechanism. This provides some evidence of the advantages of these alternatives over the single model approaches, which can be regarded as a confirmation of regime change effects on these data. We can also observe several remarkable (and suspicious) scores, namely in terms of the precision of the buy/sell signals. Obtaining 100% precision seems strange. A closer inspection of the results of these systems will reveal that this score is achieved thanks to a very small number of signals during the 5-year testing period,

```
> summary(subset(svmC,
+               stats=c('Ret','RetOverBH','PercProf','NTrades'),
+               vars=c('slide.svmC.v5','slide.svmC.v6')))

== Summary of a  Monte Carlo  Experiment ==

  20  repetitions Monte Carlo Simulation using:
        seed =  1234
        train size =  2540  cases
        test size =  1270  cases

* Datasets ::  SP500
* Learners ::  slide.svmC.v5, slide.svmC.v6

* Summary of Experiment Results:


-> Datataset:  SP500

        *Learner: slide.svmC.v5
              Ret  RetOverBH  PercProf    NTrades
```

```
avg       0.0250000  -77.10350    5.00000 0.0500000
std       0.1118034   33.12111   22.36068 0.2236068
min       0.0000000 -128.01000    0.00000 0.0000000
max       0.5000000  -33.77000  100.00000 1.0000000
invalid 0.0000000     0.00000    0.00000 0.0000000

          *Learner: slide.svmC.v6
               Ret   RetOverBH   PercProf   NTrades
avg       0.0250000  -77.10350    5.00000 0.0500000
std       0.1118034   33.12111   22.36068 0.2236068
min       0.0000000 -128.01000    0.00000 0.0000000
max       0.5000000  -33.77000  100.00000 1.0000000
invalid 0.0000000     0.00000    0.00000 0.0000000
```

In effect, at most these methods made a single trade over the testing period with an average return of 0.25%, which is −77.1% below the naive buy and hold strategy. These are clearly useless models.

A final remark on the global rankings is that the results in terms of maximum draw-down cannot be considered as too bad, while the Sharpe ratio scores are definitely disappointing.

In order to reach some conclusions on the value of all these variants, we need to add some constraints on some of the statistics. Let us assume the following minimal values: we want (1) a reasonable number of average trades, say more than 20; (2) an average return that should at least be greater than 0.5% (given the generally low scores of these systems); (3) and also a percentage of profitable trades higher than 40%. We will now see if there are some trading systems that satisfy these constraints.

```
> fullResults <- join(svmR, svmC, earth, nnetC, nnetR, by = "variants")
> nt <- statScores(fullResults, "NTrades")[[1]]
> rt <- statScores(fullResults, "Ret")[[1]]
> pp <- statScores(fullResults, "PercProf")[[1]]
> s1 <- names(nt)[which(nt > 20)]
> s2 <- names(rt)[which(rt > 0.5)]
> s3 <- names(pp)[which(pp > 40)]
> namesBest <- intersect(intersect(s1, s2), s3)

> summary(subset(fullResults,
                 stats=tgtStats,
                 vars=namesBest))


== Summary of a  Monte Carlo  Experiment ==

 20  repetitions Monte Carlo Simulation using:
          seed =  1234
          train size =  2540  cases
          test size =  1270   cases
```

```
* Datasets  ::  SP500
* Learners  ::  single.nnetR.v12, slide.nnetR.v15, grow.nnetR.v12

* Summary of Experiment Results:


-> Datataset:  SP500


          *Learner: single.nnetR.v12
               prec.sb       Ret PercProf      MaxDD SharpeRatio
avg       0.12893147   97.4240 45.88600  1595761.4 -0.01300000
std       0.06766129  650.8639 14.04880  2205913.7  0.03798892
min       0.02580645 -160.4200 21.50000   257067.4 -0.08000000
max       0.28695652 2849.8500 73.08000 10142084.7  0.04000000
invalid 0.00000000    0.0000  0.00000        0.0  0.00000000

          *Learner: slide.nnetR.v15
               prec.sb     Ret  PercProf    MaxDD SharpeRatio
avg       0.14028491 2.62300 54.360500 46786.28  0.01500000
std       0.05111339 4.93178  8.339434 23526.07  0.03052178
min       0.03030303 -7.03000 38.890000 18453.94 -0.04000000
max       0.22047244 9.85000 68.970000 99458.44  0.05000000
invalid 0.00000000 0.00000  0.000000     0.00  0.00000000

          *Learner: grow.nnetR.v12
               prec.sb       Ret PercProf     MaxDD SharpeRatio
avg       0.18774920  0.544500 52.66200  41998.26  0.00600000
std       0.07964205  4.334151 11.60824  28252.05  0.03408967
min       0.04411765 -10.760000 22.22000  18144.11 -0.09000000
max       0.33076923  5.330000 72.73000 121886.17  0.05000000
invalid 0.00000000  0.000000  0.00000      0.00  0.00000000
```

In order to obtain the names of the trading variants satisfying the constraints, we have used the `statScores()` function available in our package. This function receives a `compExp` object and the name of a statistic and, by default, provides the average scores of all systems on this statistic. The result is a list with as many components as there are datasets in the experiments (in our case, this is a single dataset). The user can specify a function on the third optional argument to obtain another numeric summary instead of the average. Using the results of this function, we have obtained the names of the variants satisfying each of the constraints. We finally obtained the names of the variants that satisfy all constraints using the `intersect()` function, which obtains the intersection between sets of values.

As we can see, only three of the 240 trading variants that were compared satisfy these minimal constraints. All of them use a regression task and all are based on neural networks. The three use the training data differently. The "single.nnetR.v12" method does not use any windowing schema and achieves an impressive 97.4% average return. However, if we look more closely at the results of this system, we see that at the same time on one of the iterations it achieved a return of −160.4%. This is clearly a system with a rather marked instability of the results obtained, as we can confirm by the standard deviation of the return (650.86%). The other two systems achieve rather similar scores. The following code carries out a statistical significance analysis of the results using the function compAnalysis():

```
> compAnalysis(subset(fullResults,
+                     stats=tgtStats,
+                     vars=namesBest))
```

```
== Statistical Significance Analysis of Comparison Results ==

Baseline Learner::          single.nnetR.v12  (Learn.1)

** Evaluation Metric::          prec.sb

- Dataset: SP500
        Learn.1    Learn.2 sig.2    Learn.3 sig.3
AVG 0.12893147 0.14028491          0.18774920    +
STD 0.06766129 0.05111339          0.07964205

** Evaluation Metric::          Ret

- Dataset: SP500
      Learn.1 Learn.2 sig.2  Learn.3 sig.3
AVG   97.4240 2.62300    -  0.544500     -
STD 650.8639 4.93178       4.334151

** Evaluation Metric::          PercProf

- Dataset: SP500
      Learn.1    Learn.2 sig.2  Learn.3 sig.3
AVG 45.88600 54.360500     +  52.66200
STD 14.04880  8.339434       11.60824

** Evaluation Metric::          MaxDD

- Dataset: SP500
      Learn.1  Learn.2 sig.2  Learn.3 sig.3
AVG 1595761 46786.28    --  41998.26    --
STD 2205914 23526.07       28252.05

** Evaluation Metric::          SharpeRatio

- Dataset: SP500
```

```
         Learn.1      Learn.2 sig.2     Learn.3 sig.3
AVG -0.01300000 0.01500000    +  0.00600000
STD  0.03798892 0.03052178       0.03408967
```

```
Legends:
Learners -> Learn.1 = single.nnetR.v12 ; Learn.2 = slide.nnetR.v15 ;
            Learn.3 = grow.nnetR.v12 ;
Signif. Codes -> 0 '++' or '--' 0.001 '+' or '-' 0.05 ' ' 1
```

Note that the above code can generate some warnings caused by the fact that some systems do not obtain a valid score on some of the statistics (e.g., no buy or sell signals lead to invalid precision scores).

Despite the variability of the results, the above Wilcoxon significance test tells us that the average return of "single.nnetR.v12" is higher than those of the other systems with 95% confidence. Yet, with respect to the other statistics, this variant is clearly worse.

We may have a better idea of the distribution of the scores on some of these statistics across all 20 repetitions by plotting the `compExp` object:

```
> plot(subset(fullResults,
+              stats=c('Ret','PercProf','MaxDD'),
+              vars=namesBest))
```

The result of this code is shown in Figure 3.8.

The scores of the two systems using windowing schemas are very similar, making it difficult to distinguish among them. On the contrary, the results of "single.nnetR.v12" are clearly distinct. We can observe that the high average return is achieved thanks to a clearly abnormal (around 2800%) return in one of the iterations of the Monte Carlo experiment. The remainder of the scores for this system seem clearly inferior to the scores of the other two. Just out of curiosity, we can check the configuration of this particular trading system using the function `getVariant()`:

```
> getVariant("single.nnetR.v12", nnetR)
```

```
Learner::   "single"
```

```
Parameter values
        learner  =  "nnetR"
        linout  =  TRUE
        trace  =  FALSE
        maxit  =  750
        size  =  10
        decay  =  0.01
        policy.func  =  "pol3"
```

As you can observe, it uses the trading policy "pol3" and learns a neural network with ten hidden units with a learning decay rate of 0.01.

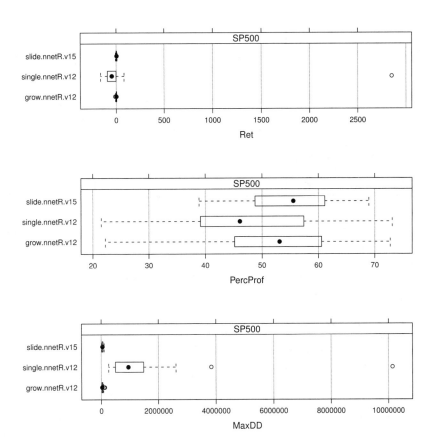

FIGURE 3.8: The scores of the best traders on the 20 repetitions.

In summary, given these results, if we were to select any of the considered alternatives, we would probably skip the "single.nnetR.v12", given its instability. Nevertheless, in the next section we will apply our three best trading systems on the final 9 years of data that were left out for the final evaluation of the best systems.

3.7   The Trading System

This section presents the results obtained by the "best" models in the final evaluation period, which was left out of the model comparison and selection stages. This period is formed by 9 years of quotes, and we will apply the five selected systems to trade during this period using our simulator.

3.7.1   Evaluation of the Final Test Data

In order to apply any of the selected systems to the evaluation period, we need the last 10 years before this evaluation period. The models will be obtained with these 10 years of data and then will be asked to make their signal predictions for the 9 years of the evaluation period. These predictions may actually involve obtaining more models in the case of the systems using windowing schemes.

The following code obtains the evaluation statistics of these systems on the 9-year test period,

```
> data <- tail(Tdata.train, 2540)
> results <- list()
> for (name in namesBest) {
+       sys <- getVariant(name, fullResults)
+       results[[name]] <- runLearner(sys, Tform, data, Tdata.eval)
+ }
> results <- t(as.data.frame(results))
```

We cycle over the three best models, obtaining their predictions by calling them with the initial training data (10 years) and with the evaluation period as test data. These calls involve the use of the functions `single()`, `slide()`, and `grow()` that we have defined before. The result of these functions is a set of evaluation metrics produced by the `eval.stats()` function that we have seen before. At the end of the loop, we transform the obtained list of results into a more appropriate table-like format.

Let us inspect the values of some of the main statistics:

```
> results[, c("Ret", "RetOverBH", "MaxDD", "SharpeRatio", "NTrades",
+       "PercProf")]
```

	Ret	RetOverBH	MaxDD	SharpeRatio	NTrades	PercProf
single.nnetR.v12	-91.13	-61.26	1256121.55	-0.03	759	44.66
slide.nnetR.v15	-6.16	23.71	107188.96	-0.01	132	48.48
grow.nnetR.v12	1.47	31.34	84881.25	0.00	89	53.93

As you can confirm, only one of the three trading systems achieves positive results in this 9-year period. All others lose money, with the "single.nnetR.v12" system confirming its instability with a very low score of −91.13% return. Among the other two, the "grow.nnetR.v12" method seems clearly better with not only a positive return but also a smaller draw-down and a percentage of profitable trades above 50%. Still, these two systems are clearly above the market in this testing period with returns over the buy and hold of 23.7% and 31.4%.

The best model has the following characteristics:

```
> getVariant("grow.nnetR.v12", fullResults)

Learner::  "grow"

Parameter values
        learner = "nnetR"
        relearn.step = 120
        linout = TRUE
        trace = FALSE
        maxit = 750
        size = 10
        decay = 0.001
        policy.func = "pol2"
```

We now proceed with a deeper analysis of the performance of this best trading system across the evaluation period. For this to be possible, we need to obtain the trading record of the system during this period. The function grow() does not return this object, so we need to obtain it by other means:

```
> model <- learner("MC.nnetR", list(maxit = 750, linout = T,
+     trace = F, size = 10, decay = 0.001))
> preds <- growingWindowTest(model, Tform, data, Tdata.eval,
+     relearn.step = 120)
> signals <- factor(preds, levels = 1:3, labels = c("s", "h",
+     "b"))
> date <- rownames(Tdata.eval)[1]
> market <- GSPC[paste(date, "/", sep = "")][1:length(signals),
+     ]
> trade.res <- trading.simulator(market, signals, policy.func = "pol2")
```

Figure 3.9 plots the trading record of the system, and was obtained as follows:

```
> plot(trade.res, market, theme = "white", name = "SP500 - final test")
```

The analysis of Figure 3.9 reveals that the system went through a long period with almost no trading activity, namely since mid-2003 until mid-2007. This is rather surprising because it was a period of significant gain in the market. This somehow shows that the system is not behaving as well as it could, despite the global results observed. It is also noteworthy that the system survived remarkably well during the generally downward tendency in the period from 2000 until 2003, and also during the 2007–2009 financial crisis.

FIGURE 3.9: The results of the final evaluation period of the "grow.nnetR.v12" system.

Package `PerformanceAnalytics` provides an overwhelming set of tools for analyzing the performance of any trading system. Here we provide a glance at some of these tools to obtain better insight into the performance of our trading system. The tools of this package work on the returns of the strategy under evaluation. The returns of our strategy can be obtained as follows:

```
> library(PerformanceAnalytics)
> rets <- Return.calculate(trade.res@trading$Equity)
```

Please note that the function `Return.calculate()` does not calculate the percentage returns we have been using up to now, yet these returns are equivalent to ours by a factor of 100.

Figure 3.10 shows the cumulative returns of the strategy across all testing periods. To obtain such a figure, it is sufficient to run the following code:

```
> chart.CumReturns(rets, main = "Cumulative returns of the strategy",
+       ylab = "returns")
```

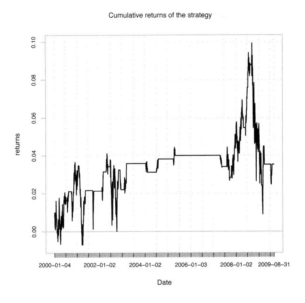

FIGURE 3.10: The cumulative returns on the final evaluation period of the "grow.nnetR.v12" system.

For most of the period, the system is on the positive side, having reached a peak of 10% return around mid-2008.

It is frequently useful to obtain information regarding the returns on an annual or even monthly basis. The package `PerformanceAnalytics` provides some tools to help with this type of analysis, namely, the function `yearlyReturn()`:

```
> yearlyReturn(trade.res@trading$Equity)
```

```
            yearly.returns
2000-12-29      0.028890251
```

2001-12-31	-0.005992597
2002-12-31	0.001692791
2003-12-31	0.013515207
2004-12-31	0.002289826
2005-12-30	0.001798355
2006-12-29	0.000000000
2007-12-31	0.007843569
2008-12-31	0.005444369
2009-08-31	-0.014785914

Figure 3.11 presents this information graphically and we can observe that there were only 2 years with negative returns.

```
> plot(100*yearlyReturn(trade.res@trading$Equity),
+        main='Yearly percentage returns of the trading system')
> abline(h=0,lty=2)
```

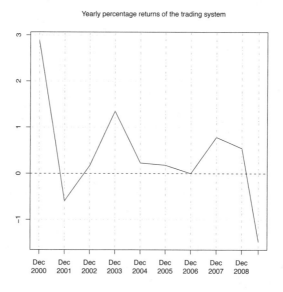

FIGURE 3.11: Yearly percentage returns of "grow.nnetR.v12" system.

The function `table.CalendarReturns()` provides even more detailed information with a table of the percentage monthly returns of a strategy (the last column is the sum over the year):

```
> table.CalendarReturns(rets)
```

	Jan	Feb	Mar	Apr	May	Jun	Jul	Aug	Sep	Oct	Nov	Dec	Equity
2000	-0.5	0.3	0.1	0.2	0	0.2	0.2	0.0	0.0	0.4	0.4	-0.2	1.0

```
2001   0.0 -0.3   0.2 -0.1    0 0.0 0.0   0.0   0.4  0.0 0.0   0.0     0.3
2002   0.0 -0.1   0.0 -0.2    0 0.0 0.2   0.0  -0.3 -0.1 0.0   0.0    -0.5
2003   0.0 -0.1   0.0  0.0    0 0.0 0.0   0.0   0.0  0.0 0.0   0.0    -0.1
2004   0.1  0.0   0.0  0.0    0 0.0 0.0   0.0   0.0  0.0 0.0   0.0     0.0
2005   0.0  0.0   0.0 -0.2    0 0.0 0.0   0.0   0.0  0.0 0.0   0.0    -0.2
2006   0.0  0.0   0.0  0.0    0 0.0 0.0   0.0   0.0  0.0 0.0   0.0     NA
2007   0.0  0.0   0.0  0.2    0 0.0 0.0  -0.2   0.0 -0.2 0.2   0.1     0.0
2008  -0.3  0.5   0.1  0.1    0 0.0 0.3   0.0   0.9  0.3 0.2   0.3     2.3
2009  -0.5  0.0  -0.2  0.0    0 0.0 0.0   0.0   NA   NA  NA    NA     -0.6
```

This table clearly shows the long period of inactivity of the system, with too many zero returns.

Finally, we present an illustration of some of the tools provided by the package PerformanceAnalytics to obtain information concerning the risk analysis of the strategy using the function table.DownsideRisk():

```
> table.DownsideRisk(rets)
```

	Equity
Semi Deviation	0.0017
Gain Deviation	0.0022
Loss Deviation	0.0024
Downside Deviation (MAR=210%)	0.0086
Downside Deviation (Rf=0%)	0.0034
Downside Deviation (0%)	0.0034
Maximum Drawdown	-0.0822
Historical VaR (95%)	-0.0036
Historical ES (95%)	-0.0056
Modified VaR (95%)	-0.0032
Modified ES (95%)	-0.0051

This function gives information on several risk measures, among which we find the percentage maximum draw-down, and also the semi-deviation that is currently accepted as a better risk measure than the more frequent Sharpe ratio. More information on these statistics can be found on the help pages of the package PerformanceAnalytics.

Overall, the analysis we have carried out shows that the "grow.nnetR.v12" trading system obtained a small return with a large risk in the 9-year testing period. Despite being clearly above the naive buy and hold strategy, this system is not ready for managing your money! Still, we must say that this was expected. This is a rather difficult problem with far too many variants/possibilities, some of which we have illustrated across this chapter. It would be rather surprising if the small set of possibilities we have tried lead to a highly successful trading system.[24] This was not the goal of this case study. Our goal was to provide the reader with procedures that are methodologically sound, and not to carry out an in-depth search for the best trading system using these methodologies.

---

[24] And it would also be surprising if we were to publish such a system!

3.7.2   An Online Trading System

Let us suppose we are happy with the trading system we have developed. How could we use it in real-time to trade on the market? In this section we present a brief sketch of a system with this functionality.

The mechanics of the system we are proposing here are the following. At the end of each day, the system will be automatically called. The system should (1) obtain whichever new data is available to it, (2) carry out any modeling steps that it may require, and (3) generate a set of orders as output of its call.

Let us assume that the code of the system we want to develop is to be stored on a file named "trader.R". The solution to call this program at the end of each day depends on the operating system you are using. On Unix-based systems there is usually a table named "crontab" to which we can add entries with programs that should be run on a regular basis by the operating system. Editing this table can be done at the command line by issuing the command:

```
shell> crontab -e
```

The syntax of the entries in this table is reasonably simple and is formed by a set of fields that describe the periodicity and finally the command to run. Below you can find an example that should run our "trader.R" program every weekday by 19:00:

```
0 19 * * 1-5 /usr/bin/R --vanilla --quiet < /home/xpto/trader.R
```

The first two entries represent the minute and the hour. The third and fourth are the day of the month and month, respectively, and an asterisk means that the program should be run for all instances of these fields. The fifth entry is the weekday, with a 1 representing Mondays, and the '-' allowing for the specification of intervals. Finally, we have the program to be run that in this case is a call to R with the source code of our trader.

The general algorithm to be implemented in the "trader.R" program is the following:

```
- Read in the current state of the trader
- Get all new data available
- Check if it is necessary to re-learn the model
- Obtain the predicted signal for today
- With this signal, call the policy function to obtain the orders
- Output the orders of today
```

The current state of the trader should be a set of data structures that stores information that is required to be memorized across the daily runs of the trader. In our case this should include the current NNET model, the learning parameters used to obtain it, the training data used to obtain the model and the associated data model specification, the "age" of the model (important to know when to re-learn it), and the information on the trading record of the system until today and its current open positions. Ideally, this information should be in a database and the trader would look for it using the interface of R with these systems (see Section 3.2.4). Please note that the information on the open positions needs to be updated from outside the system as it is the market that drives the timings for opening and closing positions, contrary to our simulator where we assumed that all orders are accomplished at the beginning of the next day.

Getting the new available data is easy if we have the data model specification. Function `getModelData()` can be used to refresh our dataset with the most recent quotes, as mentioned in Section 3.3.2.

The model will need to be re-learned if the age goes above the `relearn.step` parameter that should be memorized in conjunction with all model parameters. If that is the case, then we should call the `MC.nnetR()` function to obtain the new model with the current window of data. As our best trader uses a growing window strategy, the training dataset will constantly grow, which might start to become a problem if it gets too big to fit in the computer memory. If that occurs, we can consider forgetting the too old data, thereby pruning back the training set to an acceptable size.

Finally, we have to get a prediction for the signal of today. This means calling the `predict()` function with the current model to obtain a prediction for the last row of the training set, that is, today. Having this prediction, we can call the trading policy function with the proper parameters to obtain the set of orders to output for today. This should be the final result of the program.

This brief sketch should provide you with sufficient information for implementing such an online trading system.

3.8 Summary

The main goal of this chapter was to introduce the reader to a more real application of data mining. The concrete application that was described involved several new challenges, namely, (1) handling time series data, (2) dealing with a very dynamic system with possible changes of regime, and (3) moving from model predictions into concrete actions in the application domain.

In methodological terms we have introduced you to a few new topics:

- Time series modeling

- Handling regime shifts with windowing mechanisms

- Artificial neural networks

- Support vector machines

- Multivariate adaptive regression splines

- Evaluating time series models with the Monte Carlo method

- Several new evaluation statistics related either to the prediction of rare events or with financial trading performance

From the perspective of learning R we have illustrated

- How to handle time series data

- How to read data from different sources, such as data bases

- How to obtain several new types of models (SVMs, ANNs, and MARS)

- How to use several packages specifically dedicated to financial modeling

Chapter 4

Detecting Fraudulent Transactions

The third case study addresses an instantiation of the general problem of detecting unusual observations of a phenomena, that is, finding rare and quite different observations. The driving application has to do with transactions of a set of products that are reported by the salespeople of some company. The goal is to find "strange" transaction reports that may indicate fraud attempts by some of the salespeople. The outcome of the data mining process will support posterior inspection activities by the company. Given the limited amount of resources that can be allocated to this inspection activity, we want to provide a kind of fraud probability ranking as outcome of the process. These rankings should allow the company to apply its inspection resources in an optimal way. This general resource-bounded inspection activity is frequent in many fields, such as credit card transactions, tax declarations inspection, etc. This chapter addresses several new data mining tasks, namely, (1) outlier or anomaly detection, (2) clustering, and also (3) semi-supervised prediction models.

4.1   Problem Description and Objectives

Fraud detection is an important area for potential application of data mining techniques given the economic and social consequences that are usually associated with these illegal activities. From the perspective of data analysis, frauds are usually associated with unusual observations as these are activities that are supposed to be deviations from the norm. These deviations from normal behavior are frequently known as outliers in several data analysis disciplines. In effect, a standard definition of an outlier is that it is "an observation which deviates so much from other observations as to arouse suspicions that it was generated by a different mechanism" (Hawkins, 1980).

The data we will be using in this case study refers to the transactions reported by the salespeople of some company. These salespeople sell a set of products of the company and report these sales with a certain periodicity. The data we have available concerns these reports over a short period of time. The salespeople are free to set the selling price according to their own policy and market. At the end of each month, they report back to the company their transactions. The goal of this data mining application is to help in the task of verifying the veracity of these reports given past experience of the company that has detected both errors and fraud attempts in these transaction reports. The help we provide will take the form of a ranking of the reports according to their probability of being fraudulent. This ranking will allow to allocate the limited inspection resources of the company to the reports that our system signals as being more "suspicious".

4.2　The Available Data

The data we have available is of an undisclosed source and has been anonymized. Each of the 401,146 rows of the data table includes information on one report by some salesman. This information includes his ID, the product ID, and the quantity and total value reported by the salesman. This data has already gone through some analysis at the company. The result of this analysis is shown in the last column, which has the outcome of the inspection of some transactions by the company. Summarizing, the dataset we will be using has the following columns:

- **ID** – a factor with the ID of the salesman.

- **Prod** – a factor indicating the ID of the sold product.

- **Quant** – the number of reported sold units of the product.

- **Val** – the reported total monetary value of the sale.

- **Insp** – a factor with three possible values: ok if the transaction was inspected and considered valid by the company, fraud if the transaction was found to be fraudulent, and unkn if the transaction was not inspected at all by the company.

4.2.1　Loading the Data into R

The dataset is available in our book package or on the book Web site. At the book Web site it is available as an Rdata file, and contains a data frame with the dataset. To use this file you should download it to a local directory in your computer and then issue the command

```
> load("sales.Rdata")
```

Provided you are in the directory where you have downloaded the file, this should load from the file a data frame named sales.

If you decide to use the book package data, then you should proceed as follows:

```
> library(DMwR)
> data(sales)
```

Once again, the result is a data frame named `sales`, whose first few rows are shown below:

```
> head(sales)
```

```
  ID Prod Quant    Val Insp
1 v1   p1   182   1665 unkn
2 v2   p1  3072   8780 unkn
3 v3   p1 20393  76990 unkn
4 v4   p1   112   1100 unkn
5 v3   p1  6164  20260 unkn
6 v5   p2   104   1155 unkn
```

4.2.2   Exploring the Dataset

To get an initial overview of the statistical properties of the data, we can use the function `summary()`:[1]

```
> summary(sales)
```

```
      ID                Prod              Quant                   Val
 v431   : 10159   p1125  :  3923   Min.   :      100   Min.   :    1005
 v54    :  6017   p3774  :  1824   1st Qu.:      107   1st Qu.:    1345
 v426   :  3902   p1437  :  1720   Median :      168   Median :    2675
 v1679  :  3016   p1917  :  1702   Mean   :     8442   Mean   :   14617
 v1085  :  3001   p4089  :  1598   3rd Qu.:      738   3rd Qu.:    8680
 v1183  :  2642   p2742  :  1519   Max.   :473883883   Max.   : 4642955
 (Other):372409   (Other):388860   NA's   :    13842   NA's   :    1182
      Insp
 ok   : 14462
 unkn :385414
 fraud:  1270
```

We have a significant number of products and salespeople, as we can confirm using the function `nlevels()`:

```
> nlevels(sales$ID)
```

```
[1] 6016
```

```
> nlevels(sales$Prod)
```

```
[1] 4548
```

---

[1] An interesting alternative can be obtained using the function `describe()` from the extra package `Hmisc`. Try it!

The result of the `summary()` function reveals several relevant facts on this data. First there are a considerable number of unknown values in the columns `Quant` and `Val`. This can be particularly problematic if both happen at the same time, as this would represent a transaction report without the crucial information on the quantities involved in the sale. We can easily check if there are such situations:

```
> length(which(is.na(sales$Quant) & is.na(sales$Val)))
```

```
[1] 888
```

As you can see, this is a reasonable number of transactions. Given the large total amount of transactions, one can question whether it would not be better to simply delete these reports. We will consider this and other alternatives in Section 4.2.3.

As a side note, particularly relevant for very large datasets, there are more efficient forms of obtaining this type of information. Although the previous code using `length()` and `which()` may be considered more understandable, we can take advantage of the way logical values are coded in R (T=1 and F=0) to obtain the same number more efficiently:

```
> sum(is.na(sales$Quant) & is.na(sales$Val))
```

```
[1] 888
```

Another interesting observation from the results of the `summary()` function is the distribution of the values in the inspection column. In effect, and as expected, the proportion of frauds is relatively low, even if we only take into account the reports that were inspected, which are also a small proportion overall:

```
> table(sales$Insp)/nrow(sales) * 100
```

```
        ok       unkn       fraud
 3.6051712 96.0782359  0.3165930
```

Figure 4.1 shows the number of reports per salesperson. As you can confirm, the numbers are rather diverse across the salespeople. Figure 4.2 shows the same number but per product. Again we observe a strong variability. Both figures were obtained with the following code:

```
> totS <- table(sales$ID)
> totP <- table(sales$Prod)
> barplot(totS, main = "Transactions per salespeople", names.arg = "",
+     xlab = "Salespeople", ylab = "Amount")
> barplot(totP, main = "Transactions per product", names.arg = "",
+     xlab = "Products", ylab = "Amount")
```

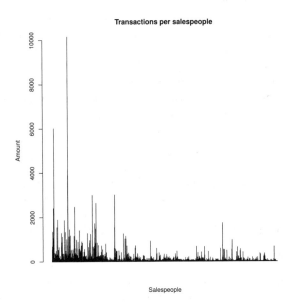

FIGURE 4.1: The number of transactions per salesperson.

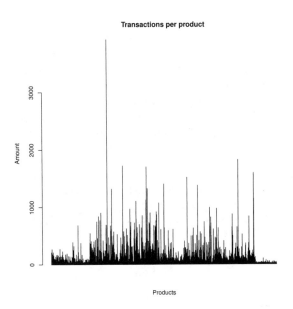

FIGURE 4.2: The number of transactions per product.

The descriptive statistics of `Quant` and `Val` show a rather marked variability. This suggests that the products may be rather different and thus it may make sense to handle them separately. In effect, if the typical prices of the products are too different, then a transaction report can only be considered abnormal in the context of the reports of the same product. Still, these two quantities may not be the ideal ones to draw this conclusion. In effect, given the different quantity of products that are sold on each transaction, it is more correct to carry out this analysis over the unit price instead. This price can be added as a new column of our data frame:

```
> sales$Uprice <- sales$Val/sales$Quant
```

The unit price should be relatively constant over the transactions of the same product. When analyzing transactions over a short period of time, one does not expect strong variations of the unit price of the products.

If we check the distribution of the unit price, for example,

```
> summary(sales$Uprice)
```

```
    Min.    1st Qu.     Median       Mean    3rd Qu.       Max.
2.4480e-06 8.4600e+00 1.1890e+01 2.0300e+01 1.9110e+01 2.6460e+04
      NA's
1.4136e+04
```

we again observe a rather marked variability.

Given these facts, it seems inevitable that we should analyze the set of transactions of each product individually, looking for suspicious transactions on each of these sets. One problem with this approach is that some products have very few transactions. In effect, of the 4,548 products, 982 have less than 20 transactions. Declaring a report as unusual based on a sample of less then 20 reports may be too risky.

It may be interesting to check what the top most expensive and cheap products are. We will use the median unit price to represent the typical price at which a product is sold. The following code obtains the information we are looking for:

```
> attach(sales)
> upp <- aggregate(Uprice,list(Prod),median,na.rm=T)
> topP <- sapply(c(T,F),function(o)
+                   upp[order(upp[,2],decreasing=o)[1:5],1])
> colnames(topP) <- c('Expensive','Cheap')
> topP
```

```
     Expensive Cheap
[1,] "p3689"   "p560"
[2,] "p2453"   "p559"
[3,] "p2452"   "p4195"
[4,] "p2456"   "p601"
[5,] "p2459"   "p563"
```

We have attached the data frame to facilitate access to the columns of the data. We then obtained the median unit price of each product using the `aggregate()` function. This applies a function that produces some scalar value (in this case the median) to subgroups of a dataset formed according to some factor (or list of factors). The result is a data frame with the values of the aggregation function for each group. From this obtained data frame we have generated the five most expensive (cheapest) products by varying the parameter `decreasing` of the function `order()`, using the `sapply()` function.

We can confirm the completely different price distribution of the top products using a box plot of their unit prices:

```
> tops <- sales[Prod %in% topP[1, ], c("Prod", "Uprice")]
> tops$Prod <- factor(tops$Prod)
> boxplot(Uprice ~ Prod, data = tops, ylab = "Uprice", log = "y")
```

The `%in%` operator tests if a value belongs to a set. The call to the function `factor()` is required because otherwise the column `Prod` of the data frame `tops` would have the same number of levels as the column in the original `sales` data frame, which would lead the `boxplot()` function to draw a box plot for each level. The scales of the prices of the most expensive and cheapest products are rather different. Because of this, we have used a log scale in the graph to avoid the values of the cheapest product becoming indistinguishable. This effect is obtained by the parameter setting `log=y`, which indicates that the Y-axis is on log scale (notice how the same distance in the axis corresponds to a different range of values of unit price). The result of this code is shown in Figure 4.3.

We can carry out a similar analysis to discover which salespeople are the ones who bring more (less) money to the company,

```
> vs <- aggregate(Val,list(ID),sum,na.rm=T)
> scoresSs <- sapply(c(T,F),function(o)
+                    vs[order(vs$x,decreasing=o)[1:5],1])
> colnames(scoresSs) <- c('Most','Least')
> scoresSs
```

```
     Most      Least
[1,] "v431"   "v3355"
[2,] "v54"    "v6069"
[3,] "v19"    "v5876"
[4,] "v4520"  "v6058"
[5,] "v955"   "v4515"
```

It may be interesting to note that the top 100 salespeople on this list account for almost 40% of the income of the company, while the bottom 2,000 out of the 6,016 salespeople generate less than 2% of the income. This may provide some insight into eventual changes that need to be carried out within the company:

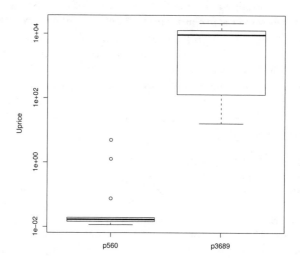

FIGURE 4.3: The distribution of the unit prices of the cheapest and most expensive products.

```
> sum(vs[order(vs$x, decreasing = T)[1:100], 2])/sum(Val, na.rm = T) *
+       100
```

```
[1] 38.33277
```

```
> sum(vs[order(vs$x, decreasing = F)[1:2000], 2])/sum(Val,
+       na.rm = T) * 100
```

```
[1] 1.988716
```

If we carry out a similar analysis in terms of the quantity that is sold for each product, the results are even more unbalanced:

```
> qs <- aggregate(Quant,list(Prod),sum,na.rm=T)
> scoresPs <- sapply(c(T,F),function(o)
+                       qs[order(qs$x,decreasing=o)[1:5],1])
> colnames(scoresPs) <- c('Most','Least')
> scoresPs
```

```
        Most    Least
[1,] "p2516" "p2442"
[2,] "p3599" "p2443"
[3,] "p314"  "p1653"
[4,] "p569"  "p4101"
[5,] "p319"  "p3678"
```

```
> sum(as.double(qs[order(qs$x,decreasing=T)[1:100],2]))/
+    sum(as.double(Quant),na.rm=T)*100
```

[1] 74.63478

```
> sum(as.double(qs[order(qs$x,decreasing=F)[1:4000],2]))/
+    sum(as.double(Quant),na.rm=T)*100
```

[1] 8.94468

You may have noticed in the code above the use of the function `as.double()`. This is required in this case because the sum of the quantities generates too large a number that must be stored as a double. This function ensures this transformation.

From the 4,548 products, 4,000 represent less than 10% of the sales volume, with the top 100 representing nearly 75%. Notice that this information is only useful in terms of the production of the products. In particular, it does not mean that the company should consider stopping the production of the products that sell too few units. In effect, these may be more profitable if they have a larger profit margin. Because we do not have any information on the production costs of the products, we cannot draw any conclusion in terms of the usefulness in continuing to produce these products that sell so few units.

One of the main assumptions we will be making in our analysis to find abnormal transaction reports is that the unit price of any product should follow a near-normal distribution. This means that we expect that the transactions of the same product will have roughly the same unit price with some small variability, possibly caused by some strategies of the salespeople to achieve their commercial goals. In this context, there are some basic statistical tests that can help us in finding deviations from this normality assumption. An example is the box plot rule. This rule serves as the basis of outlier identification in the context of box plots that we have already seen several times in this book. The rule states that an observation should be tagged as an anomaly high (low) value if it is above (below) the high (low) whisker, defined as $Q_3 + 1.5 \times IQR$ ($Q_1 - 1.5 \times IQR$), where Q_1 is the first quartile, Q_3 the third quartile, and $IQR = (Q_3 - Q_1)$ the inter-quartile range. This simple rule works rather well for normally distributed variables, and it is robust to the presence of a few outliers being based in robust statistics like the quartiles. The following code determines the number of outliers (according to the above definition) of each product:

```
> out <- tapply(Uprice,list(Prod=Prod),
+               function(x) length(boxplot.stats(x)$out))
```

The `boxplot.stats()` function obtains several statistics that are used in the construction of box plots. It returns a list with this information. The `out` component of this list contains the observations that, according to the box plot rule, are considered outliers. The above code calculates their number for the transactions of each product. The products with more outliers are the following:

```
> out[order(out, decreasing = T)[1:10]]

Prod
p1125 p1437 p2273 p1917 p1918 p4089  p538 p3774 p2742 p3338
  376   181   165   156   156   137   129   125   120   117
```

Using this very simple method, 29,446 transactions are considered outliers, which corresponds to approximately 7% of the total number of transactions,

```
> sum(out)

[1] 29446

> sum(out)/nrow(sales) * 100

[1] 7.34047
```

One might question whether this simple rule for identifying outliers would be sufficient to provide the kind of help we want in this application. In Section 4.4.1.1 we will evaluate the performance of a small variant of this rule adapted to our application.

There is a caveat to some of the conclusions we have drawn in this section. We have been using the data independently of the fact that some of the reports were found to be fraudulent and some other may also be fraudulent although not yet detected. This means that some of these "conclusions" may be biased by data that is wrong. The problem is that for the transactions that are tagged as frauds, we do not know the correct values. Theoretically, the only transactions that we are sure to be correct are the ones for which the column Insp has the value OK, but these are just 3.6% of the data. So, although the analysis is correct, the conclusions may be impaired by low-quality data. This should be taken into account in a real-world situation not to provide advice to the company based on data that includes errors. Because a complete inspection of the data is impossible, this risk will always exist. At most we can avoid using the small number of transactions already found to be errors in all exploratory analysis of the data. Another thing one can do is present the results to the company and if some result is unexpected to them, carry out a closer analysis of the data that leads to that surprising result. This means that this sort of analysis usually requires some form of interaction with the domain experts, particularly when there are doubts regarding data quality, as is the case in this problem. Moreover, this type of exploratory analysis is of key importance with low-quality data as many of the problems can be easily spotted at these stages.

4.2.3 Data Problems

This section tries to address some data quality problems that can be an obstacle to the application of the techniques we will use later in this chapter.

4.2.3.1 Unknown Values

We start by addressing the problem of unknown variable values. As mentioned in Section 2.5 (page 52), there are essentially three alternatives: (1) remove the cases, (2) fill in the unknowns using some strategy, or (3) use tools that handle these types of values. Considering the tools we will be using in this chapter, only the first two are acceptable to us.

As mentioned before, the main concern are transactions that have both the value of `Quant` and `Val` missing. Removing all 888 cases may be problematic if this leads to removing most transactions of some product or salesperson. Let us check this.

The total number of transactions per salesperson and product is given by

```
> totS <- table(ID)
> totP <- table(Prod)
```

The salespeople and products involved in the problematic transactions are the following:

```
> nas <- sales[which(is.na(Quant) & is.na(Val)), c("ID", "Prod")]
```

We now obtain the salespeople with a larger proportion of transactions with unknowns on both `Val` and `Quant`:

```
> propS <- 100 * table(nas$ID)/totS
> propS[order(propS, decreasing = T)[1:10]]
```

```
    v1237      v4254      v4038      v5248      v3666      v4433      v4170
13.793103   9.523810   8.333333   8.333333   6.666667   6.250000   5.555556
    v4926      v4664      v4642
 5.555556   5.494505   4.761905
```

It seems reasonable to delete these transactions, at least from the perspective of the salespeople, as they represent a small proportion of their transactions. Moreover, the alternative of trying to fill in both columns seems much more risky.

Wit respect to the products, these are the numbers:

```
> propP <- 100 * table(nas$Prod)/totP
> propP[order(propP, decreasing = T)[1:10]]
```

```
    p2689      p2675      p4061      p2780      p4351      p2686      p2707      p2690
39.28571   35.41667   25.00000   22.72727   18.18182   16.66667   14.28571   14.08451
    p2691      p2670
12.90323   12.76596
```

There are several products that would have more than 20% of their transactions removed; and in particular, product p2689 would have almost 40% of them removed. This seems clearly too much. On the other hand, if we decide to fill in these unknown values, the only reasonable strategy is to use the information on the "complete" transactions of the same product. This would mean to fill in 40% of the transactions of a product using the information of the remaining 60%. This also seems unreasonable. Luckly, if we look at the similarity between the unit price distribution of the products (see Section 4.2.3.2), we will observe that these products are, in effect, rather similar to other products. In this context, if we conclude that they have too few transactions after the removal, we can always join their transactions with the ones from similar products to increase the statistical reliability of any outlier detection tests. In summary, the option of removing all transactions with unknown values on both the quantity and the value is the best option we have:

```
> detach(sales)
> sales <- sales[-which(is.na(sales$Quant) & is.na(sales$Val)),]
```

We have used the `detach()` function to disable direct access to the columns of the data frame. The reason is the way the function `attach()` works. When we issue a call like `attach(sales)`, R creates a new object for each column of the `sales` data frame with copies of the data in those columns. If we start to delete data from the `sales` data frame, these changes will not be reflected in these new objects. In summary, one should not play with the facilities provided by the `attach()` function when the data we will be querying is prone to changes because we will probably end up with inconsistent views of the data: the view of the original data frame, and the views provided by the objects created by the `attach()` function. The latter are snapshots of the data frame at a certain time that become outdated if we modify the data frame after the call to `attach()`.

Let us now analyze the remaining reports with unknown values in either the quantity or the value of the transaction. We start by calculating the proportion of transactions of each product that have the quantity unknown:

```
> nnasQp <- tapply(sales$Quant,list(sales$Prod),
+                   function(x) sum(is.na(x)))
> propNAsQp <- nnasQp/table(sales$Prod)
> propNAsQp[order(propNAsQp,decreasing=T)[1:10]]

    p2442      p2443      p1653      p4101      p4243      p903       p3678
1.0000000  1.0000000  0.9090909  0.8571429  0.6842105  0.6666667  0.6666667
    p3955      p4464      p1261
0.6428571  0.6363636  0.6333333
```

There are two products (p2442 and p2443) that have all their transactions with unknown values of the quantity. Without further information it is virtually impossible to do anything with the transactions of these products because we are unable to calculate their typical unit price. These are 54 reports, and two of them are tagged as frauds while another was found to be OK. This must mean that either the inspectors had more information than given in this dataset, or we are probably facing typing errors as it seems unfeasible to conclude anything on these transactions. In this context, we will delete them:

```
> sales <- sales[!sales$Prod %in% c("p2442", "p2443"), ]
```

Given that we have just removed two products from our dataset, we should update the levels of the column `Prod`:

```
> nlevels(sales$Prod)
```

```
[1] 4548
```

```
> sales$Prod <- factor(sales$Prod)
> nlevels(sales$Prod)
```

```
[1] 4546
```

Are there salespeople with all transactions with unknown quantity?

```
> nnasQs <- tapply(sales$Quant, list(sales$ID), function(x) sum(is.na(x)))
> propNAsQs <- nnasQs/table(sales$ID)
> propNAsQs[order(propNAsQs, decreasing = T)[1:10]]
```

```
    v2925     v5537     v5836     v6058     v6065     v4368     v2923
1.0000000 1.0000000 1.0000000 1.0000000 1.0000000 0.8888889 0.8750000
    v2970     v4910     v4542
0.8571429 0.8333333 0.8095238
```

As you can see, there are several salespeople who have not filled in the information on the quantity in their reports. However, in this case the problem is not so serious. In effect, as long as we have other transactions of the same products reported by other salespeople, we can try to use this information to fill in these unknowns using the assumption that the unit price should be similar. Because of this, we will not delete these transactions.

We will now carry out a similar analysis for the transactions with an unknown value in the `Val` column. First, the proportion of transactions of each product with unknown value in this column:

```
> nnasVp <- tapply(sales$Val,list(sales$Prod),
+                  function(x) sum(is.na(x)))
> propNAsVp <- nnasVp/table(sales$Prod)
> propNAsVp[order(propNAsVp,decreasing=T)[1:10]]
```

```
     p1110      p1022      p4491      p1462        p80      p4307
0.25000000 0.17647059 0.10000000 0.07500000 0.06250000 0.05882353
     p4471      p2821      p1017      p4287
0.05882353 0.05389222 0.05263158 0.05263158
```

The numbers are reasonable so it does not make sense to delete these transactions as we may try to fill in these holes using the other transactions. With respect to salesperson, the numbers are as follows:

```
> nnasVs <- tapply(sales$Val, list(sales$ID), function(x) sum(is.na(x)))
> propNAsVs <- nnasVs/table(sales$ID)
> propNAsVs[order(propNAsVs, decreasing = T)[1:10]]
```

```
      v5647        v74      v5946      v5290      v4472      v4022
0.37500000 0.22222222 0.20000000 0.15384615 0.12500000 0.09756098
       v975      v2814      v2892      v3739
0.09574468 0.09090909 0.09090909 0.08333333
```

Once again, the proportions are not too high.

At this stage we have removed all reports that had insufficient information to be subject to a fill-in strategy. For the remaining unknown values, we will apply a method based on the assumption that transactions of the same products should have a similar unit price. We will start by obtaining this typical unit price for each product. We will skip the prices of transactions that were found to be frauds in the calculation of the typical price. For the remaining transactions we will use the median unit price of the transactions as the typical price of the respective products:

```
> tPrice <- tapply(sales[sales$Insp != "fraud", "Uprice"],
+        list(sales[sales$Insp != "fraud", "Prod"]), median, na.rm = T)
```

Having a typical unit price for each product, we can use it to calculate any of the two possibly missing values (`Quant` and `Val`). This is possible because we currently have no transactions with both values missing. The following code fills in all remaining unknown values:

```
> noQuant <- which(is.na(sales$Quant))
> sales[noQuant,'Quant'] <- ceiling(sales[noQuant,'Val'] /
+                                    tPrice[sales[noQuant,'Prod']])
> noVal <- which(is.na(sales$Val))
> sales[noVal,'Val'] <- sales[noVal,'Quant'] *
+                                    tPrice[sales[noVal,'Prod']]
```

In case you missed it, we have just filled in 12,900 unknown quantity values plus 294 total values of transaction. If you are like me, I am sure you appreciate the compactness of the above code that carries out all these operations. It is all about indexing! We have used the function `ceiling()` to avoid non-integer values of `Quant`. This function returns the smallest integer not less than the number given as argument.

Given that we now have all `Quant` and `Val` values, we can recalculate the `Uprice` column to fill in the previously unknown unit prices:

```
> sales$Uprice <- sales$Val/sales$Quant
```

After all these pre-processing steps, we have a dataset free of unknown values. For future analysis, it makes sense that you save this current state of the `sales` data frame so that you can restart your analysis from this point, without having to repeat all the steps. You can save the data frame as follows:

```
> save(sales, file = "salesClean.Rdata")
```

The `save()` function can be used to save any set of objects on a file specified in the `file` parameter. Objects saved in these files can be loaded back into R using the `load()` function, as shown in Section 4.2.1.

4.2.3.2 Few Transactions of Some Products

There are products with very few transactions. This is a problem because we need to use the information on these transactions to decide if any of them are unusual. If we have too few, it is difficult to make this decision with the required statistical significance. In this context, it makes sense to question whether we can analyze the transactions of some products together to avoid this problem.

Despite the complete lack of information on the eventual relationships between products, we can try to infer some of these relationships by observing the similarity between their distributions of unit price. If we find products with similar prices, then we can consider merging their respective transactions and analyze them together to search for unusual values. One way of comparing two distributions is to visually inspect them. Given the number of products we have, this is unfeasible. An alternative is to compare some statistical properties that summarize the distributions. Two important properties of continuous variables distributions are their central tendency and spread. As mentioned before, it is reasonable to assume that the distribution of the unit price of any product is approximately normal. This means that although variations in the price occur, they should be nicely packed around the most common price. However, we have to assume that there will be outlying values, most probably caused by fraud attempts or errors. In this context, it makes more sense to use the median as the statistic of centrality and the inter-quartile range (IQR) as the statistic of spread. These statistics are more robust to the presence of outliers when compared to the more frequently used mean and standard deviation. We can obtain both statistics for all transactions of each product as follows:

```
> attach(sales)
> notF <- which(Insp != 'fraud')
> ms <- tapply(Uprice[notF],list(Prod=Prod[notF]),function(x) {
+      bp <- boxplot.stats(x)$stats
+      c(median=bp[3],iqr=bp[4]-bp[2])
+    })
> ms <- matrix(unlist(ms),
+              length(ms),2,
```

```
+                    byrow=T,dimnames=list(names(ms),c('median','iqr')))
> head(ms)

         median       iqr
p1 11.346154 8.575599
p2 10.877863 5.609731
p3 10.000000 4.809092
p4  9.911243 5.998530
p5 10.957447 7.136601
p6 13.223684 6.685185
```

This code uses the `boxplot.stats()` function to obtain the values of the median, first and third quartiles. We calculate these values for all sets of transactions of each product, eliminating the fraudulent transactions from our analysis. With these values we obtain a matrix with the median and IQR for each product.

Figure 4.4(a) plots each product according to its respective median and IQR. The graph is difficult to read because a few products have very large values for these statistics. In particular, product p3689 (the dot at the top right) is clearly different from all other products of the company. We can overcome this visualization problem using log scales (Figure 4.4(b)). In this second graph we have used black "+" signs to indicate the products that have less than 20 transactions. The figures were obtained as follows, where the parameter `log=xy` sets log scales on both axes of the graph:

```
> par(mfrow = c(1, 2))
> plot(ms[, 1], ms[, 2], xlab = "Median", ylab = "IQR", main = "")
> plot(ms[, 1], ms[, 2], xlab = "Median", ylab = "IQR", main = "",
+      col = "grey", log = "xy")
> smalls <- which(table(Prod) < 20)
> points(log(ms[smalls, 1]), log(ms[smalls, 2]), pch = "+")
```

The first thing to note in Figure 4.4(b) is that there are many products that have approximately the same median and IQR, even taking into account that we are looking at a log scale. This provides good indications of the similarity of their distributions of unit price. Moreover, we can see that among the products with few transactions, there are many that are very similar to other products. However, there are also several products that not only have few transactions but also have a rather distinct distribution of unit prices. These are clearly the products for which we will have more difficulty declaring a transaction as fraudulent.

Despite the virtues of the visual inspection of the distribution properties of the unit prices, formal tests are required to obtain more precision when comparing the distributions of two products. We will use a nonparametric test to compare the distributions of unit prices, as these tests are more robust to the presence of outliers. The Kolmogorov-Smirnov test can be used to compare any two samples to check the validity of the null hypothesis that both come from

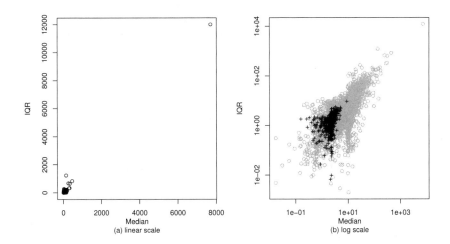

FIGURE 4.4: Some properties of the distribution of unit prices.

the same distribution. This test works by calculating a statistic that measures the maximum difference between the two empirical cumulative distribution functions. If the two distributions are similar, this distance should be rather small.

For each of the products that has less than 20 transactions, we will search for the product with the most similar unit price distribution and then use a Kolmogorov-Smirnov test to check if the similarity is statistically significant. Carrying out this task for all combinations of products would be computationally too demanding. Instead, we have decided to take advantage of the information given by the distribution properties we calculated before (median and IQR). Namely, for each of the products with few transactions, we have searched for the product with the most similar median and IQR. Given this similar product, we have carried out a Kolmogorov-Smirnov test between their respective unit price distributions, storing the results of this test. The following code obtains a matrix (`similar`) with the information on this type of test for each of the products with less than 20 transactions. It uses the `ms` object we obtained before with the information on the medians and IQRs of the unit prices of each product.

```
> dms <- scale(ms)
> smalls <- which(table(Prod) < 20)
> prods <- tapply(sales$Uprice, sales$Prod, list)
> similar <- matrix(NA, length(smalls), 7, dimnames = list(names(smalls),
+     c("Simil", "ks.stat", "ks.p", "medP", "iqrP", "medS",
+         "iqrS")))
> for (i in seq(along = smalls)) {
```

```
+      d <- scale(dms, dms[smalls[i], ], FALSE)
+      d <- sqrt(drop(d^2 %*% rep(1, ncol(d))))
+      stat <- ks.test(prods[[smalls[i]]], prods[[order(d)[2]]])
+      similar[i, ] <- c(order(d)[2], stat$statistic, stat$p.value,
+           ms[smalls[i], ], ms[order(d)[2], ])
+ }
```

The code starts by normalizing the data in the object `ms` to avoid negative scale effects when calculating the distances. After a few initializations, we have the main loop that goes over all products with few transactions. The first two statements in this loop calculate the distances between the distribution properties of the product under analysis (the current value of `i`) and all other products. The resulting object (`d`) has the values of all these distances. The second smallest distance is the product that is most similar to the product being considered. It is the second because the first is the product itself. We note again that the similarity between the products is being calculated using the information on the median and IQR of the respective unit prices. The next step is to carry out the Kolmogorov-Smirnov test to compare the two distributions of unit prices. This is done with a call to the `ks.test()` function. This function returns significant information, among which we have "extracted" the value of the statistic of the test and the respective significance level. The value of the statistic is the maximum difference between the two cumulative distribution functions. Values of the confidence level near 1 indicate strong statistical significance of the null hypothesis that both distributions are equal. Below we show the first few lines of the resulting `similar` object:

```
> head(similar)
```

	Simil	ks.stat	ks.p	medP	iqrP	medS	iqrS
p8	2827	0.4339623	0.06470603	3.850211	0.7282168	3.868306	0.7938557
p18	213	0.2568922	0.25815859	5.187266	8.0359968	5.274884	7.8894149
p38	1044	0.3650794	0.11308315	5.490758	6.4162095	5.651818	6.3248073
p39	1540	0.2258065	0.70914769	7.986486	1.6425959	8.080694	1.7668724
p40	3971	0.3333333	0.13892028	9.674797	1.6104511	9.668854	1.6520147
p47	1387	0.3125000	0.48540576	2.504092	2.5625835	2.413498	2.6402087

The row names indicate the product for which we are obtaining the most similar product. The first column has information on this latter product. The respective product ID can be obtained as shown in the following example for the first row of `similar`:

```
> levels(Prod)[similar[1, 1]]
```

```
[1] "p2829"
```

After the columns with the Kolmogorov-Smirnov statistic and confidence level, we have the medians and IQRs of the product and the most similar product, respectively.

We can check how many products have a product whose unit price distribution is significantly similar with 90% confidence:

```
> nrow(similar[similar[, "ks.p"] >= 0.9, ])
```

```
[1] 117
```

Or more efficiently,

```
> sum(similar[, "ks.p"] >= 0.9)
```

```
[1] 117
```

As you see from the 985 products with less than 20 transactions, we have only managed to find similar products for 117 of them. Nevertheless, this is useful information when it comes to analyzing which transactions are abnormal. For these 117 products we can include more transactions into the decision process to increase the statistical significance of our tests. We will save the `similar` object in case we decide to use this similarity between products later:

```
> save(similar, file = "similarProducts.Rdata")
```

4.3 Defining the Data Mining Tasks

The main goal of this application is to use data mining to provide guidance in the task of deciding which transaction reports should be considered for inspection as a result of strong suspicion of being fraudulent. Given the limited and varying resources available for this inspection task, such guidance should take the form of a ranking of fraud probability.

4.3.1 Different Approaches to the Problem

The available dataset has a column (`Insp`) that has information on previous inspection activities. The main problem we have is that the majority of the available reports have not been inspected. From the perspective of the task of deciding whether or not a report is fraudulent, the value `unkn` in the `Insp` variable has the meaning of an unknown variable value. This value represents the absence of information on whether the transaction is OK or a fraud. This means that we have two types of observations in our dataset. We have a (small) set of labeled observations for which we have the description of their characteristics plus the result of their inspection. We have another (large) set of unlabeled observations that have not been inspected, that is, have the value `unkn` in the `Insp` column. In this context, there are different types of modeling approaches that can be applied to these data, depending on which observations we use for obtaining the models.

4.3.1.1 Unsupervised Techniques

In the reports that were not inspected, the column `Insp` is in effect irrelevant as it carries no information. For these observations we only have descriptors of the transactions. This means that these sales reports are only described by a set of independent variables. This is the type of data used by unsupervised learning techniques. These methods are named this way because their goal is not to learn some "concept" with the help of a "teacher" as in supervised methods. The data used by these latter methods are examples of the concepts being learned (e.g., the concept of fraud or normal transaction). This requires that the data is preclassified (labeled) by a domain expert into one of the target concepts. This is not the case for the set of reports with unknown inspection results. We are thus facing a descriptive data mining task as opposed to predictive tasks, which are the goal of supervised methods.

Clustering is an example of a descriptive data mining technique. Clustering methods try to find the "natural" groupings of a set of observations by forming clusters of cases that are similar to each other. The notion of similarity usually requires the definition of a metric over the space defined by the variables that describe the observations. This metric is a distance function that measures how far an observation is from another. Cases that are near each other are usually considered part of the same natural group of data.

Outlier detection can also be viewed as a descriptive data mining task. Some outlier detection methods assume a certain expected distribution of the data, and tag as outliers any observations that deviate from this distribution. Another common outlier detection strategy is to assume a metric over the space of variables and use the notion of distance to tag as outliers observations that are "too far" from others.

From the above descriptions we can see that there are strong relationships between clustering and outlier detection. This is particularly true in methodologies based on the notion of distance between observations. Outliers are, by definition, rather different cases and thus they should not fit well in groups with other observations because they are too distant from them. This means that a good clustering of a dataset should not include outliers in large groups of data. At most, one can expect outliers to be similar to other outliers but by definition these are rare observations and thus should not form big groups of cases.

The use of unsupervised techniques in our problem involves some restrictions. In effect, our goal is to obtain an outlier ranking for a set of observations. This ranking is to serve as a basis for the inspection decisions within the company. This means that the unsupervised tools we select must be able to identify outliers and also rank them. Section 4.4.1 describes the unsupervised techniques we have selected to address this data mining task.

Further readings on unsupervised learning

Clustering analysis is a thoroughly explored methodology. Examples of good references are the works by Kaufman and Rousseeuw (1990) and Murtagh (1985). A more data mining-oriented perspective can be found in several reference books on data mining, for example, Han and Kamber (2006). Outlier detection has also been explored in many disciplines. Standard references include the works by Barnett and Lewis (1994) and Hawkins (1980). Good surveys of different perspectives of outlier detection are given in Austin (2004) and Chandola et al. (2007). Regarding the relationships between clustering an outlier detection, examples of works exploring it include Ng and Han (1994) and Torgo (2007).

4.3.1.2 Supervised Techniques

The set of transactions that were labeled normal or fraudulent (i.e., have been inspected) can be used with other types of modeling approaches. Supervised learning methods use this type of labeled data. The goal of these approaches is to obtain a model that relates a target variable (the concept being learned) with a set of independent variables (predictors, attributes). This model can be regarded as an approximation of an unknown function $Y = f(X_1, X_2, \cdots, X_p)$ that describes the relationship between the target variable Y and the predictors $X_1, X_2, \cdots, X_p$. The task of the modeling technique is to obtain the model parameters that optimize a certain selected criterion, for example, minimize the prediction error of the model. This search task is carried out with the help of a sample of observations of the phenomena under study, that is, it is based on a dataset containing examples of the concept being learned. These examples are particular instances of the variables $X_1, X_2, \cdots, X_p, Y$. If the target variable Y is continuous, we have a (multiple) regression problem. If Y is a nominal variable, we have a classification problem.

In the case of our dataset, the target variable is the result of the inspection task and can take two possible values: `ok` and `fraud`. This means that our goal is to learn the concepts of fraudulent and normal reports. We are thus facing a classification problem. Notice that the transactions that were not inspected cannot be used in these tasks because we are unsure whether or not they are frauds. This means that if we want to use a classification technique to obtain a model to predict whether a given report is or is not a fraud, we can only use 15,732 of the 401,146 available reports as the training sample.

The classification problem we are facing has a particularity that can impact both the way we will evaluate the performance of the models and also the models themselves. This particularity is the fact that among the two possible class values, one is much more frequent than the other. In effect, from the 15,732 inspected reports, 14,462 are normal transactions and only the remaining 1,270 are examples of frauds. Moreover, this less frequent concept is, in effect, the most important in this problem as it is related to the aim of the application: detect frauds. This means that we have to select evaluation criteria that are able to correctly measure the performance of the models on this less frequent class, and we should select modeling techniques that are able to cope with datasets with a strong class imbalance.

The use of classification tools in our problem involves a few adaptations. In effect, we are interested in obtaining a ranking of the transactions according to their probability of being frauds. This means that given a test set with new reports, we will use the model to decide which are the reports to be inspected. Some classification algorithms are only able to output the class label when given a test case. This is not enough for our problem because it does not establish a ranking among the cases classified as frauds. If these are too many for the available inspection resources, we are unable to decide which ones to handle. What we need is a probabilistic classification, that is, the model should not only predict a class label, but also an associated probability of this label. These probabilities allow us to obtain a ranking of the test cases according to the estimated probability that they are frauds.

Further readings on supervised methods

Supervised learning (also known as predictive modeling) is a well-studied subject with many different approaches to the general goal of obtaining an approximation of the unknown predictive function. Any data mining reference book will include broad coverage of many of these techniques (e.g., Han and Kamber (2006), Hand et al. (2001), or Hastie et al. (2001)). The problem of class imbalance is also the subject of many research works, for example, Chawla (2005) or Kubat and Matwin (1997).

4.3.1.3 Semi-Supervised Techniques

Semi-supervised methods are motivated by the observation that for many applications it is costly to find labeled data—that is, cases for which we have the value of the target variable. This information usually requires the work of domain experts, which increases the costs of data collection. On the other hand, unlabeled data is frequently easy to obtain, particularly with the widespread use of sensors and other types of automatic data collection devices. In this context, one frequently faces problems with a large proportion of data that is unlabeled, together with a small amount of labeled data. This is the case of our application, as we have seen before.

Semi-supervised methods are named this way exactly because they can handle this type of datasets with both labeled and unlabeled cases. There are usually two different types of semi-supervised methods. On the one hand, there are semi-supervised classification methods that try to improve the performance of standard supervised classification algorithms with the help of the extra information provided by the unlabeled cases. The alternative approach is given by semi-supervised clustering methods that try to bias the clustering process by incorporating some form of constraints based on the labeled data in the criteria used to form the groups.

In semi-supervised clustering, the idea is to use the available labels to bias the clustering process to include the cases with the same label in the same groups (*must-link* constraints), or to keep cases with different labels in different groups (*cannot-link* constraints). In search-based semi-supervised clustering, the criteria used to form the clusters is changed to bias the methods to find the appropriate groups of cases. In similarity-based semi-supervised approaches, the metric used by the algorithms is optimized to satisfy the constraints imposed by the labeled data. This means that the notion of distance is "distorted" to reflect the *must-link* and *cannot-link* constraints.

With respect to semi-supervised classification there are many alternative methodologies. A well-known method is self-training. This is an iterative approach that starts by obtaining a classification model with the given labeled data. The next step is to use this model to classify the unlabeled data. The cases for which the model has higher confidence on the classification are added together with the predicted label to the initial training set, thus extending it. Using this new set, a new model is obtained and the overall process is repeated until some convergence criterion is reached. Another example of semi-supervised classification models are transductive support vector machines (TSVMs). The goal of TSVMs is to obtain labels for a set of unlabeled data, such that a linear boundary achieves the maximum margin on both the original labeled data and on the unlabeled data (see Section 3.4.2.2 on page 127 for more details on SVMs).

Once again we should consider the particular restrictions of our application, namely in terms of obtaining outlier rankings. This can be accomplished using the same strategies outlined in the previous sections for unsupervised and supervised methods, depending on whether we use semi-supervised clustering or semi-supervised classification, respectively.

Further readings on semi-supervised methods

Semi-supervised learning has been receiving an increasing interest by the research community. Good surveys of the existing work are given in Zhu (2006), Seeger (2002), or Zhu (2005).

4.3.2 Evaluation Criteria

In this section we discuss how we will evaluate the models. When given a test set of transaction reports, each model will produce a ranking of these reports. This section discusses how to evaluate this ranking.

We also describe the experimental methodology that will be used to obtain reliable estimates of the selected evaluation metrics.

Our dataset has the particularity of including both labeled and unlabeled data. In this application the two situations translate into inspected and non-inspected transaction reports. This increases the difficulty of comparing the models because supervised and unsupervised methods are usually evaluated differently. The rankings obtained by the models will most probably include both labeled and unlabeled observations. Regarding the former, it is easy to evaluate whether or not their inclusion in the set of reports to inspect is correct. In the case of unlabeled cases, this evaluation is more difficult because we cannot be sure whether or not these cases are frauds.

4.3.2.1   Precision and Recall

In this application a successful model should obtain a ranking that includes all known frauds at the top positions of the ranking. Fraudulent reports are a minority in our data. Given a number k of reports that our resources allow to inspect, we would like that among the k top-most positions of the obtained ranking, we only have either frauds or non-inspected reports. Moreover, we would like to include in these k positions all of the known fraud cases that exist in the test set.

As we have seen in Section 3.3.4 (page 119), when our aim is to predict a small set of rare events (in this case frauds), precision and recall are the adequate evaluation metrics. Given the inspection effort limit k, we can calculate the precision and recall of the k top-most positions of the ranking. This k limit determines which reports are to be inspected according to the model. From a supervised classification perspective, this is equivalent to considering the top k positions as predictions of the class `fraud`, while the remaining are normal reports. The value of precision will tell us what proportion of these k top-most reports that are, in effect, labeled as frauds. The value of recall will measure the proportion of frauds in the test set that are included in these k top-most positions. We should note that the obtained values are pessimistic. In effect, if the k top-most positions include unlabeled reports, they will not enter the calculation of precision and recall. However, if they are inspected, we may find that they are, in effect, frauds and thus the real values of precision and recall could be higher.

Usually there is a trade-off between precision and recall. For instance, it is quite easy to achieve 100% recall if all test cases are predicted as events. However, such a strategy will inevitably also lead to a very low precision. Still, our current application has some particularities. Given the fact that there will be constraints on the resources invested in inspection activities, what we really want is to maximize the use of these resources. This means that if we can spend x hours inspecting reports and in these x hours we are able to capture all frauds, we are happy—even if in these x hours we actually inspect several normal reports, that is, even with a low precision in our ranking. Recall is actually the key issue in this application. What we want is to be able to achieve 100% recall with the resources we have available.

4.3.2.2   Lift Charts and Precision/Recall Curves

In the previous section we mentioned calculating the values of precision and recall for a given inspection effort. It is interesting to check the performance of the models at different effort levels. Different models may prevail at different levels and this may be useful information when comparing them.

Precision/recall (PR) curves are visual representations of the performance of a model in terms of the precision and recall statistics. The curves are obtained by proper interpolation of the values of the statistics at different working points. These working points can be given by different cut-off limits on a ranking of the class of interest provided by the model. In our case this would correspond to different effort limits applied to the outlier ranking produced by the models. Iterating over different limits (i.e., inspect less or more reports), we get different values of precision and recall. PR curves allow this type of analysis.

The package ROCR (Sing et al., 2009) contains several functions that are very useful for evaluating binary classifiers (i.e., classifiers for two classes problems like ours). This is an extra package that you should install before trying the code below. The package implements many evaluation metrics and it includes methods to obtain a wide range of curves. PR curves can be easily obtained with the functions in this package. The use of this package is rather simple. We start by obtaining an object of the class prediction using the predictions of the model and the true values of the test set. This is done with the prediction() function. The resulting object can be passed as an argument to the function performance() to obtain several evaluation metrics. Finally, the result of this latter function can be used with the function plot() to obtain different performance curves. The following code is an illustration of this process using some example data included in the package:

```
> library(ROCR)
> data(ROCR.simple)
> pred <- prediction(ROCR.simple$predictions, ROCR.simple$labels)
> perf <- performance(pred, "prec", "rec")
> plot(perf)
```

This code plots a PR curve that is shown on the left-most graph of Figure 4.5. The PR curves produced by the ROCR package have a sawtooth shape. This is usually considered not too clear and there are methods to overcome this effect. Namely, we can calculate the interpolated precision $Prec_{int}$ for a certain recall level r as the highest precision value found for any recall level greater than or equal to r:

$$Prec_{int}(r) = \max_{r' \geq r} Prec(r') \qquad (4.1)$$

where $Prec(x)$ is the precision at a certain recall level x.

If we take a close look at the object returned by the performance() function, we will see that it has a slot named y.values with the values of the y axis of the graph, that is, the precision values that are plotted. We can obtain a PR curve without the sawtooth effect by simply substituting this slot with the values of the interpolated precision according to Equation 4.1. The following function implements this idea for the general case:

```
> PRcurve <- function(preds, trues, ...) {
+     require(ROCR, quietly = T)
+     pd <- prediction(preds, trues)
+     pf <- performance(pd, "prec", "rec")
+     pf@y.values <- lapply(pf@y.values, function(x) rev(cummax(rev(x))))
```

```
+       plot(pf, ...)
+ }
```

The code uses the function `lapply()` because the slot `y.values` is, in effect, a list as it can include the results of several iterations of an experimental process. We will take advantage of this fact later on this chapter. For each vector of precision values, we calculate the interpolated precision using the functions `cummax()` and `rev()`. The latter simply reverses a vector, while the `cummax()` function obtains the cumulative maximum of a set of numbers. Try it with a vector of numbers if you have difficulty understanding the concept. The `PRcurve()` function is actually included in our book package, so you do not need to type the above code to use it.

We can apply the `PRcurve()` function to the example data given above, producing the right-most graph of Figure 4.5.

```
> PRcurve(ROCR.simple$predictions, ROCR.simple$labels)
```

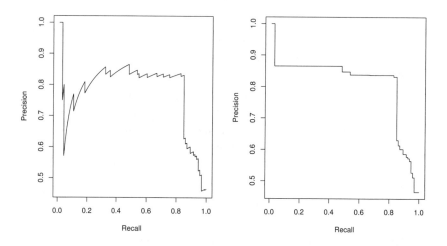

FIGURE 4.5: Smoothed (right) and non-smoothed (left) precision/recall curves.

How can we evaluate our outlier ranking models with these types of curves? We will have a test set with a variable `Insp` with possible values `unkn`, `ok`, and `fraud`, and a ranking of the observations in this set, produced by some model. We will require our models to obtain an outlier score for each observation in the test set. This score will be a value between 0 and 1. The higher the score, the higher the confidence of the model that the observation is a fraud. This score is the source of information for obtaining the ranking of the observations.

TABLE 4.1: A Confusion Matrix for the Illustrative Example.

		Predictions ok	fraud	
True	ok	3	1	4
Values	fraud	2	1	3
		5	2	7

If we order the test set observations by decreasing outlier score, we can calculate different values of precision and recall, depending on where we put our inspection effort limit. Setting this limit is equivalent to choosing a threshold on the outlier score above which we will consider the observations as fraudulent. Let us see a small example. Suppose we have seven test cases with the values $\{ok, ok, fraud, unknown, fraud, fraud, unknown\}$ in the Insp column. Imagine a certain model produces as outlier scores for these observations the values $\{0.2, 0.1, 0.7, 0.5, 0.4, 0.3, 0.25\}$, respectively. If we rank the observations by these scores, we obtain $\{fraud, unknown, fraud, fraud, unknown, ok, ok\}$. If our inspection limit only allows us to inspect two observations, it would be equivalent to a model "predicting" $\{fraud, fraud, ok, ok, ok, ok, ok\}$ for the true values $\{fraud, unknown, fraud, fraud, unknown, ok, ok\}$. This, in turn, corresponds to the confusion matrix in Table 4.1 and to the following values of precision and recall calculated according to that matrix:

$$Prec = \frac{1}{1+1} = 0.5 \qquad Rec = \frac{1}{2+1} = 0.3333$$

Notice that as mentioned in Section 4.3.2.1, we have followed a pessimistic estimate of precision and recall with respect to the reports that have not been inspected. Because of this, the prediction of fraud for the report in the second position of the ranking, which has the value unkn, is considered an error as we are not sure whether or not it is a fraud.

We will use this type of post-processing of the outlier rankings to obtain their scores in terms of precision and recall as well as the respective PR curves.

Lift charts provide a different perspective of the model predictions. These graphs give more importance to the values of recall and thus are, in a way, more adequate to our objectives, as mentioned in the end of Section 4.3.2.1. The x-axis of these graphs is the value of the rate of positive predictions (RPP), which is the probability that the model predicts a positive class. This is estimated by the proportion of positive class predictions divided by the total number of test cases. In the example of Table 4.1, this would have the value of $(1+1)/7$. In the context of our application, we can look at this statistic as the proportion of reports selected for inspection. The y-axis of lift charts is the value of recall divided by the value of RPP.

Lift charts can be obtained with the infrastructure provided by the ROCR package. The following is an illustrative example of its use with the corresponding lift chart shown in the left-most graph of Figure 4.6:

```
> pred <- prediction(ROCR.simple$predictions, ROCR.simple$labels)
> perf <- performance(pred, "lift", "rpp")
> plot(perf, main = "Lift Chart")
```

Despite their usefulness lift charts are not exactly what we search for in our particular application. A more interesting graph would be one that shows the recall values in terms of the inspection effort that is captured by the RPP. We will call this type of graph the *cumulative recall chart*; it can be implemented by the following function thanks to the ROCR package:

```
> CRchart <- function(preds, trues, ...) {
+     require(ROCR, quietly = T)
+     pd <- prediction(preds, trues)
+     pf <- performance(pd, "rec", "rpp")
+     plot(pf, ...)
+ }
```

Using again the artificial example, we obtain the right-most graph of Figure 4.6:

```
> CRchart(ROCR.simple$predictions, ROCR.simple$labels,
+          main='Cumulative Recall Chart')
```

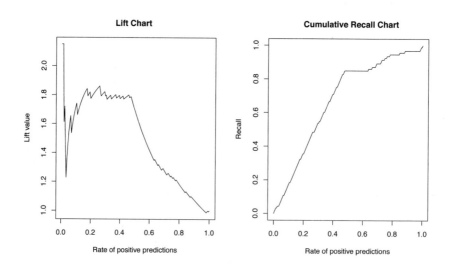

FIGURE 4.6: Lift (left) and cumulative recall (right) charts.

For cumulative recall charts, the nearer the curve of a model is to the top-left corner of the graph, the better. The CRchart() function is also included in our book package so you can use it at any time, provided you load the package.

4.3.2.3 Normalized Distance to Typical Price

The measures we have seen in previous sections only evaluate the quality of
the rankings in terms of the labeled reports. They are supervised classification
evaluation metrics. The rankings obtained by the models will most probably
also contain unlabeled reports in the top positions. Are these unlabeled cases
correctly positioned in the ranking? We cannot be sure about this as we have
not inspected them. Nevertheless, we can say something about them. For
instance, we can compare their unit price with the typical price of the reports
of the same product. We would expect that the difference between these prices
is high, as this is an indication that something is wrong with the report. In
this context, the distance between the unit price of a report and the typical
unit price of the respective product is a good indicator of the quality of the
outlier ranking obtained by a model.

Different products have a different scale of unit prices, as we have seen in
Figure 4.4. To avoid the effects of these differences in our proposed measure
of outlier ranking quality, we will normalize the distance to the typical unit
price. We use the IQR to normalize this distance:

$$NDTP_p(u) = \frac{|u - \widetilde{U_p}|}{IQR_p} \qquad (4.2)$$

where $\widetilde{U_p}$ is the typical unit price of the product p, measured by the median
unit price of its transactions, and IQR_p is the respective inter-quartile range
of the unit prices of that product.

In our experiments we will use the average value of $NDTP_p$ as one of
the evaluation metrics to characterize the performance of the models. The
following function calculates the value of this statistic:

```
> avgNDTP <- function(toInsp,train,stats) {
+   if (missing(train) && missing(stats))
+     stop('Provide either the training data or the product stats')
+   if (missing(stats)) {
+     notF <- which(train$Insp != 'fraud')
+     stats <- tapply(train$Uprice[notF],
+                 list(Prod=train$Prod[notF]),
+                 function(x) {
+                   bp <- boxplot.stats(x)$stats
+                   c(median=bp[3],iqr=bp[4]-bp[2])
+                 })
+     stats <- matrix(unlist(stats),
+                 length(stats),2,byrow=T,
+                 dimnames=list(names(stats),c('median','iqr')))
+     stats[which(stats[,'iqr']==0),'iqr'] <-
+         stats[which(stats[,'iqr']==0),'median']
+   }
+
+   mdtp <- mean(abs(toInsp$Uprice-stats[toInsp$Prod,'median']) /
```

```
+                    stats[toInsp$Prod,'iqr'])
+   return(mdtp)
+ }
```

The function receives, as the main argument, the set of transactions that a model selects for inspection. Then it must receive either the training set to obtain the median and IQR of each product, or an already prepared data structure with this information, to increase the computational efficiency of repeated calls to this function. If the training data is received, the function calculates the median and IQR values of the nonfraudulent transactions of each product in the training set. It may happen that the IQR is zero, particularly in products with very few transactions. To avoid division by zero in calculating $NDTP_p$, we have set the IQR of these cases to the value of the median.

4.3.3 Experimental Methodology

The dataset we are using has a very reasonable size. In this context, it makes sense to select the Hold Out method for our experimental comparisons. This method consists of randomly splitting the available dataset in two partitions (typically in 70%/30% proportions). One of the partitions is used for obtaining the models, while the other is used for testing them. The process can eventually be repeated a few times to ensure more reliability, if necessary. The size of our dataset ensures that the values we obtain are statistically reliable. If we select 30% of the cases for the test set, this corresponds to 120,343 reports.

One additional difficulty in this situation is the imbalance between the distributions of the different types of reports, namely on the labeled cases. A normal re-sampling strategy may lead to a test set with a different distribution of the normal/fraudulent reports. Whenever we have this type of imbalanced class distributions, it is recommended to use a stratified sampling strategy. This strategy consists of randomly sampling from bags with the observations of the different classes, ensuring that the obtained sample respects the distribution of the initial dataset. For instance, if we have 10% of cases of class X and the remaining 90% of another class Y, we will put these observations in two separate bags. If we want a random stratified sample with 100 cases, we will randomly pick ten cases from the bag with the X class cases, and the remaining 90 from the bag with the Ys, thus respecting the original proportions of the classes.

In our book package we have the function holdOut() that can be used to carry out hold-out experiments in a similar fashion to the functions used in previous chapters for cross-validation and Monte Carlo experiments. One of the parameters of the function is an object of the class hldSettings that specifies the settings of the experiment. Among other parameters, this object allows you to specify that a stratified sampling is to be used. In Section 4.4 we provide several examples of using this function to obtain hold-out estimates of our selected evaluation statistics. These statistics are precision, recall and the average $NDTP$. The following function calculates these metrics:

```
> evalOutlierRanking <- function(testSet,rankOrder,Threshold,statsProds) {
+    ordTS <- testSet[rankOrder,]
+    N <- nrow(testSet)
+    nF <- if (Threshold < 1) as.integer(Threshold*N) else Threshold
+    cm <- table(c(rep('fraud',nF),rep('ok',N-nF)),ordTS$Insp)
+    prec <- cm['fraud','fraud']/sum(cm['fraud',])
+    rec <- cm['fraud','fraud']/sum(cm[,'fraud'])
+    AVGndtp <- avgNDTP(ordTS[nF,],stats=statsProds)
+    return(c(Precision=prec,Recall=rec,avgNDTP=AVGndtp))
+ }
```

The function requires the user to supply the test set, the ranking proposed by the model for this set, a threshold specifying the inspection limit effort (either as a percentage or as a number of reports), and the statistics (median and IQR) of the products.

In Section 4.2.3.2 we observed that the products are rather different, and that some products have, in effect, few transactions. In this context, we may question whether it makes sense to analyze the transactions of all products together. An argument in favor of checking them together is that there is a variable (the product ID) that can be used to discriminate among the products, and thus the modeling techniques can use the variable if necessary. Moreover, by putting all transactions together, the models can take advantage of some eventual relationships among products. Nevertheless, an alternative would be to analyze each product in turn, ranking its transactions by some outlier score. This would require an extra step of obtaining the final global ranking from the individual product rankings but this should be simple. We will experiment with modeling approaches that follow a different strategy with respect to this issue. From the perspective of the experimental methodology, we will put all products together. With these transactions we will randomly select a test set using a stratified hold-out strategy. This test set will be given to different modeling techniques that should return a ranking of these transactions according to their estimated probability of being frauds. Internally, the models may decide to analyze the products individually or all together.

4.4   Obtaining Outlier Rankings

This section describes the different models we will try with the goal of obtaining outlier rankings. For each attempt we will estimate its results using a stratified 70%/30% hold-out strategy.

4.4.1   Unsupervised Approaches

4.4.1.1   The Modified Box Plot Rule

In Section 4.2.2 we described the box plot rule, which can be used to detect outliers of a continuous variable provided it follows a near-normal distribution. This is the case of the unit price of the products. In this context, one can think of this simple rule as the baseline method that we can apply to our data.

The application of the box plot rule to detect unusual unit price values of the transactions of each product will result in the identification of some values as potential outliers. We can use this rule on each set of transactions of the products appearing in a given test set. In the end we will have a set of potential outliers for each of the products. We have to decide how to move from these sets into an outlier ranking of all test sets. This means we have to distinguish the outliers to be able to rank them. A possibility is to use the idea of the normalized distance to the typical (median) unit price ($NDTP$) that we described in Section 4.3.2.3. This measure can be seen as a variation of the box plot rule because both use a kind of distance from the central values to decide on the "outlyingness" of a value. The advantage of the $NDTP$ is that it is a unitless metric and thus we can mix together the values for the different products and thus produce a global ranking of all test cases.

The idea outlined above can be implemented by the following function that receives a set of transactions and obtains their ranking order and score:

```
> BPrule <- function(train,test) {
+    notF <- which(train$Insp != 'fraud')
+    ms <- tapply(train$Uprice[notF],list(Prod=train$Prod[notF]),
+                 function(x) {
+                     bp <- boxplot.stats(x)$stats
+                     c(median=bp[3],iqr=bp[4]-bp[2])
+                 })
+    ms <- matrix(unlist(ms),length(ms),2,byrow=T,
+                 dimnames=list(names(ms),c('median','iqr')))
+    ms[which(ms[,'iqr']==0),'iqr'] <- ms[which(ms[,'iqr']==0),'median']
+    ORscore <- abs(test$Uprice-ms[test$Prod,'median']) /
+               ms[test$Prod,'iqr']
+    return(list(rankOrder=order(ORscore,decreasing=T),
+                rankScore=ORscore))
+ }
```

The parameters of the function are the training and test data sets. After calculating the median and IQR values per product, the function uses these statistics to obtain the outlier score using the formula of Equation (4.2). Finally, it returns a list with this score and the rank order of the test set observations. Given that this method uses the $NDTP$ values to obtain its ranking, it is foreseeable that it will score very well in terms of the average value of this metric.

As a side note, we should remark that this is the place where we could have used the information on the similarity between products. In effect, for products with very few transactions, we could consider checking if there is a product that has a distribution of unit prices that is significantly similar. If there is such a product, we could add its transactions and thus obtain the estimate of the median and IQR statistics using a larger sample. This should be done in the call to the `tapply()` function, where we could incorporate the information on the similar products that was saved in the file "similarProducts.Rdata" (see end of Section 4.2.3.2). We leave this as an exercise for the reader.

We will now evaluate this simple method using the hold-out experimental methodology. We start by calculating the values of the median and IQR for each product required to calculate the average $NDTP$ score. We will use all available data for this calculation as our goal is to have the most precise estimate of these values to correctly evaluate the outlier ranking capabilities of the models. Because this global information is not passed to the modeling techniques, this cannot be regarded as giving information from the test data to the models. It is just a form of obtaining more reliable estimates of the ability of our models for detecting unusual values.

```
> notF <- which(sales$Insp != 'fraud')
> globalStats <- tapply(sales$Uprice[notF],
+                        list(Prod=sales$Prod[notF]),
+                        function(x) {
+                            bp <- boxplot.stats(x)$stats
+                            c(median=bp[3],iqr=bp[4]-bp[2])
+                        })
> globalStats <- matrix(unlist(globalStats),
+                        length(globalStats),2,byrow=T,
+                        dimnames=list(names(globalStats),c('median','iqr')))
> globalStats[which(globalStats[,'iqr']==0),'iqr'] <-
+     globalStats[which(globalStats[,'iqr']==0),'median']
```

The `holdOut()` function needs to call a routine to obtain and evaluate the *BPrule* method for each iteration of the experimental process. In previous chapters we created similar user-defined functions for other learning systems in the context of cross-validation and Monte Carlo experiments. Those functions should return a vector with the values of the evaluation statistics of a model given the training and test sets. This time we need to return more information. To plot the PR and cumulative recall curves, the `ROCR` package functions need to know the predicted and true values of each test observation. In this context, we also need to return these predicted and true values from our function so that the curves can be plotted later. The information needed to plot the curves was illustrated by the small artificial example in Section 4.3.2.2. The following function, which will be called from the `holdOut()` routine, returns the value of the evaluation statistics with an attached attribute with the predicted and true values:

```
> ho.BPrule <- function(form, train, test, ...) {
```

```
+    res <- BPrule(train,test)
+    structure(evalOutlierRanking(test,res$rankOrder,...),
+            itInfo=list(preds=res$rankScore,
+                     trues=ifelse(test$Insp=='fraud',1,0)
+                     )
+            )
+ }
```

Most R objects can have attributes attached to them. These are, in effect, other R objects that we attach to the former. Usually they convey extra information on the object (e.g., its dimension, etc.). In this case we are attaching to the vector with the scores of the *BPrule* method, a list containing the predicted and true values that originated these scores. The function `structure()` can be used to create an object and specify the values of its attributes. These attributes must have a name and contain an R object. In this application of structures, we need to create an object with an attribute named `itInfo`. The `holdOut()` function stores this information for each iteration of the experimental process. In order for this storage to take place, we need to call the `holdOut()` function with the optional parameter `itsInfo=T`. This ensures that whatever is returned as an attribute with name `itInfo` by the user-defined function will be collected in a list and returned as an attribute named `itsInfo` of the result of the `holdOut()` function.

With this function we are ready to run the `holdOut()` function to obtain estimates of the selected statistics for the *BPrule* system. As experimental settings we will use a 70%/30% division of the full dataset using a stratified sampling strategy, and calculate the precision/recall statistics for a predefined inspection limit effort of 10% of the test set. This last setting is somewhat arbitrary and any other threshold could have been selected. A more global perspective of the performance of the system over different limits will be given by the PR and cumulative recall curves. The hold-out estimates will be obtained based on three repetitions of this process.

```
> bp.res <- holdOut(learner('ho.BPrule',
+                           pars=list(Threshold=0.1,
+                                     statsProds=globalStats)),
+                 dataset(Insp ~ .,sales),
+                 hldSettings(3,0.3,1234,T),
+                 itsInfo=TRUE
+                 )
```

Setting the fourth parameter of the `hldSettings()` function to `TRUE` indicates that a stratified sampling should be used. The other parameters specify the number of repetitions, the percentage of cases included in the hold-out set, and the random number generator seed, respectively.

The summary of the results of this experiment can be obtained as follows:

```
> summary(bp.res)
```

```
== Summary of a Hold Out Experiment ==

Stratified  3 x 70 %/ 30 % Holdout run with seed =  1234

* Dataset ::  sales
* Learner  ::  ho.BPrule  with parameters:
          Threshold  =  0.1
          statsProds  =  11.34  ...

* Summary of Experiment Results:

          Precision      Recall     avgNDTP
avg      0.016630574 0.52293272 1.87123901
std      0.000898367 0.01909992 0.05379945
min      0.015992004 0.51181102 1.80971393
max      0.017657838 0.54498715 1.90944329
invalid 0.000000000 0.00000000 0.00000000
```

The results of precision and recall are rather low. On average, only 52% of the known frauds are included in the top 10% reports of the rank produced by the *BPrule*. The low values of recall could mean that the 10% effort was not enough for including all frauds, but that is not possible given the proportion of frauds in the test set and also the low values in precision. The extremely low value of precision means that this method is putting on the top 10% positions mostly unkn or ok cases. In the case of unkn reports, this is not necessarily bad, as these may actually be fraudulent reports. Given the relatively high score of $NDTP$, we can at least be sure that the unit price of these top reports is rather different from the typical price of the respective products. In effect, an average value of 1.8 for $NDTP$ means that the difference between the unit price of these reports and the median price of the reports of the same product is around 1.8 times the value of the IQR of these prices. Given that the IQR includes 50% of the reports, this means that the unit prices of these transactions are rather unusual.

To obtain the PR and cumulative recall charts, we need access to the actual outlier scores of the method on each hold-out repetition, as well as the true "class" labels. The function we have used to apply the ranking method on each iteration (ho.BPrule()) returns these values as attributes of the vector of statistics. The function holdOut() collects this extra information for each iteration on a list. This list is returned as an attribute named itsInfo of the objected produced by the holdOut() function. To obtain the necessary information in the format required by the plotting functions, we need some extra steps as detailed below. The result of the following code are the curves shown in Figure 4.7.

```
> par(mfrow=c(1,2))
> info <- attr(bp.res,'itsInfo')
> PTs.bp <- aperm(array(unlist(info),dim=c(length(info[[1]]),2,3)),
```

```
+                        c(1,3,2)
+                        )
> PRcurve(PTs.bp[,,1],PTs.bp[,,2],
+           main='PR curve',avg='vertical')
> CRchart(PTs.bp[,,1],PTs.bp[,,2],
+           main='Cumulative Recall curve',avg='vertical')
```

The first statement allows you to divide the graph window in two to visualize both figures side by side. The second statement uses the function `attr()` to extract the list that contains the predicted and true values returned by the `ho.BPrule()` on each iteration. This function can be used to obtain the value of any attribute of an object by its name. This list is then transformed into an array with three dimensions. The first dimension is the test case and the second is the repetition of the hold-out experiment. The third dimension is the type of value (1 for the predicted values, 2 for the true values). For instance, the value `PTs.bp[3,2,1]` is the predicted value of the method for the third test case on the second repetition of the hold-out process. The function `aperm()` can be used to permute the dimensions of an array. If you are having difficulty understanding this composed statement, try calling each function in turn and inspect its output (use sub-setting to avoid huge outputs as some of these objects are rather large).

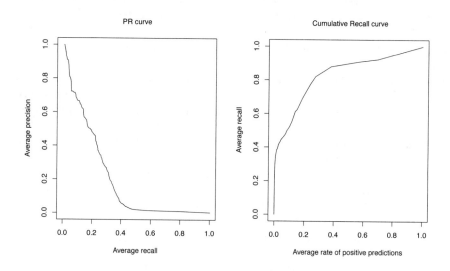

FIGURE 4.7: The PR (left) and cumulative recall (right) curves of the *BPrule* method.

Both curves are obtained by vertically averaging the curves of each repetition of the hold-out process. The cumulative recall chart gives a more global perspective of the performance of the method. We can observe that the method obtains around 40% of recall with a very low inspection effort. However, to achieve values around 80%, we already need to inspect roughly 25% to 30% of the reports.

4.4.1.2 Local Outlier Factors (LOF)

Outlier ranking is a well-studied research topic. Breunig et al. (2000) have developed the local outlier factor (LOF) system that is usually considered a state-of-the-art outlier ranking method. The main idea of this system is to try to obtain an outlyingness score for each case by estimating its degree of isolation with respect to its local neighborhood. The method is based on the notion of the local density of the observations. Cases in regions with very low density are considered outliers. The estimates of the density are obtained using the distances between cases. The authors defined a few concepts that drive the algorithm used to calculate the outlyingness score of each point. These are the (1) concept of *core distance* of a point p, which is defined as its distance to its kth nearest neighbor, (2) concept of *reachability distance* between the case p_1 and p_2, which is given by the maximum of the core distance of p_1 and the distance between both cases, and (3) *local reachability distance* of a point, which is inversely proportional to the average reachability distance of its k neighbors. The LOF of a case is calculated as a function of its local reachability distance.

Our book package includes an implementation of the LOF algorithm based on the work by (Acuna et al., 2009). Namely, we provide the function `lofactor()` that receives as arguments a dataset and the value of k that specifies the size of the neighborhood used in calculating the LOF of the observations. This implementation of the LOF system is limited to datasets described by numeric variables. This is, in effect, a frequent limitation for many modeling algorithms. As we have seen, our dataset includes several nominal variables. This means that we cannot apply this function directly to our dataset. There are several ways of overcoming this issue. A first alternative would be to change the source code of the implementation of LOF so that a mixed-mode distance function is used. There are several distance functions that can calculate the distance between observations described by variables of different type. An example is given by the function `daisy()` in the `cluster` package. Another alternative consists of re-coding the nominal variables so that the observations are described by continuous variables only. Any nominal variable with n possible values can be re-coded into $n-1$ binary (0/1) variables. These variables, frequently called dummy variables, indicate the presence (absence) of any of the n values. The application of this method to our dataset has a problem. The `ID` variable has 6,016 possible values while the variable `Prod` has 4,546. This means that if we use this strategy, we would obtain a dataset with 10,566 variables. This is an absurd increase in the dimensionality of the original data. This method is inadequate for this problem. The third alternative consists of handling each product individually, as we have done with the $BPrule$ method. By proceeding this way, not only do we decrease significantly the computational requirements to handle this problem, but we also eliminate the need for the variable `Prod`. Moreover, handling the products separately was always a plausible approach, given the observed differences between them (see Section 4.2.3.2). Nevertheless, we still have to decide what to do with the information on the salespeople (the variable `ID`). Eliminating also this variable would mean assuming the fact that we consider some report unusual is independent of the salesman reporting it. This assumption does not seem too risky. The fact is that even if some salesperson is more prone to fraud, this should also be reflected in the unit prices that he reports. In this context, the alternative of eliminating both columns and treating the products separately seems clearly more reasonable than the option of re-coding the variables. Summarizing, we will apply the *LOF* algorithm to a dataset of reports described only by the unit price:

```
> ho.LOF <- function(form, train, test, k, ...) {
+    ntr <- nrow(train)
+    all <- rbind(train,test)
+    N <- nrow(all)
+    ups <- split(all$Uprice,all$Prod)
+    r <- list(length=ups)
+    for(u in seq(along=ups))
+      r[[u]] <- if (NROW(ups[[u]]) > 3)
+                    lofactor(ups[[u]],min(k,NROW(ups[[u]]) %/% 2))
+                  else if (NROW(ups[[u]])) rep(0,NROW(ups[[u]]))
+                  else NULL
+    all$lof <- vector(length=N)
+    split(all$lof,all$Prod) <- r
+    all$lof[which(!(is.infinite(all$lof) | is.nan(all$lof)))] <-
+      SoftMax(all$lof[which(!(is.infinite(all$lof) | is.nan(all$lof)))])
+    structure(evalOutlierRanking(test,order(all[(ntr+1):N,'lof'],
+                                             decreasing=T),...),
+              itInfo=list(preds=all[(ntr+1):N,'lof'],
+                          trues=ifelse(test$Insp=='fraud',1,0))
+             )
+ }
```

The above function obtains the evaluation statistics resulting from applying the *LOF* method to the given training and test sets. Our approach was to merge the train and test datasets and use *LOF* to rank this full set of reports. From the obtained ranking we then select the outlier scores of the cases belonging to the test set. We could have ranked only the test set but this would not use the information on the training data. The alternative of ranking only the training data would also not make sense because this is an unsupervised method whose result cannot be used to make "predictions" for a test set.

The function `split()` was used to divide the unit prices of this full dataset by product. The result is a list whose components are the unit prices of the respective products. The `for` loop goes over each of these sets of prices and applies the *LOF* method to obtain an outlier factor for each of the prices. These factors are collected in a list (r) also organized by product. We only used the *LOF* method if there were at least three reports; otherwise all values were tagged as normal (score 0). After the main loop, the obtained outlier factors are "attached" to the respective transactions in the data frame all, again using the split() function. The next statement has the goal of changing the outlier factors into a 0..1 scale. It uses the function SoftMax() from our book package for this purpose. This function "squashes" a range of values into this scale. Due to the fact that the lofactor() function produced some Inf and NaN values for some transactions, we had to constrain the application of the SoftMax() function. Finally, the evaluation scores of the obtained ranking, together with the predicted and true values, are returned as the result of the function.

The next step is to use a hold-out process to obtain the estimates of our evaluation metrics, as done before for the *BPrule* method. We have used the same settings as before and, in particular, have used the same random number generator seed to ensure that the exact same data partitions are used. We have set the value of the *k* parameter of the lofactor() function to 7. Further experiments could be carried out to tune this parameter. A word of warning before you execute the following code: depending on your hardware, this may start to take a bit too long, although still on the minutes scale.

```
> lof.res <- holdOut(learner('ho.LOF',
+                             pars=list(k=7,Threshold=0.1,
+                                       statsProds=globalStats)),
+                     dataset(Insp ~ .,sales),
+                     hldSettings(3,0.3,1234,T),
+                     itsInfo=TRUE
+                     )
```

The results of the *LOF* method were the following:

```
> summary(lof.res)

== Summary of a Hold Out Experiment ==

 Stratified  3 x 70 %/ 30 % Holdout run with seed =  1234

* Dataset ::  sales
* Learner  ::  ho.LOF  with parameters:
        k  =  7
        Threshold  =  0.1
        statsProds  =  11.34   ...

* Summary of Experiment Results:

         Precision       Recall      avgNDTP
avg      0.022127825  0.69595344  2.4631856
```

```
std      0.000913681 0.02019331 0.9750265
min      0.021405964 0.67454068 1.4420851
max      0.023155089 0.71465296 3.3844572
invalid 0.000000000 0.00000000 0.0000000
```

As you may observe, the values of precision and recall for this 10% inspection effort are higher than the values obtained by the *BPrule* method. In particular, the value of recall has increased from 52% to 69%. Moreover, this is accompanied by an increase in the average value of *NDTP* (from 1.8 to 2.4).

A more global perspective can be obtained with the PR and cumulative recall curves. To enable a better comparison with the *BPrule* method, we have also plotted the curves of this method, using the parameter add=T to make more than one curve appear on the same graph (Figure 4.8):

```
> par(mfrow=c(1,2))
> info <- attr(lof.res,'itsInfo')
> PTs.lof <- aperm(array(unlist(info),dim=c(length(info[[1]]),2,3)),
+                  c(1,3,2)
+                  )
> PRcurve(PTs.bp[,,1],PTs.bp[,,2],
+         main='PR curve',lty=1,xlim=c(0,1),ylim=c(0,1),
+         avg='vertical')
> PRcurve(PTs.lof[,,1],PTs.lof[,,2],
+         add=T,lty=2,
+         avg='vertical')
> legend('topright',c('BPrule','LOF'),lty=c(1,2))
> CRchart(PTs.bp[,,1],PTs.bp[,,2],
+         main='Cumulative Recall curve',lty=1,xlim=c(0,1),ylim=c(0,1),
+         avg='vertical')
> CRchart(PTs.lof[,,1],PTs.lof[,,2],
+         add=T,lty=2,
+         avg='vertical')
> legend('bottomright',c('BPrule','LOF'),lty=c(1,2))
```

The analysis of the PR curves (Figure 4.8, left), shows that for smaller recall values, the *BPrule* generally achieves a considerably higher precision. For values of recall above 40%, the tendency is inverse although with not so marked differences. In terms of recall achieved by inspection effort (Figure 4.8, right), we can say that generally the *LOF* method dominates the *BPrule* for inspection efforts below 25% to 30%. For higher inspection efforts, the differences are not so clear, and the results are rather comparable. Given that the interest of the company is obviously on lower inspection efforts to decrease its costs (provided a good recall is achieved), we would say that the *LOF* method is more interesting. In effect, with an effort around 15% to 20%, one can capture roughly 70% to 80% of the frauds. Moreover, we should note that the values of *NDTP* of *LOF* were clearly above those obtained by the *BPrule* method for an inspection effort of 10%.

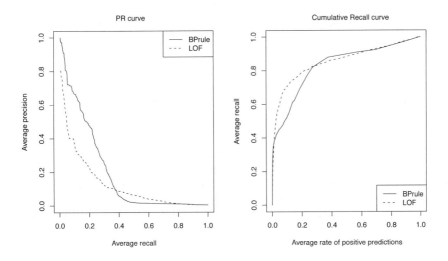

FIGURE 4.8: The PR (left) and cumulative recall (right) curves of the LOF, and $BPrule$ models.

4.4.1.3 Clustering-Based Outlier Rankings (OR_h)

The next outlier ranking method we consider is based on the results of a clustering algorithm. The OR_h method (Torgo, 2007) uses a hierarchical agglomerative clustering algorithm to obtain a dendrogram of the given data. Dendrograms are visual representations of the merging process of these clustering methods. Cutting these trees at different height levels produces different clusterings of the data. At the lowest level we have a solution with as many groups as there are observations on the given training data. This is the initial solution of the iterative algorithm used by these methods. The next steps of this algorithm decide which two groups from the previous step should be merged into a single cluster. This merging process is guided by some criterion that tries to put together observations that are more similar to each other. The iterative process is stopped when the last two groups are merged into a single cluster with all observations. The dendrogram describes the entire merging process. The function `hclust()` of the base package `stats` implements several variants of this type of clustering. The object returned by this function includes a data structure (`merge`) that includes information on which cases are involved in each merging step. The OR_h method uses the information in this data structure as the basis for the following outlier ranking method. The basic idea is that outliers should offer greater resistance to be merged and thus, when they are finally merged, the size difference between the group to which they belong and the group to which they are being merged should be very large. This reflects the idea that outliers are rather different from other observations, and thus their inclusion in groups with more "normal" observations should clearly decrease the homogeneity of the resulting group. Occasionally, outliers are merged at initial stages with other observations, but only if these are similar outliers. Otherwise, they will only be merged at later stages of the clustering process and usually with a much larger group of cases. This is the general idea that is captured by the OR_h method. This method calculates the outlier score of each case as follows. For each merging step i involving two groups ($g_{x,i}$ and $g_{y,i}$), we calculate the following value:

$$of_i(x) = \max\left(0, \frac{|g_{y,i}| - |g_{x,i}|}{|g_{y,i}| + |g_{x,i}|}\right) \tag{4.3}$$

where $g_{x,i}$ is the group to which x belongs, and $|g_{x,i}|$ is the group cardinality.

Note that the members of the larger group involved in the merge get the score 0, as we are interested in members of small groups. Each observation can be involved in several merges throughout the iterative process of the hierarchical clustering algorithm—sometimes as members of the larger group, others as members of the smaller group. The final outlier score of each case in the data sample is given by

$$OF_H(x) = \max_i of_i(x) \tag{4.4}$$

The function `outliers.ranking()` of our book package implements this method. The following function uses the OR_h method to obtain the outlier score of a test set of reports and obtains the usual evaluation statistics:

```
> ho.ORh <- function(form, train, test, ...) {
+    ntr <- nrow(train)
+    all <- rbind(train,test)
+    N <- nrow(all)
+    ups <- split(all$Uprice,all$Prod)
+    r <- list(length=ups)
+    for(u in seq(along=ups))
+      r[[u]] <- if (NROW(ups[[u]]) > 3)
+                   outliers.ranking(ups[[u]])$prob.outliers
+                else if (NROW(ups[[u]])) rep(0,NROW(ups[[u]]))
+                else NULL
+    all$orh <- vector(length=N)
+    split(all$orh,all$Prod) <- r
+    all$orh[which(!(is.infinite(all$orh) | is.nan(all$orh)))] <-
+      SoftMax(all$orh[which(!(is.infinite(all$orh) | is.nan(all$orh)))])
+    structure(evalOutlierRanking(test,order(all[(ntr+1):N,'orh'],
+                                    decreasing=T),...),
+              itInfo=list(preds=all[(ntr+1):N,'orh'],
+                          trues=ifelse(test$Insp=='fraud',1,0))
+             )
+ }
```

The function is very similar to the one presented previously for the *LOF* method. Once again we have used the approach of handling the products individually, primarily for the same reasons described for the *LOF* method. Nevertheless, the `outliers.ranking()` function can receive as argument a distance matrix of the observations being ranked, instead of the dataset. This means that we can obtain this matrix using any distance function that handles mixed-mode data (e.g., function `daisy()` in package `cluster`). However, if you decide to try this you will need large computation resources as clustering such a large dataset will require a large amount of main memory and also a fast processor. Even using this approach of handling each product separately, the following code that runs the full hold-out experiments will surely take a while to run on any normal computer.

As with *LOF*, we have not carried out any thorough exploration of the several parameter values that the OR_h method accepts, simply using its defaults:

```
> orh.res <- holdOut(learner('ho.ORh',
+                     pars=list(Threshold=0.1,
+                               statsProds=globalStats)),
+                dataset(Insp ~ .,sales),
+                hldSettings(3,0.3,1234,T),
+                itsInfo=TRUE
+                )
```

A summary of the results of the OR_h method is shown below:

```
> summary(orh.res)

== Summary of a Hold Out Experiment ==

 Stratified  3 x 70 %/ 30 % Holdout run with seed =  1234

* Dataset ::  sales
* Learner  ::  ho.ORh  with parameters:
          Threshold  =  0.1
          statsProds  =  11.34  ...

* Summary of Experiment Results:

              Precision       Recall     avgNDTP
avg         0.0220445333 0.69345072 0.5444893
std         0.0005545834 0.01187721 0.3712311
min         0.0215725471 0.67979003 0.2893128
max         0.0226553390 0.70133333 0.9703665
invalid 0.0000000000 0.00000000 0.0000000
```

The results of the OR_h system in terms of both precision and recall are very similar to the values of *BPrule* and *LOF*. With respect to the average

NDTP, the result is considerably lower than the scores of the other two methods.

The PR and cumulative recall curves of this method are shown in Figure 4.9, together with the curves of the other unsupervised methods we have tried previously. The following code was used to generate these graphs:

```
> par(mfrow=c(1,2))
> info <- attr(orh.res,'itsInfo')
> PTs.orh <- aperm(array(unlist(info),dim=c(length(info[[1]]),2,3)),
+                  c(1,3,2)
+                  )
> PRcurve(PTs.bp[,,1],PTs.bp[,,2],
+         main='PR curve',lty=1,xlim=c(0,1),ylim=c(0,1),
+         avg='vertical')
> PRcurve(PTs.lof[,,1],PTs.lof[,,2],
+         add=T,lty=2,
+         avg='vertical')
> PRcurve(PTs.orh[,,1],PTs.orh[,,2],
+         add=T,lty=1,col='grey',
+         avg='vertical')
> legend('topright',c('BPrule','LOF','ORh'),
+        lty=c(1,2,1),col=c('black','black','grey'))
> CRchart(PTs.bp[,,1],PTs.bp[,,2],
+         main='Cumulative Recall curve',lty=1,xlim=c(0,1),ylim=c(0,1),
+         avg='vertical')
> CRchart(PTs.lof[,,1],PTs.lof[,,2],
+         add=T,lty=2,
+         avg='vertical')
> CRchart(PTs.orh[,,1],PTs.orh[,,2],
+         add=T,lty=1,col='grey',
+         avg='vertical')
> legend('bottomright',c('BPrule','LOF','ORh'),
+        lty=c(1,2,1),col=c('black','black','grey'))
```

As you can see, the results of the OR_h method are comparable to those of *LOF* in terms of the cumulative recall curve. However, regarding the PR curve, the OR_h system clearly dominates the score of *LOF*, with a smaller advantage over *BPrule*.

4.4.2 Supervised Approaches

In this section we explore several supervised classification approaches to our problem. Given our goal of obtaining a ranking for a set of transaction reports, we will have to constrain the selection of models. We will use only systems that are able to produce probabilistic classifications. For each test case, these methods output the probability of belonging to each of the possible classes. This type of information will allow us to rank the test reports according to their probability of belonging to our "target" class: the fraudulent reports.

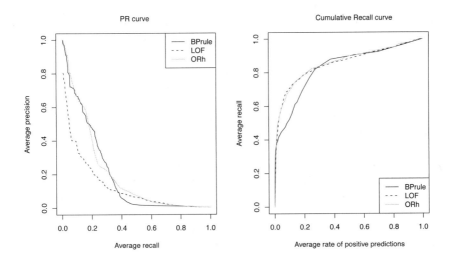

FIGURE 4.9: The PR (left) and cumulative recall (right) curves of the OR_h, LOF, and $BPrule$ models.

Before describing a few concrete classification algorithms that we will use, we address a particular problem of our dataset: the imbalanced distribution of the class labels.

4.4.2.1 The Class Imbalance Problem

Our dataset has a very imbalanced proportion of normal and fraudulent reports. The latter are a clear minority, roughly 8.1% of the inspected reports (i.e., supervised cases). Problems of this type can create all sorts of difficulties in the task of obtaining predictive models. First, they require proper evaluation metrics as it is well known that the standard accuracy (or its complement error rate) is clearly inadequate for these domains. In effect, for our application it would be easy to obtain around 90% accuracy by predicting that all reports are normal. Given the prevalence of this class, this would get us to this apparently very high accuracy level. Another problem with class imbalance is that it has a strong impact on the performance of the learning algorithms that tend to disregard the minority class given its lack of statistical support. This is particularly problematic in situations where this minority class is exactly the most relevant class, as is the case in our domain.

There are several techniques that have been developed with the purpose of helping the learning algorithms overcome the problems raised by class imbalance. They generally group in two families: (1) methods that bias the learning process by using specific evaluation metrics that are more sensitive to minority class examples; and (2) sampling methods that manipulate the training data to change the class distribution. In our attempt to use supervised classification methods in our problem, we will use a method belonging to this second group.

Several sampling methods have been proposed to change the class imbalance of a dataset. Under-sampling methods select a small part of the majority class examples and add them to the minority class cases, thereby building a dataset with a more balanced class distribution. Over-sampling methods work the other way around, using some process to replicate the minority class examples. Many variants of these two general sampling approaches exist. A successful example is the SMOTE method (Chawla et al., 2002). The general idea of this method is to artificially generate new examples of the minority class using the nearest neighbors of these cases. Furthermore, the majority class examples are also under-sampled, leading to a more balanced dataset. We have implemented this sampling method in a function called SMOTE(), which is included in our book package. Given an imbalanced sample, this function generates a new data set with a more balanced class distribution. The following code shows a simple illustration of its use:

```
> data(iris)
> data <- iris[, c(1, 2, 5)]
> data$Species <- factor(ifelse(data$Species == "setosa", "rare",
+     "common"))
> newData <- SMOTE(Species ~ ., data, perc.over = 600)
> table(newData$Species)

common   rare
   600    350
```

This small example uses the iris data to create an artificial dataset with two predictor variables (for easier visualization) and a new target variable that has an unbalanced class distribution. The code calls the function SMOTE() with the value 600 for the parameter perc.over, which means that six new examples will be created for each case in the initial dataset that belongs to the minority class. These new cases are created by some form of random interpolation between the case and its nearest neighbors (by default, 5). Our implementation uses a mixed-mode distance function so you can use SMOTE() on datasets with both continuous and nominal variables.

We can get a better idea of what was done by plotting the original and SMOTE'd datasets. This is the purpose of the following code, with the results shown in Figure 4.10:

```
> par(mfrow = c(1, 2))
> plot(data[, 1], data[, 2], pch = 19 + as.integer(data[, 3]),
+     main = "Original Data")
> plot(newData[, 1], newData[, 2], pch = 19 + as.integer(newData[,
+     3]), main = "SMOTE'd Data")
```

In our experiments with supervised classification algorithms, we will try variants of the methods using training sets balanced by this SMOTE method.

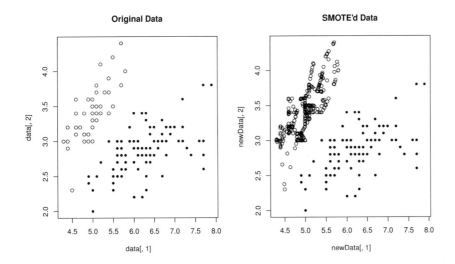

FIGURE 4.10: Using SMOTE to create more rare class examples.

Further readings on class imbalance

Class imbalance is a well-studied subject. Examples of this research can be found in several workshops on this specific topic, such as the AAAI'2000 and ICML'2003 Workshops on Imbalanced datasets, or the special issue on Learning from Imbalanced Datasets in SIGKDD (Chawla et al., 2004). A good overview of the existent work can be found in Chawla (2005). Class imbalance has implications in several relevant subjects of predictive modeling. Examples include the evaluation of prediction models (e.g., Provost and Fawcett (1997, 2001); Provost et al. (1998)), or cost sensitive learning (e.g., Domingos (1999); Drummond and Holte (2006); Elkan (2001)). Regarding sampling-based approaches to class imbalance, some reference works include Kubat and Matwin (1997), Japkowicz (2000), and Weiss and Provost (2003), among others. Specifically on SMOTE, the main references are Chawla et al. (2002) and Chawla et al. (2003).

4.4.2.2   Naive Bayes

Naive Bayes is a probabilistic classifier based on the Bayes theorem that uses very strong assumptions on the independence between the predictors. These assumptions rarely hold for real-world problems—and thus the name naive. Nevertheless, this method has been successfully applied to a large number of real-world applications.

The Bayes theorem specifies that $P(A|B) = \frac{P(B|A)P(A)}{P(B)}$. Using this theorem, the Naive Bayes classifier calculates the probability of each class for a given test case as

$$P(c|X_1, \cdots, X_p) = \frac{P(c)P(X_1, \cdots, X_p|c)}{P(X_1, \cdots, X_p)} \tag{4.5}$$

where c is a class and $X_1, \cdots, X_p$ are the observed values of the predictors for the given test case.

The probability $P(c)$ can be seen as the prior expectation of the class c. $P(X_1, \cdots, X_p|c)$ is the likelihood of the test case given the class c. Finally, the denominator is the probability of the observed evidence. This equation is calculated for all possible class values to determine the most probable class of the test case. This decision only depends on the numerator of the equation, as the denominator will be constant over all classes. Using some statistical definitions on conditional probabilities and assuming (naively) conditional independence between the predictors, we reduce the numerator of the fraction to

$$P(c)P(X_1, \cdots, X_p|c) = P(c) \prod_{i=1}^{p} P(X_i|c) \qquad (4.6)$$

Naive Bayes implementations estimate these probabilities from the training sample using relative frequencies. Using these estimates, the method outputs the class probabilities for each test case according to Equation 4.5.

R has several implementations in the Naive Bayes method. We will use the function `naiveBayes()` from package `e1071`. Package `klaR` (Weihs et al., 2005) also includes an implementation of this classifier, together with interesting visualization functions.

The following function uses Naive Bayes to obtain the ranking scores of a test set of reports. It uses the inspected reports from the given training sample to obtain a Naive Bayes model. The outlier ranking is obtained using the estimated probabilities of the class being `fraud`:

```
> nb <- function(train, test) {
+      require(e1071, quietly = T)
+      sup <- which(train$Insp != "unkn")
+      data <- train[sup, c("ID", "Prod", "Uprice", "Insp")]
+      data$Insp <- factor(data$Insp, levels = c("ok", "fraud"))
+      model <- naiveBayes(Insp ~ ., data)
+      preds <- predict(model, test[, c("ID", "Prod", "Uprice",
+          "Insp")], type = "raw")
+      return(list(rankOrder = order(preds[, "fraud"], decreasing = T),
+          rankScore = preds[, "fraud"]))
+ }
```

The next function is to be called from the hold-out routines and obtains the selected evaluation statistics for the Naive Bayes predictions:

```
> ho.nb <- function(form, train, test, ...) {
+    res <- nb(train,test)
+    structure(evalOutlierRanking(test,res$rankOrder,...),
+             itInfo=list(preds=res$rankScore,
+                    trues=ifelse(test$Insp=='fraud',1,0)
+                  )
```

```
+                )
+ }
```

Finally, we call our `holdOut()` function to carry out the experiments with this model using the same settings as for the unsupervised models of previous sections:

```
> nb.res <- holdOut(learner('ho.nb',
+                           pars=list(Threshold=0.1,
+                                     statsProds=globalStats)),
+                   dataset(Insp ~ .,sales),
+                   hldSettings(3,0.3,1234,T),
+                   itsInfo=TRUE
+                   )
```

The results of the Naive Bayes model for the 10% inspection effort are the following:

```
> summary(nb.res)

== Summary of a Hold Out Experiment ==

 Stratified  3 x 70 %/ 30 % Holdout run with seed =   1234

 * Dataset ::   sales
 * Learner  ::   ho.nb  with parameters:
          Threshold  =  0.1
          statsProds  =  11.34  ...

 * Summary of Experiment Results:

           Precision      Recall     avgNDTP
 avg       0.013715365 0.43112103 0.8519657
 std       0.001083859 0.02613164 0.2406771
 min       0.012660336 0.40533333 0.5908980
 max       0.014825920 0.45758355 1.0650114
 invalid 0.000000000 0.00000000 0.0000000
```

The scores are considerably worse than the best scores obtained previously with the unsupervised methods.

Next we obtain the usual curves to get a better overall perspective of the performance of the model. We compare Naive Bayes with one of the best unsupervised models, OR_h:

```
> par(mfrow=c(1,2))
> info <- attr(nb.res,'itsInfo')
> PTs.nb <- aperm(array(unlist(info),dim=c(length(info[[1]]),2,3)),
+                 c(1,3,2)
+                 )
```

```
> PRcurve(PTs.nb[,,1],PTs.nb[,,2],
+         main='PR curve',lty=1,xlim=c(0,1),ylim=c(0,1),
+         avg='vertical')
> PRcurve(PTs.orh[,,1],PTs.orh[,,2],
+         add=T,lty=1,col='grey',
+         avg='vertical')
> legend('topright',c('NaiveBayes','ORh'),
+         lty=1,col=c('black','grey'))
> CRchart(PTs.nb[,,1],PTs.nb[,,2],
+         main='Cumulative Recall curve',lty=1,xlim=c(0,1),ylim=c(0,1),
+         avg='vertical')
> CRchart(PTs.orh[,,1],PTs.orh[,,2],
+         add=T,lty=1,col='grey',
+         avg='vertical')
> legend('bottomright',c('NaiveBayes','ORh'),
+         lty=1,col=c('black','grey'))
```

The graphs of Figure 4.11 show very clearly that the Naive Bayes method is inferior to the OR_h method for this particular application. Both curves indicate that the latter method dominates over all possible setups.

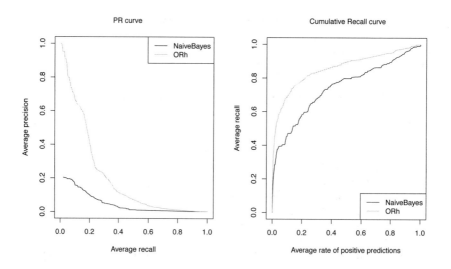

FIGURE 4.11: The PR (left) and cumulative recall (right) curves of the Naive Bayes and OR_h methods.

A possible cause for the poor performance of the Naive Bayes may be the class imbalance of this problem. In Section 4.4.2.1 we discussed several methods for addressing this problem and, in particular, the SMOTE algorithm. We will now apply the Naive Bayes classifier using a training set obtained using SMOTE.

The main difference from the previous code lies in the following function where we call the `naiveBayes()` function but this time with a modified training set:

```
> nb.s <- function(train, test) {
+     require(e1071, quietly = T)
+     sup <- which(train$Insp != "unkn")
+     data <- train[sup, c("ID", "Prod", "Uprice", "Insp")]
+     data$Insp <- factor(data$Insp, levels = c("ok", "fraud"))
+     newData <- SMOTE(Insp ~ ., data, perc.over = 700)
+     model <- naiveBayes(Insp ~ ., newData)
+     preds <- predict(model, test[, c("ID", "Prod", "Uprice",
+         "Insp")], type = "raw")
+     return(list(rankOrder = order(preds[, "fraud"], decreasing = T),
+         rankScore = preds[, "fraud"]))
+ }
```

The following statements obtain the hold-out estimates for this SMOTE'd version of Naive Bayes:

```
> ho.nbs <- function(form, train, test, ...) {
+   res <- nb.s(train,test)
+   structure(evalOutlierRanking(test,res$rankOrder,...),
+             itInfo=list(preds=res$rankScore,
+                         trues=ifelse(test$Insp=='fraud',1,0)
+                         )
+             )
+ }
```

```
> nbs.res <- holdOut(learner('ho.nbs',
+                     pars=list(Threshold=0.1,
+                               statsProds=globalStats)),
+                 dataset(Insp ~ .,sales),
+                 hldSettings(3,0.3,1234,T),
+                 itsInfo=TRUE
+                 )
```

The results of this version of the Naive Bayes model for the 10% inspection effort are the following:

```
> summary(nbs.res)

== Summary of a Hold Out Experiment ==

 Stratified  3 x 70 %/ 30 % Holdout run with seed =  1234

* Dataset ::  sales
* Learner  ::  ho.nbs  with parameters:
          Threshold  =  0.1
          statsProds =  11.34  ...
```

```
* Summary of Experiment Results:

        Precision      Recall   avgNDTP
avg     0.014215115 0.44686510 0.8913330
std     0.001109167 0.02710388 0.8482740
min     0.013493253 0.43044619 0.1934613
max     0.015492254 0.47814910 1.8354999
invalid 0.000000000 0.00000000 0.0000000
```

These results are almost indistinguishable from the results of the "normal" Naive Bayes. The scores are only slightly superior but still very far from the best results of the unsupervised models. It seems that despite the oversampling of the minority class carried out by SMOTE, Naive Bayes is still not able to correctly predict which are the fraudulent reports. Let us check the graphs for a more global perspective of the performance of this variant:

```
> par(mfrow=c(1,2))
> info <- attr(nbs.res,'itsInfo')
> PTs.nbs <- aperm(array(unlist(info),dim=c(length(info[[1]]),2,3)),
+                  c(1,3,2)
+                  )
> PRcurve(PTs.nb[,,1],PTs.nb[,,2],
+         main='PR curve',lty=1,xlim=c(0,1),ylim=c(0,1),
+         avg='vertical')
> PRcurve(PTs.nbs[,,1],PTs.nbs[,,2],
+         add=T,lty=2,
+         avg='vertical')
> PRcurve(PTs.orh[,,1],PTs.orh[,,2],
+         add=T,lty=1,col='grey',
+         avg='vertical')
> legend('topright',c('NaiveBayes','smoteNaiveBayes','ORh'),
+        lty=c(1,2,1),col=c('black','black','grey'))
> CRchart(PTs.nb[,,1],PTs.nb[,,2],
+         main='Cumulative Recall curve',lty=1,xlim=c(0,1),ylim=c(0,1),
+         avg='vertical')
> CRchart(PTs.nbs[,,1],PTs.nbs[,,2],
+         add=T,lty=2,
+         avg='vertical')
> CRchart(PTs.orh[,,1],PTs.orh[,,2],
+         add=T,lty=1,col='grey',
+         avg='vertical')
> legend('bottomright',c('NaiveBayes','smoteNaiveBayes','ORh'),
+        lty=c(1,2,1),col=c('black','black','grey'))
```

The graphs of Figure 4.12 confirm the disappointing results of the SMOTE'd version of Naive Bayes. In effect, it shows the same poor results as the standard Naive Bayes when compared to OR_h and, moreover, its performance is almost always surpassed by the standard version.

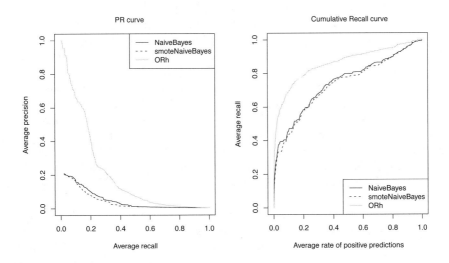

FIGURE 4.12: The PR (left) and cumulative recall (right) curves for the two versions of Naive Bayes and OR_h methods.

Given these results, we might question whether the fact that we have not split the model construction by product, as done in the unsupervised methods, may be causing difficulties with this model. As an exercise you can try to follow this approach with Naive Bayes. You need to adapt the code used for the unsupervised models that splits the transactions by product to the Naive Bayes model. An additional difficulty that you will meet, if you decide to carry out this exercise, is the fact that you will have very few supervised reports by product. In effect, even without the restriction of being labeled, we have observed that several products have too few transactions. If we add the restriction of only using the labeled transactions, this problem will surely increase.

Further readings on Naive Bayes

Naive Bayes is a well-known classification algorithm studied in many research areas. Some interesting additional references on this topic include the works by Domingos and Pazzani (1997), Rish (2001), Hand and Yu (2001); and Kononenko (1991).

4.4.2.3 AdaBoost

AdaBoost (Freund and Shapire, 1996) is a learning algorithm that belongs to the class of ensemble models. These types of models are, in effect, formed by a set of base models that contribute to the prediction of the algorithm using some form of aggregation. *AdaBoost* uses an adaptive boosting method to obtain the set of base models. Boosting is a general method that can be used to improve the performance of any base algorithm provided it is better than the random classifier. The construction of the *AdaBoost* model is obtained sequentially. Each new member of the sequence is obtained by improving on the errors of the previous model of the sequence. The improvements are obtained using a weighting schema that increases the weights of the cases that are incorrectly classified by the previous model. This means that the base learner is used on different distributions of the training data. After some number of iterations of this process, the result is a set of base models obtained on different training samples. This ensemble can be used to obtain predictions for test cases of the original problem. The predictions are obtained by a weighted average of the predictions of the individual base models. These weights are defined so that larger values are given to the last models in the sequence (theoretically the ones with lower error).

The case weighting schema used by *AdaBoost* is interesting from the perspective of learning with imbalance class distributions. Even if at the initial iterations the cases of the minority class are disregarded by the models, their weight is increased and the models are "forced" to focus on learning them. Theoretically, this should lead the resulting ensemble to be more accurate at predicting these rare cases.

AdaBoost.M1 is a particular instantiation of the *AdaBoost* method. It uses as base learners classification trees with a small number of nodes. This method is implemented in function `adaboost.M1()` of the extra package `adabag` (Cortes et al., 2010). Unfortunately, the `predict` method that is provided for these models is unable to return class probabilities. This is a serious limitation for our application. As mentioned before, we need these class probabilities because we use the probability of each report being of class `fraud` to obtain an outlier ranking. In this context, we will not use this implementation of the *AdaBoost.M1* algorithm. At the time of writing this book, this was the only package providing such implementation. However, we have an alternative using the Weka[2] data mining software. Weka is an open source software for data mining and machine learning. This excellent tool provides many learning algorithms with a nice graphical user interface. Compared to R, it offers several algorithms that are not available in R, and it offers an easy and nice user interface. R, on the other hand, offers much more flexibility in terms of software development/prototyping and many more available modeling tools spanning a much wider set of research areas. Thanks to the R extra package `RWeka` (Hornik et al., 2009), we can easily use most Weka facilities within R. Installing this package will also install Weka on your computer, provided you already have Java installed on it. The installation process will complain and give you clear instructions on what to do if that is not your case. We strongly suggest that after installing the package, you read its help pages to get an idea of the many methods that are available through `RWeka`.

The function `AdaBoostM1()` provided in package `RWeka` obtains

[2]http://www.cs.waikato.ac.nz/ml/weka/.

AdaBoost.M1 classification models using the Weka implementation of this algorithm. Contrary to the implementation of package adabag, the predict method of this algorithm is able to output a probabilistic classification and thus can be used to obtain outlier rankings for our problem. By default, the Weka implementation uses decision stumps as the base learners. These models are a special type of classification trees formed by a single test node. This and other settings are parameters of the function that can be changed if required. The function WOW() allows you to check which parameters are available for a particular Weka learning algorithm. The following is an example of its use for our target model:

```
> library(RWeka)
> WOW(AdaBoostM1)
```

```
-P         Percentage of weight mass to base training on.  (default
           100, reduce to around 90 speed up)
           Number of arguments: 1.
-Q         Use resampling for boosting.
-S         Random number seed.  (default 1)
           Number of arguments: 1.
-I         Number of iterations.  (default 10)
           Number of arguments: 1.
-D         If set, classifier is run in debug mode and may output
           additional info to the console
-W         Full name of base classifier.  (default:
           weka.classifiers.trees.DecisionStump)
           Number of arguments: 1.
-
-D         If set, classifier is run in debug mode and may output
           additional info to the console
```

The value of some parameter can be changed when we call the respective function, with the help of the parameter control and the function Weka_control(). Here is a small illustrative example of applying AdaBoostM1() to the well-known iris data set, using 100 iterations instead of the default 10:

```
> data(iris)
> idx <- sample(150,100)
> model <- AdaBoostM1(Species ~ .,iris[idx,],
+                       control=Weka_control(I=100))
> preds <- predict(model,iris[-idx,])
> head(preds)
```

```
[1] setosa setosa setosa setosa setosa setosa
Levels: setosa versicolor virginica
```

```
> table(preds,iris[-idx,'Species'])
```

```
preds           setosa versicolor virginica
   setosa         19          0         0
   versicolor      0         13         1
   virginica       0          2        15
```

```
> prob.preds <- predict(model,iris[-idx,],type='probability')
> head(prob.preds)
```

```
       setosa    versicolor     virginica
2   0.9999942 5.846673e-06 2.378153e-11
4   0.9999942 5.846673e-06 2.378153e-11
7   0.9999942 5.846673e-06 2.378153e-11
9   0.9999942 5.846673e-06 2.378153e-11
10  0.9999942 5.846673e-06 2.378153e-11
12  0.9999942 5.846673e-06 2.378153e-11
```

This small example also illustrates how to obtain probabilistic classifications with this model.

We now provide the functions necessary to apply this type of model to our outlier ranking problem. As with the Naive Bayes algorithm, we will apply the *AdaBoost.M1* method to all transactions—and not individually by product. The following function obtains the report rankings for the given train and test sets:

```
> ab <- function(train,test) {
+    require(RWeka,quietly=T)
+    sup <- which(train$Insp != 'unkn')
+    data <- train[sup,c('ID','Prod','Uprice','Insp')]
+    data$Insp <- factor(data$Insp,levels=c('ok','fraud'))
+    model <- AdaBoostM1(Insp ~ .,data,
+                        control=Weka_control(I=100))
+    preds <- predict(model,test[,c('ID','Prod','Uprice','Insp')],
+                     type='probability')
+    return(list(rankOrder=order(preds[,'fraud'],decreasing=T),
+                rankScore=preds[,'fraud'])
+          )
+ }
```

The function to be called from the hold-out routines is the following:

```
> ho.ab <- function(form, train, test, ...) {
+    res <- ab(train,test)
+    structure(evalOutlierRanking(test,res$rankOrder,...),
+             itInfo=list(preds=res$rankScore,
+                         trues=ifelse(test$Insp=='fraud',1,0)
+                        )
+            )
+ }
```

Finally, we have the code to run the hold-out experiments:

```
> ab.res <- holdOut(learner('ho.ab',
+                           pars=list(Threshold=0.1,
+                                     statsProds=globalStats)),
+                   dataset(Insp ~ .,sales),
+                   hldSettings(3,0.3,1234,T),
+                   itsInfo=TRUE
+                   )
```

The results of *AdaBoost* for the 10% effort are the following:

```
> summary(ab.res)

== Summary of a Hold Out Experiment ==

 Stratified  3 x 70 %/ 30 % Holdout run with seed =  1234

* Dataset ::  sales
* Learner  ::  ho.ab  with parameters:
        Threshold  =  0.1
        statsProds  =  11.34  ...

* Summary of Experiment Results:

            Precision       Recall    avgNDTP
avg     0.0220722972 0.69416565 1.5182034
std     0.0008695907 0.01576555 0.5238575
min     0.0214892554 0.68241470 0.9285285
max     0.0230717974 0.71208226 1.9298286
invalid 0.0000000000 0.00000000 0.0000000
```

These results are among the best we have seen thus far. In effect, these scores compare well with the best scores we have obtained with both *LOF* and OR_h. Moreover, we note that this model is using only a very small part of the given reports (the inspected ones) to obtain its rankings. Despite this, it achieved a robust 69% of recall with a good 1.5 score in terms of average *NDTP*.

The PR and cumulative recall curves can be obtained as before:

```
> par(mfrow=c(1,2))
> info <- attr(ab.res,'itsInfo')
> PTs.ab <- aperm(array(unlist(info),dim=c(length(info[[1]]),2,3)),
+                 c(1,3,2)
+                 )
> PRcurve(PTs.nb[,,1],PTs.nb[,,2],
+         main='PR curve',lty=1,xlim=c(0,1),ylim=c(0,1),
+         avg='vertical')
> PRcurve(PTs.orh[,,1],PTs.orh[,,2],
+         add=T,lty=1,col='grey',
+         avg='vertical')
```

```
> PRcurve(PTs.ab[,,1],PTs.ab[,,2],
+         add=T,lty=2,
+         avg='vertical')
> legend('topright',c('NaiveBayes','ORh','AdaBoostM1'),
+        lty=c(1,1,2),col=c('black','grey','black'))
> CRchart(PTs.nb[,,1],PTs.nb[,,2],
+         main='Cumulative Recall curve',lty=1,xlim=c(0,1),ylim=c(0,1),
+         avg='vertical')
> CRchart(PTs.orh[,,1],PTs.orh[,,2],
+         add=T,lty=1,col='grey',
+         avg='vertical')
> CRchart(PTs.ab[,,1],PTs.ab[,,2],
+         add=T,lty=2,
+         avg='vertical')
> legend('bottomright',c('NaiveBayes','ORh','AdaBoostM1'),
+        lty=c(1,1,2),col=c('black','grey','black'))
```

The graphs in Figure 4.13 confirm the excellent performance of the *AdaBoost.M1* algorithm, particularly in terms of the cumulative recall curve. This curve shows that for most effort levels, *AdaBoost.M1* matches the score obtained by OR_h. In terms of precision/recall, the performance of *AdaBoost.M1* is not that interesting, particularly for low levels of recall. However, for higher recall levels, it clearly matches the precision of the best scores we have obtained thus far. Moreover, we note that these higher recall levels are exactly what matters for this application.

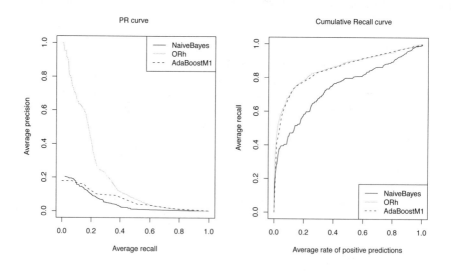

FIGURE 4.13: The PR (left) and cumulative recall (right) curves of the Naive Bayes, OR_h, and *AdaBoost.M1* methods.

Summarizing, we have seen that *AdaBoost.M1* is a very competitive algorithm for this application. Despite the difficulties of class imbalance, this ensemble method has managed to achieve top performance with the rankings it produces.

Further readings on boosting

The *AdaBoost.M1* algorithm is an example of a wider class of boosting algorithms that try to obtain good predictive performance using an ensemble of weak learners (learners that are marginally better than random guessing). The reference work on *AdaBoost* is the paper by Freund and Shapire (1996). Other important historical references on boosting are the works by Shapire (1990) and Freund (1990). Some important analyses can also be found in Breiman (1998), Friedman (2002), and Rätsch et al. (2001). A very good description of boosting can be found in Chapter 10 of the book by Hastie et al. (2001).

4.4.3 Semi-Supervised Approaches

This section describes an attempt to use both inspected and non-inspected reports to obtain a classification model to detect fraudulent reports. This means we need some form of semi-supervised classification method (see Section 4.3.1.3).

Self-training (e.g., Rosenberg et al. (2005); Yarowsky (1995)) is a well-known form of semi-supervised classification. This approach consists of building an initial classifier using the given labeled cases. This classifier is then used to predict the labels of the unlabeled cases in the given training set. The cases for which the classifier has higher confidence in the predicted label are added to the labeled set, together with their predicted labels. With this larger dataset, a new classifier is obtained and so on. This iterative process is continued until some criteria are met. The last classifier is the result of the learning process. This methodology can be applied to any base classification algorithm, provided it is able to output some indication of its confidence in the predictions. This is the case of probabilistic classifiers like the two we described in Section 4.4.2. The self-training method has three relevant parameters: (1) the base learner, (2) the threshold on the confidence of classifications that determines which cases are added to the new training set, and (3) the criteria to decide when to terminate the self-training process. In our book package we have included a general function (`SelfTrain()`) that can be used with any probabilistic classifier to learn a model based on a training set with both labeled and unlabeled cases.

Below you can find a simple example that illustrates its use with the `iris` dataset. We have artificially created a few unlabeled examples in this dataset to make semi-supervised classification potentially useful:

```
> library(DMwR)
> library(e1071)
> data(iris)
> idx <- sample(150, 100)
> tr <- iris[idx, ]
```

```
> ts <- iris[-idx, ]
> nb <- naiveBayes(Species ~ ., tr)
> table(predict(nb, ts), ts$Species)
```

	setosa	versicolor	virginica
setosa	12	0	0
versicolor	0	21	1
virginica	0	0	16

```
> trST <- tr
> nas <- sample(100, 90)
> trST[nas, "Species"] <- NA
> func <- function(m, d) {
+       p <- predict(m, d, type = "raw")
+       data.frame(cl = colnames(p)[apply(p, 1, which.max)],
+           p = apply(p, 1, max))
+ }
> nbSTbase <- naiveBayes(Species ~ ., trST[-nas, ])
> table(predict(nbSTbase, ts), ts$Species)
```

	setosa	versicolor	virginica
setosa	12	0	0
versicolor	0	18	2
virginica	0	3	15

```
> nbST <- SelfTrain(Species ~ ., trST, learner("naiveBayes",
+       list()), "func")
> table(predict(nbST, ts), ts$Species)
```

	setosa	versicolor	virginica
setosa	12	0	0
versicolor	0	20	2
virginica	0	1	15

The above code obtains three different Naive Bayes models. The first (nb) is obtained with a sample of 100 labeled cases. This set of 100 cases is then transformed in another set where 90 of the cases were unlabeled by setting the target variable to NA. Using the remaining ten labeled cases we obtain the second Naive Bayes model (nbSTbase). Finally, the dataset with the mixed labeled and unlabeled cases are given to the SelfTrain() function and another model (nbST) obtained. As you can observe, in this small example, the self-trained model is able to almost reach the same level of performance as the initial model obtained with all 100 labeled cases.

In order to use SelfTrain(), the user must create a function (func() on the code above) that given a model and a test set is able to return a data frame with two columns and the same number of rows as the test set. The first column of this data frame contains the labels predicted for the cases, while the second column has the respective probability of that classification.

This needs to be defined outside the `SelfTrain()` function because not all `predict` methods use the same syntax to obtain probabilistic classifications.

The `SelfTrain()` function has several parameters that control the iterative process. Parameter `thrConf` (defaulting to 0.9) sets the required probability for an unlabeled case to be merged into the labeled set. Parameter `maxIts` (default value of 10) allows the user to indicate a maximum number of self-training iterations, while parameter `percFull` (default value of 1) indicates that the process should stop if the labeled set reaches a certain percentage of the given dataset. The self-training iterative process finishes if either there are no classifications that reach the required probability level, if the maximum number of iterations is reached, or if the size of the current labeled training set is already the target percentage of the given dataset. A final note on the fact that the `SelfTrain()` function requires that the unlabeled cases be signaled as such by having the value `NA` on the target variable.

We have applied this self-training strategy with the Naive Bayes model as base classifier. The following functions implement and run the hold-out experiments with this self-trained Naive Bayes. A word of warning is in order concerning the computational resources that are necessary for carrying out these experiments. Depending on your hardware, this can take some time, although always on the order of minutes (at least on my average computer):

```
> pred.nb <- function(m,d) {
+    p <- predict(m,d,type='raw')
+    data.frame(cl=colnames(p)[apply(p,1,which.max)],
+               p=apply(p,1,max)
+              )
+ }
> nb.st <- function(train,test) {
+    require(e1071,quietly=T)
+    train <- train[,c('ID','Prod','Uprice','Insp')]
+    train[which(train$Insp == 'unkn'),'Insp'] <- NA
+    train$Insp <- factor(train$Insp,levels=c('ok','fraud'))
+    model <- SelfTrain(Insp ~ .,train,
+                       learner('naiveBayes',list()),'pred.nb')
+    preds <- predict(model,test[,c('ID','Prod','Uprice','Insp')],
+                     type='raw')
+    return(list(rankOrder=order(preds[,'fraud'],decreasing=T),
+               rankScore=preds[,'fraud'])
+          )
+ }
> ho.nb.st <- function(form, train, test, ...) {
+    res <- nb.st(train,test)
+    structure(evalOutlierRanking(test,res$rankOrder,...),
+              itInfo=list(preds=res$rankScore,
+                          trues=ifelse(test$Insp=='fraud',1,0)
+                         )
+             )
+ }
```

```
> nb.st.res <- holdOut(learner('ho.nb.st',
+                                 pars=list(Threshold=0.1,
+                                     statsProds=globalStats)),
+                          dataset(Insp ~ .,sales),
+                          hldSettings(3,0.3,1234,T),
+                          itsInfo=TRUE
+                          )
```

The results of this self-trained model are the following:

```
> summary(nb.st.res)

== Summary of a Hold Out Experiment ==

 Stratified  3 x 70 %/ 30 % Holdout run with seed =  1234

* Dataset ::  sales
* Learner  ::  ho.nb.st  with parameters:
        Threshold  =  0.1
        statsProds  =  11.34  ...

* Summary of Experiment Results:

              Precision       Recall      avgNDTP
avg        0.013521017 0.42513271 1.08220611
std        0.001346477 0.03895915 1.59726790
min        0.012077295 0.38666667 0.06717087
max        0.014742629 0.46456693 2.92334375
invalid 0.000000000 0.00000000 0.00000000
```

These results are rather disappointing. They are very similar to the results obtained with a Naive Bayes model learned only on the labeled data. With the exception of the average $NDTP$, which has improved slightly, all other statistics are roughly the same, and thus still far from the best scores we have obtained thus far. Moreover, even this better score is accompanied by a large standard deviation.

Figure 4.14 shows the PR and cumulative recall curves of this model as well as those of the standard Naive Bayes and OR_h methods. They were obtained with the following code:

```
> par(mfrow=c(1,2))
> info <- attr(nb.st.res,'itsInfo')
> PTs.nb.st <- aperm(array(unlist(info),dim=c(length(info[[1]]),2,3)),
+                     c(1,3,2)
+                     )
> PRcurve(PTs.nb[,,1],PTs.nb[,,2],
+          main='PR curve',lty=1,xlim=c(0,1),ylim=c(0,1),
+          avg='vertical')
> PRcurve(PTs.orh[,,1],PTs.orh[,,2],
```

```
+            add=T,lty=1,col='grey',
+            avg='vertical')
> PRcurve(PTs.nb.st[,,1],PTs.nb.st[,,2],
+            add=T,lty=2,
+            avg='vertical')
> legend('topright',c('NaiveBayes','ORh','NaiveBayes-ST'),
+          lty=c(1,1,2),col=c('black','grey','black'))
> CRchart(PTs.nb[,,1],PTs.nb[,,2],
+            main='Cumulative Recall curve',lty=1,xlim=c(0,1),ylim=c(0,1),
+            avg='vertical')
> CRchart(PTs.orh[,,1],PTs.orh[,,2],
+            add=T,lty=1,col='grey',
+            avg='vertical')
> CRchart(PTs.nb.st[,,1],PTs.nb.st[,,2],
+            add=T,lty=2,
+            avg='vertical')
> legend('bottomright',c('NaiveBayes','ORh','NaiveBayes-ST'),
+          lty=c(1,1,2),col=c('black','grey','black'))
```

The graphs confirm the disappointing performance of the self-trained Naive Bayes classifier. For this particular problem, this semi-supervised classifier is clearly not competitive even with the standard Naive Bayes model obtained with a considerable smaller dataset.

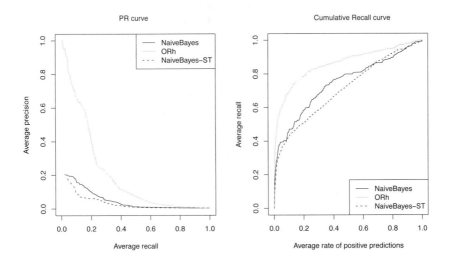

FIGURE 4.14: The PR (left) and cumulative recall (right) curves of the self-trained Naive Bayes, together with the standard Naive Bayes and OR_h methods.

We have also used the self-training approach with the *AdaBoost.M1* algorithm. The following code carries out these experiments:

```
> pred.ada <- function(m,d) {
+     p <- predict(m,d,type='probability')
+     data.frame(cl=colnames(p)[apply(p,1,which.max)],
+                 p=apply(p,1,max)
+                 )
+ }
> ab.st <- function(train,test) {
+     require(RWeka,quietly=T)
+     train <- train[,c('ID','Prod','Uprice','Insp')]
+     train[which(train$Insp == 'unkn'),'Insp'] <- NA
+     train$Insp <- factor(train$Insp,levels=c('ok','fraud'))
+     model <- SelfTrain(Insp ~ .,train,
+                     learner('AdaBoostM1',
+                             list(control=Weka_control(I=100))),
+                     'pred.ada')
+     preds <- predict(model,test[,c('ID','Prod','Uprice','Insp')],
+                     type='probability')
+     return(list(rankOrder=order(preds[,'fraud'],decreasing=T),
+             rankScore=preds[,'fraud'])
+             )
+ }
> ho.ab.st <- function(form, train, test, ...) {
+     res <- ab.st(train,test)
+     structure(evalOutlierRanking(test,res$rankOrder,...),
+             itInfo=list(preds=res$rankScore,
+                         trues=ifelse(test$Insp=='fraud',1,0)
+                         )
+             )
+ }
> ab.st.res <- holdOut(learner('ho.ab.st',
+                         pars=list(Threshold=0.1,
+                                 statsProds=globalStats)),
+                     dataset(Insp ~ .,sales),
+                     hldSettings(3,0.3,1234,T),
+                     itsInfo=TRUE
+                     )
```

The results of the self-trained *AdaBoost* for the 10% effort are the following:

```
> summary(ab.st.res)

== Summary of a Hold Out Experiment ==

 Stratified  3 x 70 %/ 30 % Holdout run with seed =   1234

* Dataset ::   sales
* Learner  ::   ho.ab.st  with parameters:
        Threshold  =   0.1
        statsProds  =   11.34   ...
```

```
* Summary of Experiment Results:

           Precision      Recall   avgNDTP
avg       0.022377700 0.70365350 1.6552619
std       0.001130846 0.02255686 1.5556444
min       0.021322672 0.68266667 0.5070082
max       0.023571548 0.72750643 3.4257016
invalid   0.000000000 0.00000000 0.0000000
```

Although not impressive, these scores represent a slight improvement over the *AdaBoost.M1* model obtained using only the labeled data. While precision stayed basically the same, there were small improvements in recall and average *NDTP*. The value of recall is the highest value we have observed across all tried models for a 10% effort level.

Figure 4.15 shows the curves of this self-trained model, together with the standard *AdaBoost.M1* and OR_h methods. The curves were obtained as usual.

```
> par(mfrow = c(1, 2))
> info <- attr(ab.st.res, "itsInfo")
> PTs.ab.st <- aperm(array(unlist(info), dim = c(length(info[[1]]),
+     2, 3)), c(1, 3, 2))
> PRcurve(PTs.ab[, , 1], PTs.ab[, , 2], main = "PR curve",
+     lty = 1, xlim = c(0, 1), ylim = c(0, 1), avg = "vertical")
> PRcurve(PTs.orh[, , 1], PTs.orh[, , 2], add = T, lty = 1,
+     col = "grey", avg = "vertical")
> PRcurve(PTs.ab.st[, , 1], PTs.ab.st[, , 2], add = T, lty = 2,
+     avg = "vertical")
> legend("topright", c("AdaBoostM1", "ORh", "AdaBoostM1-ST"),
+     lty = c(1, 1, 2), col = c("black", "grey", "black"))
> CRchart(PTs.ab[, , 1], PTs.ab[, , 2], main = "Cumulative Recall curve",
+     lty = 1, xlim = c(0, 1), ylim = c(0, 1), avg = "vertical")
> CRchart(PTs.orh[, , 1], PTs.orh[, , 2], add = T, lty = 1,
+     col = "grey", avg = "vertical")
> CRchart(PTs.ab.st[, , 1], PTs.ab.st[, , 2], add = T, lty = 2,
+     avg = "vertical")
> legend("bottomright", c("AdaBoostM1", "ORh", "AdaBoostM1-ST"),
+     lty = c(1, 1, 2), col = c("black", "grey", "black"))
```

The cumulative recall curve confirms that the self-trained *AdaBoost.M1* is the best model from the ones we have considered for this fraud detection problem. In particular, for inspection efforts above 15% to 20% it clearly dominates the other systems in terms of the proportion of frauds that it detects. In terms of precision, the scores are not that interesting, but as we mentioned before, this is not necessarily bad if the unlabeled reports that the model puts on higher positions in the ranking are confirmed as frauds.

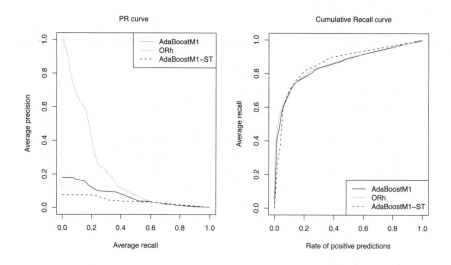

FIGURE 4.15: The PR (left) and cumulative recall (right) curves of *Ad-aBoost.M1* with self-training together with OR_h and standard *AdaBoost.M1* methods.

4.5   Summary

The main goal of this chapter was to introduce the reader to a new class of data mining problems: outliers ranking. In particular, we have used a dataset that enabled us to tackle this task from different perspectives. Namely, we used supervised, unsupervised- and semi-supervised approaches to the problem. The application used in this chapter can be regarded as an instantiation of the general problem of finding unusual observations of a phenomenon having a limited amount of resources. Several real-world applications map into this general framework, such as detecting frauds in credit card transactions, telecommunications, tax declarations, etc. In the area of security, there are also several applications of this general concept of outlier ranking.

In methodological terms we have introduced the reader to a few new topics:

- Outlier detection and ranking

- Clustering methods

- Semi-supervised learning

- Semi-supervised classification through self-training

- Imbalanced class distributions and methods for handling this type of problems

- Naive Bayes classifiers

- *AdaBoost* classifiers

- Precision/recall and cumulative recall curves

- Hold-out experiments

From the perspective of learning R, we have illustrated,

- How to obtain several evaluation statistics and how to visualize them using the ROCR package

- How to obtain hold-out estimates of evaluation metrics

- How to obtain local outlier factors with the *LOF* method

- How to obtain outlier rankings using the OR_h method

- How to fight class imbalance through SMOTE

- How to obtain Naive Bayes classification models

- How to obtain *AdaBoost.M1* classifiers

- How to use methods from the Weka data mining system with the RWeka package

- How to apply a classifier to a semi-supervised dataset using self-training

Chapter 5

Classifying Microarray Samples

The fourth case study is from the area of bioinformatics. Namely, we will address the problem of classifying microarray samples into a set of alternative classes. More specifically, given a microarray probe that describes the gene expression level of a patient, we aim to classify this patient into a pre-defined set of genetic mutations of acute lymphoblastic leukemia. This case study addresses several new data mining topics. The main focus, given the characteristics of this type of datasets, is on feature selection, that is, how to reduce the number of features that describe each observation. In our approach to this particular application we will illustrate several general methods for feature selection. Other new data mining topics addressed in this chapter include k-nearest neighbors classifiers, leave one out cross-validation, and some new variants of ensemble models.

5.1   Problem Description and Objectives

Bioinformatics is one of the main areas of application of R. There is even an associated project based on R, with the goal of providing a large set of analysis tools for this domain. The project is called Bioconductor.[1] This case study will use the tools provided by this project to address a supervised classification problem.

5.1.1   Brief Background on Microarray Experiments

One of the main difficulties faced by someone coming from a nonbiological background is the huge amount of "new" terms used in this field. In this very brief background section, we try to introduce the reader to some of the "jargon" in this field and also to provide some mapping to more "standard" data mining terminology.

The analysis of differential gene expression is one of the key applications of DNA microarray experiments. Gene expression microarrays allow us to characterize a set of samples (e.g., individuals) according to their expression levels

---

[1]http://www.bioconductor.org.

on a large set of genes. In this area a sample is thus an observation (case) of some phenomenon under study. Microarray experiments are the means used to measure a set of "variables" for these observations. The variables here are a large set of genes. For each variable (gene), these experiments measure an expression value. In summary, a dataset is formed by a set of samples (the cases) for which we have measured expression levels on a large set of genes (the variables). If these samples have some disease state associated with them, we may try to approximate the unknown function that maps gene expression levels into disease states. This function can be approximated using a dataset of previously analyzed samples. This is an instantiation of supervised classification tasks, where the target variable is the disease type. The observations in this problem are samples (microarrays, individuals), and the predictor variables are the genes for which we measure a value (the expression level) using a microarray experiment. The key hypothesis here is thus that different disease types can be associated with different gene expression patterns and, moreover, that by measuring these patterns using microarrays we can accurately predict what the disease type of an individual is.

There are several types of technologies created with the goal of obtaining gene expression levels on some sample. Short oligonucleotide arrays are an example of these technologies. The output of oligonucleotide chips is an image that after several pre-processing steps can be mapped into a set of gene expression levels for quite a large set of genes. The bioconductor project has several packages devoted to these pre-processing steps that involve issues like the analysis of the images resulting from the oligonucleotide chips, normalization tasks, and several other steps that are necessary until we reach a set of gene expression scores. In this case study we do not address these initial steps. The interested reader is directed to several informative sources available at the bioconductor site as well as several books (e.g., Hahne et al. (2008)).

In this context, our starting point will be a matrix of gene expression levels that results from these pre-processing steps. This is the information on the predictor variables for our observations. As we will see, there are usually many more predictor variables being measured than samples; that is, we have more predictors than observations. This is a typical characteristic of microarray data sets. Another particularity of these expression matrices is that they appear transposed when compared to what is "standard" for data sets. This means that the rows will represent the predictors (i.e., genes), while the columns are the observations (the samples). For each of the samples we will also need the associated classification. In our case this will be an associated type of mutation of a disease. There may also exist information on other co-variates (e.g., sex and age of the individuals being sampled, etc.).

5.1.2 The ALL Dataset

The dataset we will use comes from a study on acute lymphoblastic leukemia (Chiaretti et al., 2004; Li, 2009). The data consists of microarray samples from 128 individuals with this type of disease. Actually, there are two different types of tumors among these samples: T-cell ALL (33 samples) and B-cell ALL (95 samples).

We will focus our study on the data concerning the B-cell ALL samples. Even within this latter group of samples we can distinguish different types of mutations. Namely, ALL1/AF4, BCR/ABL, E2A/PBX1, p15/p16 and also individuals with no cytogenetic abnormalities. In our analysis of the B-cell ALL samples we will discard the p15/p16 mutation as we only have one sample. Our modeling goal is to be able to predict the type of mutation of an individual given its microarray assay. Given that the target variable is nominal with 4 possible values, we are facing a supervised classification task.

5.2 The Available Data

The ALL dataset is part of the bioconductor set of packages. To use it, we need to install at least a set of basic packages from bioconductor. We have not included the dataset in our book package because the dataset is already part of the R "universe".

To install a set of basic bioconductor packages and the ALL dataset, we need to carry out the following instructions that assume we have a working Internet connection:

```
> source("http://bioconductor.org/biocLite.R")
> biocLite()
> biocLite("ALL")
```

This only needs to be done for the first time. Once you have these packages installed, if you want to use the dataset, you simply need to do

```
> library(Biobase)
> library(ALL)
> data(ALL)
```

These instructions load the **Biobase** (Gentleman et al., 2004) and the **ALL** (Gentleman et al., 2010) packages. We then load the ALL dataset, that creates an object of a special class (**ExpressionSet**) defined by Bioconductor. This class of objects contains significant information concerning a microarray dataset. There are several associated methods to handle this type of object. If you ask R about the content of the **ALL** object, you get the following information:

```
> ALL
```

```
ExpressionSet (storageMode: lockedEnvironment)
assayData: 12625 features, 128 samples
  element names: exprs
phenoData
  sampleNames: 01005, 01010, ..., LAL4  (128 total)
  varLabels and varMetadata description:
    cod:  Patient ID
    diagnosis:  Date of diagnosis
    ...:  ...
    date last seen:  date patient was last seen
    (21 total)
featureData
  featureNames: 1000_at, 1001_at, ..., AFFX-YEL024w/RIP1_at  (12625 total)
  fvarLabels and fvarMetadata description: none
experimentData: use 'experimentData(object)'
  pubMedIds: 14684422 16243790
Annotation: hgu95av2
```

The information is divided in several groups. First we have the assay data with the gene expression levels matrix. For this dataset we have 12,625 genes and 128 samples. The object also contains a lot of meta-data about the samples of the experiment. This includes the **phenoData** part with information on the sample names and several associated co-variates. It also includes information on the features (i.e., genes) as well as annotations of the genes from biomedical databases. Finally, the object also contains information that describes the experiment.

There are several methods that facilitate access to all information in the **ExpressionSet** objects. We give a few examples below. We start by obtaining some information on the co-variates associated to each sample:

```
> pD <- phenoData(ALL)
> varMetadata(pD)
```

```
                                                         labelDescription
cod                                                            Patient ID
diagnosis                                               Date of diagnosis
sex                                                   Gender of the patient
age                                          Age of the patient at entry
BT                          does the patient have B-cell or T-cell ALL
remission       Complete remission(CR), refractory(REF) or NA. Derived from CR
CR                                               Original remisson data
date.cr                              Date complete remission if achieved
t(4;11)         did the patient have t(4;11) translocation. Derived from citog
t(9;22)         did the patient have t(9;22) translocation. Derived from citog
cyto.normal                    Was cytogenetic test normal? Derived from citog
citog           original citogenetics data, deletions or t(4;11), t(9;22) status
mol.biol                                               molecular biology
fusion protein          which of p190, p210 or p190/210 for bcr/able
mdr                                                  multi-drug resistant
kinet                          ploidy: either diploid or hyperd.
ccr                      Continuous complete remission? Derived from f.u
```

relapse   Relapse? Derived from f.u
transplant   did the patient receive a bone marrow transplant? Derived from f.u
f.u   follow up data available
date last seen   date patient was last seen

```
> table(ALL$BT)
```

```
 B  B1 B2 B3 B4  T  T1 T2 T3 T4
 5  19 36 23 12  5  1  15 10  2
```

```
> table(ALL$mol.biol)
```

```
ALL1/AF4  BCR/ABL E2A/PBX1     NEG   NUP-98  p15/p16
      10       37        5      74        1        1
```

```
> table(ALL$BT, ALL$mol.bio)
```

	ALL1/AF4	BCR/ABL	E2A/PBX1	NEG	NUP-98	p15/p16
B	0	2	1	2	0	0
B1	10	1	0	8	0	0
B2	0	19	0	16	0	1
B3	0	8	1	14	0	0
B4	0	7	3	2	0	0
T	0	0	0	5	0	0
T1	0	0	0	1	0	0
T2	0	0	0	15	0	0
T3	0	0	0	9	1	0
T4	0	0	0	2	0	0

The first two statements obtain the names and descriptions of the existing co-variates. We then obtain some information on the distribution of the samples across the two main co-variates: the BT variable that determines the type of acute lymphoblastic leukemia, and the mol.bio variable that describes the cytogenetic abnormality found on each sample (NEG represents no abnormality).

We can also obtain some information on the genes and samples:

```
> featureNames(ALL)[1:10]
```

```
[1] "1000_at"   "1001_at"   "1002_f_at" "1003_s_at" "1004_at"
[6] "1005_at"   "1006_at"   "1007_s_at" "1008_f_at" "1009_at"
```

```
> sampleNames(ALL)[1:5]
```

```
[1] "01005" "01010" "03002" "04006" "04007"
```

This code shows the names of the first 10 genes and the names of the first 5 samples.

As mentioned before, we will focus our analysis of this data on the B-cell ALL cases and in particular on the samples with a subset of the mutations, which will be our target class. The code below obtains the subset of data that we will use:

```
> tgt.cases <- which(ALL$BT %in% levels(ALL$BT)[1:5] &
+                     ALL$mol.bio %in% levels(ALL$mol.bio)[1:4])
> ALLb <- ALL[,tgt.cases]
> ALLb
```

```
ExpressionSet (storageMode: lockedEnvironment)
assayData: 12625 features, 94 samples
  element names: exprs
phenoData
  sampleNames: 01005, 01010, ..., LAL5  (94 total)
  varLabels and varMetadata description:
    cod:  Patient ID
    diagnosis:  Date of diagnosis
    ...: ...
    date last seen:  date patient was last seen
    (21 total)
featureData
  featureNames: 1000_at, 1001_at, ..., AFFX-YEL024w/RIP1_at  (12625 total)
  fvarLabels and fvarMetadata description: none
experimentData: use 'experimentData(object)'
  pubMedIds: 14684422 16243790
Annotation: hgu95av2
```

The first statement obtains the set of cases that we will consider. These are the samples with specific values of the BT and mol.bio variables. Check the calls to the **table()** function we have shown before to see which ones we are selecting. We then subset the original ALL object to obtain the 94 samples that will enter our study. This subset of samples only contains some of the values of the BT and mol.bio variables. In this context, we should update the available levels of these two factors on our new ALLb object:

```
> ALLb$BT <- factor(ALLb$BT)
> ALLb$mol.bio <- factor(ALLb$mol.bio)
```

The ALLb object will be the dataset we will use throughout this chapter. It may eventually be a good idea to save this object in a local file on your computer, so that you do not need to repeat these pre-processing steps in case you want to start the analysis from scratch:

```
> save(ALLb, file = "myALL.Rdata")
```

5.2.1   Exploring the Dataset

The function **exprs()** allows us to access the gene expression levels matrix:

```
> es <- exprs(ALLb)
> dim(es)
```

```
[1] 12625    94
```

The matrix of our dataset has 12,625 rows (the genes/features) and 94 columns (the samples/cases).

In terms of dimensionality, the main challenge of this problem is the fact that there are far too many variables (12,625) for the number of available cases (94). With these dimensions, most modeling techniques will have a hard time obtaining any meaningful result. In this context, one of our first goals will be to reduce the number of variables, that is, eliminate some genes from our analysis. To help in this task, we start by exploring the expression levels data.

The following instruction tells us that most expression values are between 4 and 7:

```
> summary(as.vector(es))

   Min. 1st Qu.  Median    Mean 3rd Qu.     Max.
  1.985   4.122   5.469   5.624   6.829   14.040
```

A better overview of the distribution of the expression levels can be obtained graphically. We will use a function from package **genefilter** Gentleman et al. (2010). This package must be installed before using it. Please notice that this is a Bioconductor package, and these packages are not installed from the standard R repository. The easiest way to install a Bioconductor package is through the script provided by this project for this effect:

```
> source("http://bioconductor.org/biocLite.R")
> biocLite("genefilter")
```

The first instruction loads the script and then we use it do download and install the package. We can now proceed with the above-mentioned graphical display of the distribution of the expression levels:

```
> library(genefilter)
> hist(as.vector(es),breaks=80,prob=T,
+       xlab='Expression Levels',
+       main='Histogram of Overall Expression Levels')
> abline(v=c(median(as.vector(es)),
+            shorth(as.vector(es)),
+            quantile(as.vector(es),c(0.25,0.75))),
+         lty=2,col=c(2,3,4,4))
> legend('topright',c('Median','Shorth','1stQ','3rdQ'),
+         lty=2,col=c(2,3,4,4))
```

The results are shown in Figure 5.1. We have changed the default number of intervals of the function hist() that obtains histograms. With the value 80 on the parameter **breaks**, we obtain a fine-grained approximation of the distribution, which is possible given the large number of expression levels we have. On top of the histogram we have plotted several lines showing the median, the first and third quartiles, and the shorth. This last statistic is a robust estimator of the centrality of a continuous distribution that is implemented by the function `shorth()` of package `genefilter`. It is calculated as the mean of the values in a central interval containing 50% of the observations (i.e., the inter-quartile range).

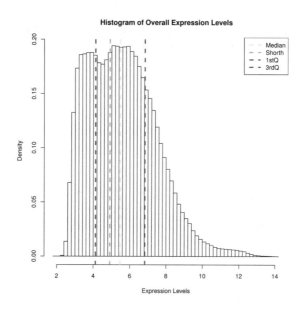

FIGURE 5.1: The distribution of the gene expression levels.

Are the distributions of the gene expression levels of the samples with a particular mutation different from each other? The following code answers this question:

```
> sapply(levels(ALLb$mol.bio), function(x) summary(as.vector(es[,
+     which(ALLb$mol.bio == x)]])))
```

	ALL1/AF4	BCR/ABL	E2A/PBX1	NEG
Min.	2.266	2.195	2.268	1.985
1st Qu.	4.141	4.124	4.152	4.111
Median	5.454	5.468	5.497	5.470
Mean	5.621	5.627	5.630	5.622
3rd Qu.	6.805	6.833	6.819	6.832
Max.	14.030	14.040	13.810	13.950

As we see, things are rather similar across these subsets of samples and, moreover, they are similar to the global distribution of expression levels.

5.3   Gene (Feature) Selection

Feature selection is an important task in many data mining problems. The general problem is to select the subset of features (variables) of a problem that is more relevant for the analysis of the data. This can be regarded as an instantiation of the more general problem of deciding the weights (importance) of the features in the subsequent modeling stages. Generally, there are two types of approaches to feature selection: (1) filters and (2) wrappers. As mentioned in Section 3.3.2 the former use statistical properties of the features to select the final set, while the latter include the data mining tools in the selection process. Filter approaches are carried out in a single step, while wrappers typically involve a search process where we iteratively look for the set of features that is more adequate for the data mining tools we are applying. Feature wrappers have a clear overhead in terms of computational resources. They involve running the full filter+model+evaluate cycle several times until some convergence criteria are met. This means that for very large data mining problems, they may not be adequate if time is critical. Yet, they will find a solution that is theoretically more adequate for the used modeling tools. The strategies we use and describe in this section can be seen as filter approaches.

5.3.1   Simple Filters Based on Distribution Properties

The first gene filtering methods we describe are based on information concerning the distribution of the expression levels. This type of experimental data usually includes several genes that are not expressed at all or show very small variability. The latter property means that these genes can hardly be used to differentiate among samples. Moreover, this type of microarray usually has several control probes that can be safely removed from our analysis. In the case of this study, which uses Affymetric U95Av2 microarrays, these probes have their name starting with the letters "AFFX".

We can get an overall idea of the distribution of the expression levels of each gene across all individuals with the following graph. We will use the median and inter-quartile range (IQR) as the representatives of these distributions. The following code obtains these scores for each gene and plots the values producing the graph in Figure 5.2:

```
> rowIQRs <- function(em)
+    rowQ(em,ceiling(0.75*ncol(em))) - rowQ(em,floor(0.25*ncol(em)))
> plot(rowMedians(es),rowIQRs(es),
+       xlab='Median expression level',
+       ylab='IQR expression level',
+       main='Main Characteristics of Genes Expression Levels')
```

The function rowMedians() from package Biobase obtains a vector of the medians per row of a matrix. This is an efficient implementation of this task. A less efficient alternative would be to use the function `apply()`.[2] The `rowQ()` function is another efficient implementation provided by this package with the goal of obtaining quantiles of a distribution from the rows of a matrix. The second argument of this function is an integer ranging from 1 (that would give us the minimum) to the number of columns of the matrix (that would result in the maximum). In this case we are using this function to obtain the IQR by subtracting the 3rd quartile from the 1st quartile. These statistics correspond to 75% and 25% of the data, respectively. We have used the functions `floor()` and `ceiling()` to obtain the corresponding order in the number of values of each row. Both functions take the integer part of a floating point number, although with different rounding procedures. Experiment with both to see the difference. Using the function `rowQ()`, we have created the function `rowIQRs()` to obtain the IQR of each row.

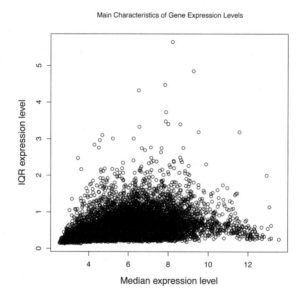

FIGURE 5.2: The median and IQR of the gene expression levels.

Figure 5.2 provides interesting information. Namely, we can observe that a large proportion of the genes have very low variability (IQRs near 0). As mentioned above, if a gene has a very low variability across all samples, then it is reasonably safe to conclude that it will not be useful in discriminating among the different types of mutations of B-cell ALL. This means that we can safely remove these genes from our classification task. We should note

[2]As an exercise, time both alternatives using function `system.time()` to observe the difference.

that there is a caveat on this reasoning. In effect, we are looking at the genes individually. This means that there is some risk that some of these genes with low variability, when put together with other genes, could actually be useful for the classification task. Still, the gene-by-gene approach that we will follow is the most common for these problems as exploring the interactions among genes with datasets of this dimension is not easy. Nevertheless, there are methods that try to estimate the importance of features, taking into account their dependencies. That is the case of the RELIEF method (Kira and Rendel, 1992; Kononenko et al., 1997).

We will use a heuristic threshold based on the value of the IQR to eliminate some of the genes with very low variability. Namely, we will remove any genes with a variability that is smaller than 1/5 of the global IQR. The function `nsFilter()` from the package `genefilter` can be used for this type of filtering:

```
> library(genefilter)
> ALLb <- nsFilter(ALLb,
+                  var.func=IQR,
+                  var.cutoff=IQR(as.vector(es))/5,
+                  feature.exclude="^AFFX")
> ALLb

$eset
ExpressionSet (storageMode: lockedEnvironment)
assayData: 4035 features, 94 samples
  element names: exprs
phenoData
  sampleNames: 01005, 01010, ..., LAL5  (94 total)
  varLabels and varMetadata description:
    cod:  Patient ID
    diagnosis:  Date of diagnosis
    ...:  ...
    mol.bio:  molecular biology
    (22 total)
featureData
  featureNames: 41654_at, 35430_at, ..., 34371_at  (4035 total)
  fvarLabels and fvarMetadata description: none
experimentData: use 'experimentData(object)'
  pubMedIds: 14684422 16243790
Annotation: hgu95av2

$filter.log
$filter.log$numLowVar
[1] 4764

$filter.log$numDupsRemoved
[1] 2918

$filter.log$feature.exclude
[1] 19
```

```
$filter.log$numRemoved.ENTREZID
[1] 889
```

As you see, we are left with only 4,035 genes from the initial 12,625. This is a rather significant reduction. Nevertheless, we are still far from a dataset that is "manageable" by most classification models, given that we only have 94 observations.

The result of the `nsFilter()` function is a list with several components. Among these we have several containing information on the removed genes, and also the component `eset` with the "filtered" object. Now that we have seen the result of this filtering, we can update our `ALLb` and `es` objects to contain the filtered data:

```
> ALLb <- ALLb$eset
> es <- exprs(ALLb)
> dim(es)

[1] 4035   94
```

5.3.2 ANOVA Filters

If a gene has a distribution of expression values that is similar across all possible values of the target variable, then it will surely be useless to discriminate among these values. Our next approach builds on this idea. We will compare the mean expression level of genes across the subsets of samples belonging to a certain B-cell ALL mutation, that is, the mean conditioned on the target variable values. Genes for which we have high statistical confidence of having the same mean expression level across the groups of samples belonging to each mutation will be discarded from further analysis.

Comparing means across more than two groups can be carried out using an ANOVA statistical test. In our case study, we have four groups of cases, one for each of the gene mutations of B-cell ALL we are considering. Filtering of genes based on this test is rather easy in R, thanks to the facilities provided by the `genefilter` package. We can carry out this type of filtering as follows:

```
> f <- Anova(ALLb$mol.bio, p = 0.01)
> ff <- filterfun(f)
> selGenes <- genefilter(exprs(ALLb), ff)

> sum(selGenes)

[1] 752

> ALLb <- ALLb[selGenes, ]
> ALLb
```

```
ExpressionSet (storageMode: lockedEnvironment)
assayData: 752 features, 94 samples
  element names: exprs
phenoData
  sampleNames: 01005, 01010, ..., LAL5  (94 total)
  varLabels and varMetadata description:
    cod:  Patient ID
    diagnosis:  Date of diagnosis
    ...:  ...
    mol.bio:  molecular biology
    (22 total)
featureData
  featureNames: 266_s_at, 33047_at, ..., 40698_at  (752 total)
  fvarLabels and fvarMetadata description: none
experimentData: use 'experimentData(object)'
  pubMedIds: 14684422 16243790
Annotation: hgu95av2
```

The function `Anova()` creates a new function for carrying out ANOVA filtering. It requires a factor that determines the subgroups of our dataset and a statistical significance level. The resulting function is stored in the variable f. The `filterfun()` function works in a similar manner. It generates a filtering function that can be applied to an expression matrix. This application is carried out with the `genefilter()` function that produces a vector with as many elements as there are genes in the given expression matrix. The vector contains logical values. Genes that are considered useful according to the ANOVA statistical test have the value TRUE. As you can see, there are only 752. Finally, we can use this vector to filter our `ExpressionSet` object.

Figure 5.3 shows the median and IQR of the genes selected by the ANOVA test. The figure was obtained as follows:

```
> es <- exprs(ALLb)
> plot(rowMedians(es),rowIQRs(es),
+      xlab='Median expression level',
+      ylab='IQR expression level',
+      main='Distribution Properties of the Selected Genes')
```

The variability in terms of IQR and median that we can observe in Figure 5.3 provides evidence that the genes are expressed in different scales of values. Several modeling techniques are influenced by problems where each case is described by a set of variables using different scales. Namely, any method relying on distances between observations will suffer from this type of problem as distance functions typically sum up differences between variable values. In this context, variables with a higher average value will end up having a larger influence on the distance between observations. To avoid this effect, it is usual to standardize (normalize) the data. This transformation consists of subtracting the typical value of the variables and dividing the result by a measure of

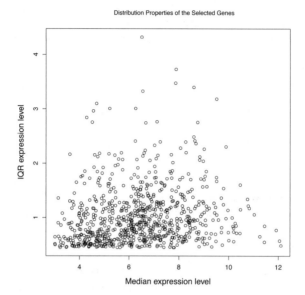

FIGURE 5.3: The median and IQR of the final set of genes.

spread. Given that not all modeling techniques are affected by this data characteristic we will leave this transformation to the modeling stages, making it depend on the tool to be used.

5.3.3   Filtering Using Random Forests

The expression level matrix resulting from the ANOVA filter is already of manageable size, although we still have many more features than observations. In effect, in our modeling attempts described in Section 5.4, we will apply the selected models to this matrix. Nevertheless, one can question whether better results can be obtained with a dataset with a more "standard" dimensionality. In this context, we can try to further reduce the number of features and then compare the results obtained with the different datasets.

Random forests can be used to obtain a ranking of the features in terms of their usefulness for a classification task. In Section 3.3.2 (page 112) we saw an example of using random forests to obtain a ranking of importance of the variables in the context of a prediction problem.

Before proceeding with an illustration of this approach, we will change the names of the genes. The current names are non-standard in terms of what is expected in data frames that are used by many modeling techniques. The function `make.names()` can be used to "solve" this problem as follows:

```
> featureNames(ALLb) <- make.names(featureNames(ALLb))
> es <- exprs(ALLb)
```

The function `featureNames()` provides access to the names of the genes in an `ExpressionSet`.

Random forests can be used to obtain a ranking of the genes as follows,

```
> library(randomForest)
> dt <- data.frame(t(es), Mut = ALLb$mol.bio)
> rf <- randomForest(Mut ~ ., dt, importance = T)
> imp <- importance(rf)
> imp <- imp[, ncol(imp) - 1]
> rf.genes <- names(imp)[order(imp, decreasing = T)[1:30]]
```

We construct a training set by adding the mutation information to the transpose of the expression matrix.[3] We then obtain a random forest with the parameter `importance` set to `TRUE` to obtain estimates of the importance of the variables. The function `importance()` is used to obtain the relevance of each variable. This function actually returns several scores on different columns, according to different criteria and for each class value. We select the column with the variable scores measured as the estimated mean decrease in classification accuracy when each variable is removed in turn. Finally, we obtain the genes that appear at the top 30 positions of the ranking generated by these scores.

We may be curious about the expression levels distribution of theses 30 genes across the different mutations. We can obtain the median level for these top 30 genes as follows:

```
> sapply(rf.genes, function(g) tapply(dt[, g], dt$Mut, median))
```

```
          X40202_at X1674_at X1467_at X1635_at X37015_at X34210_at
ALL1/AF4   8.550639 3.745752 3.708985 7.302814  3.752649  5.641130
BCR/ABL    9.767293 5.833510 4.239306 8.693082  4.857105  9.204237
E2A/PBX1   7.414635 3.808258 3.411696 7.562676  6.579530  8.198781
NEG        7.655605 4.244791 3.515020 7.324691  3.765741  8.791774
          X32116_at X34699_at X40504_at X41470_at X41071_at X36873_at
ALL1/AF4   7.115400  4.253504  3.218079  9.616743  7.698420  7.040593
BCR/ABL    7.966959  6.315966  4.924310  5.205797  6.017967  3.490262
E2A/PBX1   7.359097  6.102031  3.455316  3.931191  6.058185  3.634471
NEG        7.636213  6.092511  3.541651  4.157748  6.573731  3.824670
          X35162_s_at X38323_at X1134_at X32378_at X1307_at X1249_at
ALL1/AF4     4.398885  4.195967 7.846189  8.703860 3.368915 3.582763
BCR/ABL      4.924553  4.866452 8.475578  9.694933 4.945270 4.477659
E2A/PBX1     4.380962  4.317550 8.697500 10.066073 4.678577 3.257649
NEG          4.236335  4.286104 8.167493  9.743168 4.863930 3.791764
          X33774_at X40795_at X36275_at X34850_at X33412_at X37579_at
ALL1/AF4   6.970072  3.867134  3.618819  5.426653 10.757286  7.614200
```

---

[3]Remember that expression matrices have genes (variables) on the rows.

BCR/ABL	8.542248	4.544239	6.259073	6.898979	6.880112	8.231081
E2A/PBX1	7.385129	4.151637	3.635956	5.928574	5.636466	9.494368
NEG	7.348818	3.909532	3.749953	6.327281	5.881145	8.455750
	X37225_at	X39837_s_at	X37403_at	X37967_at	X2062_at	X35164_at
ALL1/AF4	5.220668	6.633188	5.888290	8.130686	9.409753	5.577268
BCR/ABL	3.460902	7.374046	5.545761	9.274695	7.530185	6.493672
E2A/PBX1	7.445655	6.708400	4.217478	8.260236	7.935259	7.406714
NEG	3.387552	6.878846	4.362275	8.986204	7.086033	7.492440

We can observe several interesting differences between the median expression level across the types of mutations, which provides a good indication of the discriminative power of these genes. We can obtain even more detail by graphically inspecting the concrete expression values of these genes for the 94 samples:

```
> library(lattice)
> ordMut <- order(dt$Mut)
> levelplot(as.matrix(dt[ordMut,rf.genes]),
+           aspect='fill', xlab='', ylab='',
+           scales=list(
+             x=list(
+               labels=c('+','-','*','|')[as.integer(dt$Mut[ordMut])],
+               cex=0.7,
+               tck=0
+             ),
+           main=paste(paste(c('"+"','"-"','"*"','"|"'),
+                         levels(dt$Mut)
+                       ),
+                     collapse='; '),
+           col.regions=colorRampPalette(c('white','orange','blue'))
+           )
```

The graph obtained with this code is shown in Figure 5.4. We observe that there are several genes with marked differences in expression level across the different mutations. For instance, there are obvious differences in expression level at gene X36275_at between ALL1/AF4 and BCR/ABL. To obtain this graph we used the function levelplot() of the lattice package. This function can plot a color image of a matrix of numbers. In this case we have used it to plot our expression level matrix with the samples ordered by type of mutation.

5.3.4   Filtering Using Feature Clustering Ensembles

The approach described in this section uses a clustering algorithm to obtain 30 groups of variables that are supposed to be similar. These 30 variable clusters will then be used to obtain an ensemble classification model where m models will be obtained with 30 variables, each one randomly chosen from one of the 30 clusters.

Ensembles are learning methods that build a set of predictive models and

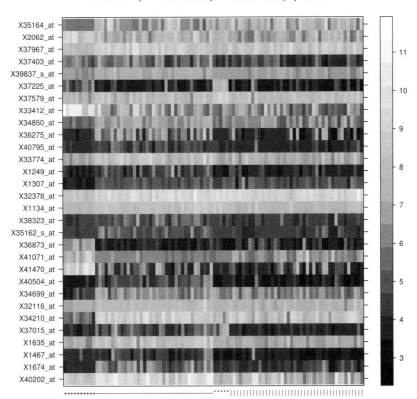

FIGURE 5.4: The expression level of the 30 genes across the 94 samples.

then classify new observations using some form of averaging of the predictions of these models. They are known for often outperforming the individual models that form the ensemble. Ensembles are based on some form of diversity among the individual models. There are many forms of creating this diversity. It can be through different model parameter settings or by different samples of observations used to obtain each model, for instance. Another alternative is to use different predictors for each model in the ensemble. The ensembles we use in this section follow this latter strategy. This approach works better if the pool of predictors from which we obtain different sets is highly redundant. We will assume that there is some degree of redundancy on our set of features generated by the ANOVA filter. We will try to model this redundancy by clustering the variables. Clustering methods are based on distances, in this case distances between variables. Two variables are near (and thus similar) each other if their expression values across the 94 samples are similar. By clustering the variables we expect to find groups of genes that are similar to each other. The Hmisc package contains a function that uses a hierarchical clustering algorithm to cluster the variables of a dataset. The name of this function is varclus(). We can use it as follows:

```
> library(Hmisc)
> vc <- varclus(t(es))
> clus30 <- cutree(vc$hclust, 30)
> table(clus30)

clus30
  1  2  3  4  5  6  7  8  9 10 11 12 13 14 15 16 17 18 19 20 21 22 23 24 25
 27 26 18 30 22 18 24 46 22 20 24 18 56 28 47 32 22 31 18 22 18 33 20 20 21
 26 27 28 29 30
 17  9 19 30 14
```

We used the function cutree() to obtain a clustering formed by 30 groups of variables. We then checked how many variables (genes) belong to each cluster. Based on this clustering we can create sets of predictors by randomly selecting one variable from each cluster. The reasoning is that members of the same cluster will be similar to each other and thus somehow redundant.

The following function facilitates the process by generating one set of variables via randomly sampling from the selected number of clusters (defaulting to 30):

```
> getVarsSet <- function(cluster,nvars=30,seed=NULL,verb=F)
+ {
+    if (!is.null(seed)) set.seed(seed)
+
+    cls <- cutree(cluster,nvars)
+    tots <- table(cls)
+    vars <- c()
+    vars <- sapply(1:nvars,function(clID)
+      {
```

```
+        if (!length(tots[clID])) stop('Empty cluster! (',clID,')')
+        x <- sample(1:tots[clID],1)
+        names(cls[cls==clID])[x]
+      })
+    if (verb)   structure(vars,clusMemb=cls,clusTots=tots)
+    else        vars
+ }
> getVarsSet(vc$hclust)
```

```
 [1] "X41346_at"   "X33047_at"   "X1044_s_at"   "X38736_at"   "X39814_s_at"
 [6] "X649_s_at"   "X41672_at"   "X36845_at"    "X40771_at"   "X38370_at"
[11] "X36083_at"   "X34964_at"   "X35228_at"    "X40855_at"   "X41038_at"
[16] "X40495_at"   "X40419_at"   "X1173_g_at"   "X40088_at"   "X879_at"
[21] "X39135_at"   "X34798_at"   "X39649_at"    "X39774_at"   "X39581_at"
[26] "X37024_at"   "X32585_at"   "X41184_s_at"  "X33305_at"   "X41266_at"
```

```
> getVarsSet(vc$hclust)
```

```
 [1] "X40589_at"   "X33598_r_at"  "X41015_at"   "X38999_s_at"  "X37027_at"
 [6] "X32842_at"   "X37951_at"    "X35693_at"   "X36874_at"    "X41796_at"
[11] "X1462_s_at"  "X31751_f_at"  "X34176_at"   "X40855_at"    "X1583_at"
[16] "X38488_s_at" "X32542_at"    "X32961_at"   "X32321_at"    "X879_at"
[21] "X38631_at"   "X37718_at"    "X948_s_at"   "X38223_at"    "X34256_at"
[26] "X1788_s_at"  "X38271_at"    "X37610_at"   "X33936_at"    "X36899_at"
```

Each time we call this function, we will get a "new" set of 30 variables. Using this function it is easy to generate a set of datasets formed by different predictors and then obtain a model using each of these sets. In Section 5.4 we present a function that obtains ensembles using this strategy.

Further readings on feature selection

Feature selection is a well-studied topic in many disciplines. Good overviews and references of the work in the area of data mining can be obtained in Liu and Motoda (1998), Chizi and Maimon (2005), and Wettschereck et al. (1997).

5.4   Predicting Cytogenetic Abnormalities

This section describes our modeling attempts for the task of predicting the type of cytogenetic abnormalities of the B-cell ALL cases.

5.4.1   Defining the Prediction Task

The data mining problem we are facing is a predictive task. More precisely, it is a classification problem. Predictive classification consists of obtaining models designed with the goal of forecasting the value of a nominal target variable using information on a set of predictors. The models are obtained using a set of labeled observations of the phenomenon under study, that is, observations for which we know both the values of the predictors and of the target variable.

In this case study our target variable is the type of cytogenetic abnormality of a B-cell ALL sample. In our selected dataset, this variable will take four possible values: ALL1/AF4, BCR/ABL, E2A/PBX1, and NEG. Regarding the predictors, they will consist of a set of selected genes for which we have measured an expression value. In our modeling attempts we will experiment with different sets of selected genes, based on the study described in Section 5.3. This means that the number of predictors (features) will vary depending on these trials. Regarding the number of observations, they will consist of 94 cases of B-cell ALL.

5.4.2   The Evaluation Metric

The prediction task is a multi-class classification problem. Predictive classification models are usually evaluated using the error rate or its complement, the accuracy. Nevertheless, there are several alternatives, such as the area under the ROC curve, pairs of measures (e.g., precision and recall), and also measures of the accuracy of class probability estimates (e.g., the Brier score). The package ROCR provides a good sample of these measures.

The selection of the evaluation metric for a given problem often depends on the goals of the user. This is a difficult decision that is often impaired by incomplete information such as the absence of information on the costs of misclassifying a class i case with class j (known as the misclassification costs).

In our case study we have no information on the misclassification costs, and thus we assume that it is equally serious to misclassify, for instance, an E2A/PBX1 mutation as NEG, as it is to misclassify ALL1/AF4 as BCR/ABL. Moreover, we have more than two classes, and generalizations of ROC analysis to multi-class problems are not so well established, not to mention recent drawbacks discovered in the use of the area under the ROC curve (Hand, 2009). In this context, we will resort to the use of the standard accuracy that is measured as

$$\overline{acc} = 1 - \frac{1}{N} \sum_{i=1}^{N} L_{0/1}(y_i, \hat{y}_i) \tag{5.1}$$

where N is the size of test sample, and $L_{0/1}()$ is a loss function defined as

$$L_{0/1}(y_i, \hat{y}_i) = \begin{cases} 0 & \text{if } y_i = \hat{y}_i \\ 1 & \text{otherwise} \end{cases} \tag{5.2}$$

5.4.3   The Experimental Procedure

The number of observations of the dataset we will use is rather small: 94 cases. In this context, the more adequate experimental methodology to obtain reliable estimates of the error rate is the Leave-One-Out Cross-Validation (LOOCV) method. LOOCV is a special case of the k-fold cross-validation experimental methodology that we have used before, namely, when k equals the number of observations. Briefly, LOOCV consists of obtaining N models, where N is the dataset size, and each model is obtained using $N-1$ cases and tested on the observation that was left out. In the book package you may find the function loocv() that implements this type of experiment. This function uses a process similar to the other functions we have described in previous chapters for experimental comparisons. Below is a small illustration of its use with the iris dataset:

```
> data(iris)
> rpart.loocv <- function(form,train,test,...) {
+    require(rpart,quietly=T)
+    m <- rpart(form,train,...)
+    p <- predict(m,test,type='class')
+    c(accuracy=ifelse(p == resp(form,test),100,0))
+ }
> exp <- loocv(learner('rpart.loocv',list()),
+              dataset(Species~.,iris),
+              loocvSettings(seed=1234,verbose=F))

> summary(exp)

== Summary of a Leave One Out Cross Validation  Experiment ==

 LOOCV experiment with verbose =  FALSE  and seed = 1234

* Dataset ::  iris
* Learner  ::  rpart.loocv  with parameters:

* Summary of Experiment Results:

          accuracy
avg       93.33333
std       25.02795
min        0.00000
max      100.00000
invalid    0.00000
```

The function loocv() takes the usual three arguments: the learner, the dataset, and the settings of the experiment. It returns an object of class loocvRun that we can use with the function summary() to obtain the results of the experiment.

The user-defined function (`rpart.loocv()` in the example above) should run the learner, use it for obtaining predictions for the test set, and return a vector with whatever evaluation statistics we wish to estimate by LOOCV. In this small illustration it simply calculates the accuracy of the learner. We should recall that in LOOCV the test set is formed by a single observation on each iteration of the experimental process so in this case we only need to check whether the prediction is equal to the true value.

5.4.4   The Modeling Techniques

As discussed before we will use three different datasets that differ in the predictors that are used. One will have all genes selected by an ANOVA test, while the other two will select 30 of these genes. All datasets will contain 94 cases of B-cell ALL. With the exception of the target variable, all information is numeric.

To handle this problem we have selected three different modeling techniques. Two of them have already been used before in this book. They are random forests and support vector machines (SVMs). They are recognized as some of the best off-the-shelf prediction methods. The third algorithm we will try on this problem is new. It is a method based on distances between observations, known as k-nearest neighbors.

The use of random forests is motivated by the fact that these models are particularly adequate to handle problems with a large number of features. This property derives from the algorithm used by these methods (see Section 5.4.4.1) that randomly selects subsets of the full set of features of a problem. Regarding the use of k-nearest neighbors, the motivation lies on the assumption that samples with the same mutation should have a similar gene "signature," that is, should have similar expression values on the genes we use to describe them. The validity of this assumption is strongly dependent on the genes selected to describe the samples. Namely, they should have good discrimination properties across the different mutations. As we will see in Section 5.4.4.2, k-nearest neighbors methods work by assessing similarities between cases, and thus they seem adequate for this assumption. Finally, the use of SVMs is justified with the goal of trying to explore nonlinear relationships that may eventually exist between gene expression and cytogenetic abnormalities.

SVMs were described in Section 3.4.2.2 (page 127). They are highly non-linear models that can be used on both regression and classification problems. Once again, among the different implementations of SVMs that exist in R, we will use the `svm()` function of package `e1071`.

5.4.4.1   Random Forests

Random forests (Breiman, 2001) are an example of an ensemble model, that is, a model that is formed by a set of simpler models. In particular, random forests consist of a set of decision trees, either classification or regression trees, depending on the problem being addressed. The user decides the number of trees in the ensemble. Each tree is learned using a bootstrap sample obtained by randomly drawing N cases with replacement from the original dataset, where N is the number of cases in that dataset. With each of these training sets, a different tree is obtained. Each node of these trees is chosen considering only a random subset of the predictors of the original problem. The size of these subsets should be much smaller than the number of predictors in the dataset. The trees are fully grown, that is, they are obtained without any post-pruning step. More details on how tree-based models are obtained appear in Section 2.6.2 (page 71).

The predictions of these ensembles are obtained by averaging over the predictions of each tree. For classification problems this consists of a voting mechanism. The class that gets more votes across all trees is the prediction of the ensemble. For regression, the values predicted by each tree are averaged to obtain the random forest prediction.

In R, random forests are implemented in the package `randomForest`. We have already seen several examples of the use of the functions provided by this package throughout the book, namely, for feature selection.

Further readings on random forests

The reference on Random Forests is the original work by Breiman (2001). Further information can also be obtained at the site `http://stat-www.berkeley.edu/users/breiman/RandomForests/`.

5.4.4.2 k-Nearest Neighbors

The k-nearest neighbors algorithm belongs to the class of so-called *lazy learners*. These types of techniques do not actually obtain a model from the training data. They simply store this dataset. Their main work happens at prediction time. Given a new test case, its prediction is obtained by searching for similar cases in the training data that was stored. The k most similar training cases are used to obtain the prediction for the given test case. In classification problems, this prediction is usually obtained by voting and thus an odd number for k is desirable. However, more elaborate voting mechanisms that take into account the distance of the test case to each of the k neighbors are also possible. For regression, instead of voting we have an average of the target variable values of the k neighbors.

This type of model is strongly dependent on the notion of similarity between cases. This notion is usually defined with the help of a metric over the input space defined by the predictor variables. This metric is a distance function that can calculate a number representing the "difference" between any two observations. There are many distance functions, but a rather frequent selection is the Euclidean distance function that is defined as

$$d(\mathbf{x}_i, \mathbf{x}_j) = \sqrt{\sum_{k=1}^{p}(X_{i,k} - X_{j,k})^2} \qquad (5.3)$$

where p is the number of predictors, and $\mathbf{x}_i$ and $\mathbf{x}_j$ are two observations.

These methods are thus very sensitive to both the selected metric and also to the presence of irrelevant variables that may distort the notion of similarity. Moreover, the scale of the variables should be uniform; otherwise we might underestimate some of the differences in variables with lower average values.

The choice of the number of neighbors (k) is also an important parameter of these methods. Frequent values include the numbers in the set $\{1, 3, 5, 7, 11\}$, but obviously these are just heuristics. However, we can say that larger values of k should be avoided because there is the risk of using cases that are already far away from the test case. Obviously, this depends on the density of the training data. Too sparse datasets incur more of this risk. As with any learning model, the "ideal" parameter settings can be estimated through some experimental methodology.

In R, the package `class` (Venables and Ripley, 2002) includes the function `knn()` that implements this idea. Below is an illustrative example of its use on the `iris` dataset:

```
> library(class)
> data(iris)
> idx <- sample(1:nrow(iris), as.integer(0.7 * nrow(iris)))
> tr <- iris[idx, ]
> ts <- iris[-idx, ]
> preds <- knn(tr[, -5], ts[, -5], tr[, 5], k = 3)
> table(preds, ts[, 5])
```

```
preds         setosa versicolor virginica
  setosa          14          0         0
  versicolor       0         14         2
  virginica        0          1        14
```

As you see, the function `knn()` uses a nonstandard interface. The first argument is the training set with the exception of the target variable column. The second argument is the test set, again without the target. The third argument includes the target values of the training data. Finally, there are several other parameters controlling the method, among which the parameter k determines the number of neighbors. We can create a small function that enables the use of this method in a more standard formula-type interface:

```
> kNN <- function(form, train, test, norm = T, norm.stats = NULL,
+        ...) {
+        require(class, quietly = TRUE)
+        tgtCol <- which(colnames(train) == as.character(form[[2]]))
+        if (norm) {
```

```
+          if (is.null(norm.stats))
+              tmp <- scale(train[, -tgtCol], center = T, scale = T)
+          else tmp <- scale(train[, -tgtCol], center = norm.stats[[1]],
+              scale = norm.stats[[2]])
+          train[, -tgtCol] <- tmp
+          ms <- attr(tmp, "scaled:center")
+          ss <- attr(tmp, "scaled:scale")
+          test[, -tgtCol] <- scale(test[, -tgtCol], center = ms,
+              scale = ss)
+      }
+      knn(train[, -tgtCol], test[, -tgtCol], train[, tgtCol],
+          ...)
+ }
> preds.norm <- kNN(Species ~ ., tr, ts, k = 3)
> table(preds.norm, ts[, 5])
```

preds.norm	setosa	versicolor	virginica
setosa	14	0	0
versicolor	0	14	3
virginica	0	1	13

```
> preds.notNorm <- kNN(Species ~ ., tr, ts, norm = F, k = 3)
> table(preds.notNorm, ts[, 5])
```

preds.notNorm	setosa	versicolor	virginica
setosa	14	0	0
versicolor	0	14	2
virginica	0	1	14

This function allows the user to indicate if the data should be normalized prior to the call to the knn() function. This is done through parameter norm. In the example above, you see two examples of its use. A third alternative is to provide the centrality and spread statistics as a list with two components in the argument norm.stats. If this is not done, the function will use the means as centrality estimates and the standard deviations as statistics of spread. In our experiments we will use this facility to call the function with medians and IQRs. The function kNN() is actually included in our book package so you do not need to type its code.

Further readings on *k*-nearest neighbors

The standard reference on this type of methods is the work by Cover and Hart (1967). Good overviews can be found in the works by Aha et al. (1991) and Aha (1997). Deeper analysis can be found in the PhD theses by Aha (1990) and Wettschereck (1994). A different, but related, perspective of lazy learning is the use of so-called local models (Nadaraya, 1964; Watson, 1964). Good references on this vast area are Atkeson et al. (1997) and Cleveland and Loader (1996).

5.4.5   Comparing the Models

This section describes the process we have used to compare the selected models using a LOOCV experimental methodology.

In Section 5.3, we have seen examples of several feature selection methods. We have used some basic filters to eliminate genes with low variance and also control probes. Next, we applied a method based on the conditioned distribution of the expression levels with respect to the target variable. This method was based on an ANOVA statistical test. Finally, from the results of this test we tried to further reduce the number of genes using random forests and clustering of the variables. With the exception of the first simple filters, all other methods depend somehow on the target variable values. We may question whether these filtering stages should be carried out before the experimental comparisons, or if we should integrate these steps into the processes being compared. If our goal is to obtain an unbiased estimate of the classification accuracy of our methodology on new samples, then we should include these filtering stages as part of the data mining processes being evaluated and compared. Not doing so would mean that the estimates we obtain are biased by the fact that the genes used to obtain the models were selected using information of the test set. In effect, if we use all datasets to decide which genes to use, then we are using information on this selection process that should be unknown as it is part of the test data. In this context, we will include part of the filtering stages within the user-defined functions that implement the models we will compare.

For each iteration of the LOOCV process, a feature selection process, is carried out, prior to the predictive model construction, using only the training data provided by the LOOCV routines. The initial simple filtering step will be carried out before the LOOCV comparison. The genes removed by this step would not change if we do it inside the LOOCV process. Control probes would always be removed, and the genes removed due to very low variance would most probably still be removed if a single sample is not given (which is what the LOOCV process does at each iteration).

We will now describe the user-defined functions that need to be supplied to the LOOCV routines for running the experiments. For each of the modeling techniques, we will evaluate several variants. These alternatives differ not only on several parameters of the techniques themselves, but also on the feature selection process that is used. The following list includes the information on these variants for each modeling technique:

```
> vars <- list()
> vars$randomForest <- list(ntree=c(500,750,100),
+                           mtry=c(5,15,30),
+                           fs.meth=list(list('all'),
+                                        list('rf',30),
+                                        list('varclus',30,50)))
> vars$svm <- list(cost=c(1,100,500),
+                  gamma=c(0.01,0.001,0.0001),
```

```
+                        fs.meth=list(list('all'),
+                                     list('rf',30),
+                                     list('varclus',30,50)))
> vars$knn <- list(k=c(3,5,7,11),
+                  norm=c(T,F),
+                  fs.meth=list(list('all'),
+                               list('rf',30),
+                               list('varclus',30,50)))
```

The list has three components, one for each of the algorithms being compared. For each model the list includes the parameters that should be used. For each of the parameters a set of values is given. The combinations of all these possible values will determine the different variants of the systems. Regarding random forests, we will consider three values for the parameter `ntree` that sets the number of trees in the ensemble, and three values for the `mtry` parameter that determines the size of the random subset of features to use when deciding the test for each tree node. The last parameter (`fs.meth`) provides the alternatives for the feature selection phase that we describe below. With respect to SVMs, we consider three different values for both the `cost` and `gamma` parameters. Finally, for the k-nearest neighbors, we try four values for k and two values for the parameter that determines if the predictors data is to be normalized or not.

As mentioned above, for each of the learners we consider three alternative feature sets (the parameter `fs.meth`). The first alternative (`list('all')`) uses all the features resulting from the ANOVA statistical test. The second (`list('rf',30)`) selects 30 genes from the set obtained with the ANOVA test, using the feature ranking obtained with a random forest. The final alternative select 30 genes using the variable clustering ensemble strategy that we described previously and then builds an ensemble using 50 models with 30 predictors randomly selected from the variable clusters. In order to implement the idea of the ensembles based on different variable sets generated by a clustering of the genes, we have created the following function:

```
> varsEnsembles <- function(tgt,train,test,
+                           varsSets,
+                           baseLearner,blPars,
+                           verb=F)
+ {
+   preds <- matrix(NA,ncol=length(varsSets),nrow=NROW(test))
+   for(v in seq(along=varsSets)) {
+     if (baseLearner=='knn')
+       preds[,v] <- knn(train[,-which(colnames(train)==tgt)],
+                        test[,-which(colnames(train)==tgt)],
+                        train[,tgt],blPars)
+     else {
+       m <- do.call(baseLearner,
+                    c(list(as.formula(paste(tgt,
+                                            paste(varsSets[[v]],
```

```
+                                               collapse='+'),
+                                        sep='~')),
+                            train[,c(tgt,varsSets[[v]])]),
+                        blPars)
+                  )
+        if (baseLearner == 'randomForest')
+          preds[,v] <- do.call('predict',
+                               list(m,test[,c(tgt,varsSets[[v]])],
+                                    type='response'))
+        else
+          preds[,v] <- do.call('predict',
+                               list(m,test[,c(tgt,varsSets[[v]])]))
+      }
+   }
+   ps <- apply(preds,1,function(x)
+                     levels(factor(x))[which.max(table(factor(x)))])
+   ps <- factor(ps,
+                levels=1:nlevels(train[,tgt]),
+                labels=levels(train[,tgt]))
+   if (verb) structure(ps,ensemblePreds=preds) else ps
+ }
```

The first arguments of this function are the name of the target variable, the training set, and the test set. The next argument (varsSets) is a list containing the sets of variable names (the obtained clusters) from which we should sample a variable to generate the predictors of each member of the ensemble. Finally, we have two arguments (baseLearner and blPars) that provide the name of the function that implements the learner to be used on each member of the ensemble and respective list of learning arguments. The result of the function is the set of predictions of the ensemble for the given test set. These predictions are obtained by a voting mechanism among the members of the ensemble. The difference between the members of the ensemble lies only in the predictors that are used, which are determined by the varsSets parameters. These sets result from a variable clustering process, as mentioned in Section 5.3.4.

Given the similarity of the tasks to be carried out by each of the learners, we have created a single user-defined modeling function that will receive as one of the parameters the learner that is to be used. The function genericModel() that we present below implements this idea:

```
> genericModel <- function(form,train,test,
+                          learner,
+                          fs.meth,
+                          ...)
+   {
+      cat('=')
+      tgt <- as.character(form[[2]])
+      tgtCol <- which(colnames(train)==tgt)
```

```
+
+        # Anova filtering
+        f <- Anova(train[,tgt],p=0.01)
+        ff <- filterfun(f)
+        genes <- genefilter(t(train[,-tgtCol]),ff)
+        genes <- names(genes)[genes]
+        train <- train[,c(tgt,genes)]
+        test <- test[,c(tgt,genes)]
+        tgtCol <- 1
+
+        # Specific filtering
+        if (fs.meth[[1]]=='varclus') {
+          require(Hmisc,quietly=T)
+          v <- varclus(as.matrix(train[,-tgtCol]))
+          VSs <- lapply(1:fs.meth[[3]],function(x)
+                        getVarsSet(v$hclust,nvars=fs.meth[[2]]))
+          pred <- varsEnsembles(tgt,train,test,VSs,learner,list(...))
+
+        } else {
+          if (fs.meth[[1]]=='rf') {
+            require(randomForest,quietly=T)
+            rf <- randomForest(form,train,importance=T)
+            imp <- importance(rf)
+            imp <- imp[,ncol(imp)-1]
+            rf.genes <- names(imp)[order(imp,decreasing=T)[1:fs.meth[[2]]]]
+            train <- train[,c(tgt,rf.genes)]
+            test <- test[,c(tgt,rf.genes)]
+          }
+
+          if (learner == 'knn')
+            pred <- kNN(form,
+                    train,
+                    test,
+                    norm.stats=list(rowMedians(t(as.matrix(train[,-tgtCol]))),
+                                    rowIQRs(t(as.matrix(train[,-tgtCol])))),
+                    ...)
+          else {
+            model <- do.call(learner,c(list(form,train),list(...)))
+            pred <- if (learner != 'randomForest') predict(model,test)
+                    else predict(model,test,type='response')
+          }
+
+        }
+
+        c(accuracy=ifelse(pred == resp(form,test),100,0))
+      }
```

This user-defined function will be called from within the LOOCV routines for each iteration of the process. The experiments with all these variants on the microarray data will take a long time to complete.[4] In this context, we do not recommend that you run the following experiments unless you are aware of this temporal constraint. The objects resulting from this experiment are available at the book Web page so that you are able to proceed with the rest of the analysis without having to run all these experiments. The code to run the full experiments is the following:

```
> require(class,quietly=TRUE)
> require(randomForest,quietly=TRUE)
> require(e1071,quietly=TRUE)
> load('myALL.Rdata')
> es <- exprs(ALLb)
> # simple filtering
> ALLb <- nsFilter(ALLb,
+                      var.func=IQR,var.cutoff=IQR(as.vector(es))/5,
+                      feature.exclude="^AFFX")
> ALLb <- ALLb$eset
> # the dataset
> featureNames(ALLb) <- make.names(featureNames(ALLb))
> dt <- data.frame(t(exprs(ALLb)),Mut=ALLb$mol.bio)
> DSs <- list(dataset(Mut ~ .,dt,'ALL'))
> # The learners to evaluate
> TODO <- c('knn','svm','randomForest')
> for(td in TODO) {
+    assign(td,
+              experimentalComparison(
+                   DSs,
+                   c(
+                      do.call('variants',
+                              c(list('genericModel',learner=td),
+                                vars[[td]],
+                                varsRootName=td))
+                   ),
+                   loocvSettings(seed=1234,verbose=F)
+                   )
+              )
+    save(list=td,file=paste(td,'Rdata',sep='.'))
+ }
```

This code uses the function `experimentalComparison()` to test all variants using the LOOCV method. The code uses the function `variants()` to generate all `learner` objects from the variants provided by the components of list `vars` that we have seen above. Each of these variants will be evaluated by an LOOCV process. The results of the code are three `compExp` objects with the names `knn`, `svm`, and `randomForest`. Each of these objects contains the results of the variants of the respective learner. All of them are saved in a file with the same name as the object and extension ".Rdata". These are

---

[4]On my standard desktop computer it takes approximately 3 days.

the files that are available at the book Web site, so in case you have not run all these experiments, you can download them into your computer, and load them into R using the `load()` function (indicating the name of the respective file as argument):

```
> load("knn.Rdata")
> load("svm.Rdata")
> load("randomForest.Rdata")
```

The results of all variants of a learner are contained in the respective object. For instance, if you want to see which were the best SVM variants, you may issue

```
> rankSystems(svm, max = T)
```

```
$ALL
$ALL$accuracy
  system    score
1 svm.v2 86.17021
2 svm.v3 86.17021
3 svm.v5 86.17021
4 svm.v6 86.17021
5 svm.v9 86.17021
```

The function `rankSystems()` takes an object of class `compExp` and obtains the best performing variants for each of the statistics that were estimated in the experimental process. By default, the function assumes that "best" means smaller values. In case of statistics that are to be maximized, like accuracy, we can use the parameter `max` as we did above.[5]

In order to have an overall perspective of all trials, we can join the three objects:

```
> all.trials <- join(svm, knn, randomForest, by = "variants")
```

With the resulting `compExp` object we can check the best overall score of our trials:

```
> rankSystems(all.trials, top = 10, max = T)
```

```
$ALL
$ALL$accuracy
           system    score
1          knn.v2 88.29787
2          knn.v3 87.23404
3 randomForest.v4 87.23404
4 randomForest.v6 87.23404
```

---

[5]In case we measure several statistics, some that are to be minimized and others maximized, the parameter `max` accepts a vector of Boolean values.

```
5            svm.v2 86.17021
6            svm.v3 86.17021
7            svm.v5 86.17021
8            svm.v6 86.17021
9            svm.v9 86.17021
10          svm.v23 86.17021
```

The top score is obtained by a variant of the k-nearest neighbor method. Let us check its characteristics:

```
> getVariant("knn.v2", all.trials)

Learner::  "genericModel"

Parameter values
        learner  =  "knn"
        k = 5
        norm  =  TRUE
        fs.meth  =  list("rf", 30)
```

This variant uses 30 genes filtered by a random forest, five neighbors and normalization of the gene expression values. It is also interesting to observe that among the top ten scores, only the last one ("svm.v23") does not use the 30 genes filtered with a random forest. This tenth best model uses all genes resulting from the ANOVA filtering. However, we should note that the accuracy scores among these top ten models are rather similar. In effect, given that we have 94 test cases, the accuracy of the best model means that it made 11 mistakes, while the model on the tenth position makes 13 errors.

It may be interesting to know which errors were made by the models, for instance, the best model. Confusion matrices (see page 120) provide this type of information. To obtain a confusion matrix we need to know what the actual predictions of the models are. Our user-defined function does not output the predicted classes, only the resulting accuracy. As a result, the compExp objects do not have this information. In case we need this sort of extra information, on top of the evaluation statistics measured on each iteration of the experimental process, we need to make the user-defined functions return it back to the experimental comparison routines. These are prepared to receive and store this extra information, as we have seen in Chapter 4. Let us imagine that we want to know the predictions of the best model on each iteration of the LOOCV process. The following code allows us to obtain such information. The code focuses on the best model but it should be easily adaptable to any other model.

```
> bestknn.loocv <- function(form,train,test,...) {
+     require(Biobase,quietly=T)
+     require(randomForest,quietly=T)
+     cat('=')
+     tgt <- as.character(form[[2]])
```

```
+    tgtCol <- which(colnames(train)==tgt)
+    # Anova filtering
+    f <- Anova(train[,tgt],p=0.01)
+    ff <- filterfun(f)
+    genes <- genefilter(t(train[,-tgtCol]),ff)
+    genes <- names(genes)[genes]
+    train <- train[,c(tgt,genes)]
+    test <- test[,c(tgt,genes)]
+    tgtCol <- 1
+    # Random Forest filtering
+    rf <- randomForest(form,train,importance=T)
+    imp <- importance(rf)
+    imp <- imp[,ncol(imp)-1]
+    rf.genes <- names(imp)[order(imp,decreasing=T)[1:30]]
+    train <- train[,c(tgt,rf.genes)]
+    test <- test[,c(tgt,rf.genes)]
+    # knn prediction
+    ps <- kNN(form,train,test,norm=T,
+          norm.stats=list(rowMedians(t(as.matrix(train[,-tgtCol]))),
+                          rowIQRs(t(as.matrix(train[,-tgtCol])))),
+          k=5,...)
+    structure(c(accuracy=ifelse(ps == resp(form,test),100,0)),
+          itInfo=list(ps)
+          )
+ }
> resTop <- loocv(learner('bestknn.loocv',pars=list()),
+               dataset(Mut~.,dt),
+               loocvSettings(seed=1234,verbose=F),
+               itsInfo=T)
```

The `bestknn.loocv()` function is essentially a specialization of the function `genericModel()` we have seen before, but focused on 5-nearest neighbors with random forest filtering and normalization using medians and IQRs. Most of the code is the same as in the `genericModel()` function, the only exception being the result that is returned. This new function, instead of returning the vector with the accuracy of the model, returns a structure. We have seen before that structures are R objects with appended attributes. The `structure()` function allows us to create such "enriched" objects by attaching to them a set of attributes. In the case of our user-defined functions, if we want to return some extra information to the `loocv()` function, we should do it on an attribute named `itInfo`. In the function above we are using this attribute to return the actual predictions of the model. The `loocv()` function stores this information for each iteration of the experimental process. In order for this storage to take place, we need to call the `loocv()` function with the optional parameter `itsInfo=T`. This ensures that whatever is returned as an attribute with name `itInfo` by the user-defined function, it will be collected in a list and returned as an attribute named `itsInfo` of the result of the `loocv()`

function. In the end, we can inspect this information and in this case see what were the actual predictions of the best model on each iteration.

We can check the content of the attribute containing the wanted information as follows (we are only showing the first 4 predictions):

```
> attr(resTop, "itsInfo")[1:4]

[[1]]
[1] BCR/ABL
Levels: ALL1/AF4 BCR/ABL E2A/PBX1 NEG

[[2]]
[1] NEG
Levels: ALL1/AF4 BCR/ABL E2A/PBX1 NEG

[[3]]
[1] BCR/ABL
Levels: ALL1/AF4 BCR/ABL E2A/PBX1 NEG

[[4]]
[1] ALL1/AF4
Levels: ALL1/AF4 BCR/ABL E2A/PBX1 NEG
```

The function `attr()` allows us to obtain the value of any attribute of an R object. As you see, the `itsInfo` attribute contains the predictions of each iteration of the LOOCV process. Using this information together with the true value of the class of the dataset, we can obtain the confusion matrix:

```
> preds <- unlist(attr(resTop, "itsInfo"))
> table(preds, dt$Mut)

preds       ALL1/AF4 BCR/ABL E2A/PBX1 NEG
  ALL1/AF4        10       0        0   0
  BCR/ABL          0      33        0   4
  E2A/PBX1         0       0        3   1
  NEG              0       4        2  37
```

The confusion matrix can be used to inspect the type of errors that the model makes. For instance, we can observe that the model correctly predicts all cases with the ALL1/AF4 mutation. Moreover, we can also observe that most of the errors of the model consist of predicting the class NEG for a case with some mutation. Nevertheless, the reverse also happens with five samples with no mutation, incorrectly predicted as having some abnormality.

5.5 Summary

The primary goal of this chapter was to introduce the reader to an important range of applications of data mining that receives a lot of attention from the R community: bioinformatics. In this context, we explored some of the tools of the project Bioconductor, which provides a large set of R packages specialized for this type of applications. As a concrete example, we addressed a bioinformatics predictive task: to forecast the type of genetic mutation associated with samples of patients with B-cell acute lymphoblastic leukemia. Several classification models were obtained based on information concerning the expression levels on a set of genes resulting from microarray experiments. In terms of data mining concepts, this chapter focused on the following main topics:

- Feature selection methods for problems with a very large number of predictors

- Classification methods

- Random forests

- k-Nearest neighbors

- SVMs

- Ensembles using different subsets of predictors

- Leave-one-out cross-validation experiments

With respect to R, we have learned a few new techniques, namely,

- How to handle microarray data

- Using ANOVA tests to compare means across groups of data

- Using random forests to select variables in classification problems

- Clustering the variables of a problem

- Obtaining ensembles with models learned using different predictors

- Obtaining k-nearest neighors models

- Estimating the accuracy of models using leave-one-out cross-validation.

Bibliography

Acuna, E., and Members of the CASTLE group at UPR-Mayaguez, (2009). *dprep: Data preprocessing and visualization functions for classification.* R package version 2.1.

Adler, D., Glaser, C., Nenadic, O., Oehlschlagel, J., and Zucchini, W. (2010). *ff: Memory-efficient storage of large data on disk and fast access functions.* R package version 2.1-2.

Aha, D. (1990). *A Study of Instance-Based Learning Algorithms for Supervised Learning Tasks: Mathematical, Empirical, and Psychological Evaluations.* Ph.D. thesis, University of California at Irvine, Department of Information and Computer Science.

Aha, D. (1997). Lazy learning. *Artificial Intelligence Review*, 11, 7–10.

Aha, D., Kibler, D., and Albert, M. (1991). Instance-based learning algorithms. *Machine Learning*, 6(1):37–66.

Atkeson, C. G., Moore, A., and Schaal, S. (1997). Locally weighted learning. *Artificial Intelligence Review*, 11:11–73.

Austin, J. and Hodge, V. (2004). A survey of outlier detection methodologies. *Artificial Intelligence Review*, 22:85–126.

Barnett, V. and Lewis, T. (1994). *Outliers in statistical data (3rd edition).* John Wiley.

Bontempi, G., Birattari, M., and Bersini, H. (1999). Lazy learners at work: The lazy learning toolbox. In *Proceedings of the 7th European Congress on Intelligent Tecnhiques & Soft Computing (EUFIT'99).*

Breiman, L. (1996). Bagging predictors. *Machine Learning*, 24:123–140.

Breiman, L. (1998). Arcing classifiers (with discussion). *Annals of Statistics*, 26:801–849.

Breiman, L. (2001). Random forests. *Machine Learning*, 45(1):5–32.

Breiman, L., Friedman, J., Olshen, R., and Stone, C. (1984). *Classification and regression trees.* Statistics/Probability Series. Wadsworth & Brooks/Cole Advanced Books & Software.

Breunig, M., Kriegel, H., Ng, R., and Sander, J. (2000). LOF: identifying density-based local outliers. In *ACM Int. Conf. on Management of Data*, pages 93–104.

Carl, P. and Peterson, B. G. (2009). *PerformanceAnalytics: Econometric tools for performance and risk analysis*. R package version 1.0.0.

Chambers, J. (2008). *Software for data analysis: Programming with R*. Springer.

Chan, R. (1999). Protecting rivers & streams by monitoring chemical concentrations and algae communities. In *Proceedings of the 7th European Congress on Intelligent Tecnhiques & Soft Computing (EUFIT'99)*.

Chandola, V., Banerjee, A., and Kumar, V. (2007). Outlier detection: A survey. Technical Report TR 07-017, Department of Computer Science and Engineering, University of Minnesota.

Chatfield, C. (1983). *Statistics for technology*. Chapman and Hall, 3rd edition.

Chawla, N. (2005). *The data mining and knowledge discovery handbook*, chapter on data mining for imbalanced datasets: an overview, pages 853–867. Springer.

Chawla, N., Japkowicz, N., and Kokz, A. (2004). SIGKDD *Explorations* special issue on learning from imbalanced datasets.

Chawla, N., Lazarevic, A., Hall, L., and Bowyer, K. (2003). Smote-boost: Improving prediction of the minority class in boosting. In *Seventh European Conference on Principles and Practice of Knowledge Discovery in Databases*, pages 107–119.

Chawla, N. V., Bowyer, K. W., Hall, L. O., and Kegelmeyer, W. P. (2002). Smote: Synthetic minority over-sampling technique. *Journal of Artificial Intelligence Research*, 16:321–357.

Chen, C., Hardle, W., and Unwin, A., Editors (2008). *Handbook of data visualization*. Springer.

Chiaretti, S., Li, X., Gentleman, R., Vitale, A., Vignetti, M., Mandelli, F., Ritz, J., and Foa, R. (2004). Gene expression profile of adult T-cell acute lymphocytic leukemia identifies distinct subsets of patients with different response to therapy and survival. *Blood*, 103(7), 2771–2778.

Chizi, B. and Maimon, O. (2005). *The data mining and knowledge discovery handbook*, chapter on dimension reduction and feature selection, pages 93–111. Springer.

Cleveland, W. (1993). *Visualizing data*. Hobart Press.

Cleveland, W. (1995). *The elements of graphing data.* Hobart Press.

Cleveland, W. and Loader, C. (1996). Smoothing by local regression: Principles and methods, statistical theory and computational aspects of smoothing. Edited by W. Haerdle and M. G. Schimek, Springer, 10–49.

Cortes, E. A., Martinez, M. G., and Rubio, N. G. (2010). *adabag: Applies Adaboost.M1 and Bagging.* R package version 1.1.

Cover, T. M. and Hart, P. E. (1967). Nearest neighbor pattern classification. *IEEE Transactions on Information Theory,* 13(1):21–27.

Dalgaard, P. (2002). *Introductory statistics with R.* Springer.

Deboeck, G., Editor. (1994). *Trading on the edge.* John Wiley & Sons.

Demsar, J. (2006). Statistical comparisons of classifiers over multiple data sets. *Journal of Machine Learning Research,* 7:1–30.

Devogelaere, D., Rijckaert, M., and Embrechts, M. J. (1999). 3rd international competition: Protecting rivers and streams by monitoring chemical concentrations and algae communities solved with the use of gadc. In *Proceedings of the 7th European Congress on Intelligent Tecnhiques & Soft Computing (EUFIT'99).*

Dietterich, T. G. (1998). Approximate statistical tests for comparing supervised classification learning algorithms. *Neural Computation,* 10:1895–1923.

Dietterich, T. G. (2000). Ensemble methods in machine learning. *Lecture Notes in Computer Science,* 1857:1–15.

Dimitriadou, E., Hornik, K., Leisch, F., Meyer, D., and Weingessel, A. (2009). *e1071: Misc Functions of the Department of Statistics (e1071), TU Wien.* R package version 1.5-19.

Domingos, P. (1999). Metacost: A general method for making classifiers cost-sensitive. In *KDD'99: Proceedings of the 5th International Conference on Knowledge Discovery and Data Mining,* pages 155–164. ACM Press.

Domingos, P. and Pazzani, M. (1997). On the optimality of the simple Bayesian classifier under zero-one loss. *Machine Learning,* 29:103–137.

Drapper, N. and Smith, H. (1981). *Applied Regression Analysis.* John Wiley & Sons, 2nd edition.

Drummond, C. and Holte, R. (2006). Cost curves: An improved method for visualizing classifier performance. *Machine Learning,* 65(1):95–130.

DuBois, P. (2000). *MySQL.* New Riders.

Elkan, C. (2001). The foundations of cost-sensitive learning. In *IJCAI'01: Proceedings of 17th International Joint Conference of Artificial Intelligence*, pages 973–978. Morgan Kaufmann Publishers Inc.

Fox, J. (2009). *car: Companion to Applied Regression*. R package version 1.2-16.

Freund, Y. (1990). Boosting a weak learning algorithm by majority. In *Proceedings of the Third Annual Workshop on Computational Learning Theory*.

Freund, Y. and Shapire, R. (1996). Experiments with a new boosting algorithm. In *Proceedings of the 13th International Conference on Machine Learning*. Morgan Kaufmann.

Friedman, J. (1991). Multivariate adaptive regression splines. *The Annals of Statistics*, 19(1):1–144.

Friedman, J. (2002). Stochastic gradient boosting. *Computational Statistics and Data Analysis*, 38(4):367–378.

Gama, J. and Gaber, M., Editors. (2007). *Learning from data streams*. Springer.

Gama, J., Medas, P., Castillo, G., and Rodrigues, P. (2004). Learning with drift detection. In Bazzan, A. and Labidi, S., Editors, *Advances in artificial intelligence-SBIA 2004*, volume 3171 of *Lecture Notes in Computer Science*, pages 286–295. Springer.

Gentleman, R., Carey, V., Huber, W., and Hahne, F. (2010). *genefilter: genefilter: methods for filtering genes from microarray experiments*. R package version 1.28.2.

Gentleman, R. C., Carey, V. J., Bates, D. M., et al. (2004). Bioconductor: Open software development for computational biology and bioinformatics. *Genome Biology*, 5:R80.

Hahne, F., Huber, W., Gentleman, R., and Falcon, S. (2008). *Bioconductor case studies*. Springer.

Han, J. and Kamber, M. (2006). *Data mining: concepts and techniques (2nd edition)*. Morgan Kaufmann Publishers.

Hand, D., Mannila, H., and Smyth, P. (2001). *Principles of data mining*. MIT Press.

Hand, D. and Yu, K. (2001). Idiot's Bayes — Not so stupid after all? *International Statistical Review*, 69(3):385–399.

Hand, D. J. (2009). Measuring classifier performance: A coherent alternative to the area under the roc curve. *Machine Learning*, 77(1):103–123.

Harrell, Jr., F. E. (2009). *Hmisc: Harrell miscellaneous.* R package version 3.7-0. With contributions from many other users.

Hastie, T. and Tibshirani, R. (1990). *Generalized additive models.* Chapman & Hall.

Hastie, T., Tibshirani, R., and Friedman, J. (2001). *The elements of statistical learning: data mining, inference and prediction.* Springer.

Hawkins, D. M. (1980). *Identification of outliers.* Chapman and Hall.

Hong, S. (1997). Use of contextual information for feature ranking and discretization. *IEEE Transactions on Knowledge and Data Engineering,* 9(5):718–730.

Hornik, K., Buchta, C., and Zeileis, A. (2009). Open-source machine learning: R meets Weka. *Computational Statistics,* 24(2):225–232.

Ihaka, R. and Gentleman, R. (1996). R: A language for data analysis and graphics. *Journal of Computational and Graphical Statistics,* 5(3):299–314.

James, D. A. and DebRoy, S. (2009). *RMySQL: R interface to the MySQL database.* R package version 0.7-4.

Japkowicz, N. (2000). The class imbalance problem: Significance and strategies. In *Proceedings of the 2000 International Conference on Artificial Intelligence (IC-A1'2000):Special Track on Inductive Learning.*

Karatzoglou, A., Smola, A., Hornik, K., and Zeileis, A. (2004). kernlab — an S4 package for kernel methods in R. *Journal of Statistical Software,* 11(9):1–20.

Kaufman, L. and Rousseeuw, P. (1990). *Finding groups in data: An introduction to cluster analysis.* John Wiley & Sons, New York.

Kifer, D., Ben-David, S., and Gehrke, J. (2004). Detecting change in data streams. In *VLDB 04: Proceedings of the 30th International Conference on Very Large Data Bases,* pages 180–191. Morgan Kaufmann.

Kira, K. and Rendel, L. (1992). The feature selection problem: Traditional methods and a new algorithm. In *Proc. Tenth National Conference on Artificial Intelligence,* pages 129–134. MIT Press.

Klinkenberg, R. (2004). Learning drifting concepts: example selection vs. example weighting. *Intelligent Data Analysis,* 8(3):281–300.

Kononenko, I. (1991). Semi-naive Bayesian classifier. In *EWSL-91: Proceedings of the European Working Session on Learning on Machine Learning,* pages 206–219. Springer.

Kononenko, I., Simec, E., and Robnik-Sikonja, M. (1997). Overcoming the myopia of induction learning algorithms with relieff. *Applied Intelligence*, 17(1):39–55.

Kubat, M. and Matwin, S. (1997). Addressing the curse of imbalanced training sets: one-sided selection. In *Proceedings of the Fourteenth International Conference on Machine Learning*, pages 179–186.

Leisch, F., Hornik, K., and Ripley., B. D. (2009). *mda: Mixture and flexible discriminant analysis, S original by Trevor Hastie and Robert Tibshirani*. R package version 0.3-4.

Li, X. (2009). *ALL: A data package.* R package version 1.4.7.

Liaw, A. and Wiener, M. (2002). Classification and regression by randomforest. *R News*, 2(3):18–22.

Liu, H. and Motoda, H. (1998). *Feature selection for knowledge discovery and data mining.* Kluwer Academic Publishers.

McCulloch, W. and Pitts, W. (1943). A logical calculus of the ideas immanent in nervous activity. *Bulletin of Mathematical Biophysics*, 5:115–133.

Milborrow, S. (2009). *Earth: Multivariate adaptive regression spline models, derived from mda:mars by Trevor Hastie and Rob Tibshirani*. R package version 2.4-0.

Minsky, M. and Papert, S. (1969). *Perceptrons: an introduction to computational geometry.* MIT Press.

Murrell, P. (2006). *R graphics.* Chapman & Hall/CRC.

Murtagh, F. (1985). Multidimensional clustering algorithms. *COMPSTAT Lectures 4*, Wuerzburg: Physica-Verlag.

Myers, R. (1990). *Classical and modern regression with applications.* 2nd edition. Duxbury Press.

Nadaraya, E. (1964). On estimating regression. *Theory of Probability and its Applications*, 9:141–142.

Nemenyi, P. (1969). Distribution-free Multiple Comparisons. Ph.D. thesis, Princeton University.

Ng, R. and Han, J. (1994). Efficient and effective clustering method for spatial data mining. In *Proceedings of the 20th International Conference on Very Large Data Bases*, page 144. Morgan Kaufmann.

Oakland, J. (2007). *Statistical process control, 6th edition.* Butterworth-Heinemann.

Provost, F. and Fawcett, T. (1997). Analysis and visualization of classifier performance: Comparison under imprecise class and cost distributions. In *KDD'97: Proceedings of the 3rd International Conference on Knowledge Discovery and Data Mining*, pages 43–48. AAAI Press.

Provost, F. and Fawcett, T. (2001). Robust classification for imprecise environments. *Machine Learning*, 42(3), 203–231.

Provost, F., Fawcett, T., and Kohavi, R. (1998). The case against accuracy estimation for comparing induction algorithms. In *Proc. 15th International Conf. on Machine Learning*, pages 445–453. Morgan Kaufmann, San Francisco, CA.

Pyle, D. (1999). *Data preparation for data mining*. Morgan Kaufmann.

Quinlan, R. (1993). *C4.5: programs for machine learning*. Morgan Kaufmann.

R Special Interest Group on Databases, R.-S.-D. (2009). *DBI: R Database Interface*. R package version 0.2-5.

Rätsch, G., Onoda, T., and Müller, K. (2001). Soft margins for *AdaBoost*. *Machine Learning*, 42(3):287–320.

Rijsbergen, C. V. (1979). *Information retrieval*. 2nd edition. Dept. of Computer Science, University of Glasgow.

Rish, I. (2001). An empirical study of the Naive Bayes classifier. In *IJCAI 2001 Workshop on Empirical Methods in Artificial Intelligence*, pages 41–46.

Rogers, R. and Vemuri, V. (1994). *Artificial neural networks forecasting time series*. IEEE Computer Society Press.

Rojas, R. (1996). *Neural networks*. Springer-Verlag.

Ronsenblatt, F. (1958). The perceptron: A probabilistic models for information storage and organization in the brain. *Psychological Review*, 65:386–408.

Rosenberg, C., Hebert, M., and Schneiderman, H. (2005). Semi-supervised self-training of object detection models. In *Proceedings of the 7th IEEE Workshop on Applications of Computer Vision*, pages 29–36. IEEE Computer Society.

Rumelhart, D., Hinton, G., and Williams, R. (1986). Learning internal representations by error propagation. In Rumelhart, D.E. et al., Editors, *Parallel distributed processing*, volume 1. MIT Press.

Ryan, J. A. (2009). *quantmod: Quantitative financial modelling framework*. R package version 0.3-13.

Ryan, J. A. and Ulrich, J. M. (2010). *xts: Extensible time series.* R package version 0.7-0.

Sarkar, D. (2010). *lattice: Lattice graphics.* R package version 0.18-3.

Seeger, M. (2002). Learning with Labeled and Unlabeled Data. Technical report, Institute for Adaptive and Neural Computation, University of Edinburgh.

Shapire, R. (1990). The strength of weak learnability. *Machine Learning,* 5:197–227.

Shawe-Taylor, J. and Cristianini, N. (2000). *An introduction to support vector machines.* Cambridge University Press.

Sing, T., Sander, O., Beerenwinkel, N., and Lengauer, T. (2009). *ROCR: Visualizing the performance of scoring classifiers.* R package version 1.0-4.

Smola, A. and Schölkopf, B. (2004). A tutorial on support vector regression. *Statistics and Computing,* 14:199–222.

Smola, A. J. and Schölkopf, B. (1998). A tutorial on support vector regression. NeuroCOLT Technical Report TR-98-030.

Therneau, T. M. and Atkinson, B.; port by Brian Ripley. (2010). *rpart: Recursive Partitioning.* R package version 3.1-46.

Torgo, L. (1999a). Inductive Learning of Tree-based Regression Models. Ph.D. thesis, Faculty of Sciences, University of Porto.

Torgo, L. (1999b). Predicting the density of algae communities using local regression trees. In *Proceedings of the 7th European Congress on Intelligent Tecnhiques & Soft Computing (EUFIT'99).*

Torgo, L. (2000). Partial linear trees. In Langley, P., Editor, *Proceedings of the 17th International Conference on Machine Learning (ICML 2000),* pages 1007–1014. Morgan Kaufmann.

Torgo, L. (2007). Resource-bounded fraud detection. In Neves, J. et. al, Editors, *Proceedings of the 13th Portuguese Conference on Artificial Intelligence (EPIA'07),* pages 449–460, Springer.

Trapletti, A. and Hornik, K. (2009). *tseries: Time series analysis and computational finance.* R package version 0.10-22.

Ulrich, J. (2009). *TTR: Technical trading rules.* R package version 0.20-1.

Vapnik, V. (1995). *The nature of statistical learning theory.* Springer.

Vapnik, V. (1998). *Statistical Learning Theory.* John Wiley & Sons.

Venables, W. N. and Ripley, B. D. (2002). *Modern applied statistics with S.* fourth edition, Springer.

Watson, G. S. (1964). Smooth regression analysis. *Sankhya: The Indian Journal of Statistics, Series A*, 26:359–372.

Weihs, C., Ligges, U., Luebke, K., and Raabe, N. (2005). klar analyzing German business cycles. In Baier, D., Decker, R., and Schmidt-Thieme, L., Editors, *Data analysis and decision support*, pages 335–343, Springer-Verlag.

Weiss, G. and F. Provost (2003). Learning when training data are costly: The effect of class distribution on tree induction. *Journal of Artificial Intelligence Research*, 19:315–354.

Weiss, S. and Indurkhya, N. (1999). *Predictive data mining.* Morgan Kaufmann.

Werbos, P. (1974). *Beyond Regression — New Tools for Prediction and Analysis in the Behavioral Sciences.* Ph.D. thesis, Harvard University.

Werbos, P. (1996). *The roots of backpropagation — from observed derivatives to neural networks and political forecasting.* John Wiley & Sons.

Wettschereck, D. (1994). *A Study of Distance-Based Machine Learning Algorithms.* Ph.D. thesis, Oregon State University.

Wettschereck, D., Aha, D., and Mohri, T. (1997). A review and empirical evaluation of feature weighting methods for a class of lazy learning algorithms. *Artificial Intelligence Review*, 11:11–73.

Wilson, D. and Martinez, T. (1997). Improved heterogeneous distance functions. *Journal of Artificial Intelligence Research*, 6:1–34.

Yarowsky, D. (1995). Unsupervised word sense disambiguation rivaling supervised methods. In *Proceedings of the 33rd Annual Meeting of the Association for Computational Linguistics (ACL)*, pages 189–196.

Zeileis, A. and Grothendieck, G. (2005). zoo: S3 infrastructure for regular and irregular time series. *Journal of Statistical Software*, 14(6):1–27.

Zhu, X. (2005). Semi-Supervised Learning with Graphs. Ph.D. thesis, School of Computer Science, Carnegie Mellon University.

Zhu, X. (2006). Semi-Supervised Literature Survey. Technical report TR 1530, University of Wisconsin–Madison.

Zirilli, J. (1997). *Financial prediction using neural networks.* International Thomson Computer Press.

Subject Index

Index of Data Mining Topics

Index of **R** Functions